ASK FOR IT

ALSO BY LINDA BABCOCK AND SARA LASCHEVER

Women Don't Ask: The High Cost of
Avoiding Negotiation—and Positive Strategies for Change

ASK FOR IT

How Women Can Use the Power of Negotiation to Get What They Really Want

LINDA BABCOCK

and

SARA LASCHEVER

BANTAM BOOKS

ASK FOR IT
A Bantam Book / March 2008

Published by Bantam Dell
A Division of Random House, Inc.
New York, New York

Book design by Helene Berinsky

Bantam Books is a registered trademark of Random House, Inc., and the colophon
is a trademark of Random House, Inc.

Library of Congress Cataloging-in-Publication Data

Babcock, Linda, 1961–
Ask for it : how women can use the power of negotiation to get what they really want /
Linda Babcock and Sara Laschever.
p. cm.
"A Bantam Book."
ISBN 978-0-553-38375-1 (hardcover)
1. Negotiation in business. 2. Negotiation. 3. Assertiveness in women. 4. Achievement
motivation in women. 5. Women—Life skills guides. I. Laschever, Sara, 1957– II. Title.
III. Title: How women can use the power of negotiation to get what they really want.
HD58.6.B32 2008
158'.5—dc22
2007036278

Printed in the United States of America
Published simultaneously in Canada

www.bantamdell.com

BVG   10 9 8 7 6 5 4 3 2 1

Linda dedicates this book to her mom,
for her support, guidance, and encouragement

Sara dedicates it to her husband Tim:
unvarying source of inspiration, lively debate,
and loving support

CONTENTS

ASK FOR IT

I

WHY YOU NEED TO ASK

IF YOU'RE A WOMAN, you probably have a voice inside your head that whispers:

"Are you sure you're as good as you think you are?"

Or maybe it says:

"Why can't you be happy with what you've got? Don't you have enough already?"

Or perhaps, even though you're very successful, you hear that voice warning:

"Watch out. Don't get pushy. . . ."

This voice probably talks the loudest when you're thinking about asking for something you want—a raise, a better title, more power or responsibility, or even more help around the house. And the odds are, you listen to this voice. You may think it's the voice of experience, or maybe your common sense preventing you from doing something rash. Or perhaps you think you should be grateful for what you've got—you should feel lucky—and not mess things up by reaching for more.

We've written this book to help you talk back to that voice. Because that voice is not the voice of experience and it's not your common sense. It's not even *your* voice. It's the voice of a society that hasn't progressed nearly as far as we'd like to think, a society that's *still* trying to tell women how they should and shouldn't behave. It's a voice whose message is conveyed, often unwittingly, by our parents, teachers, colleagues, and friends—and then repeated and amplified by the media and popular culture.

If you have that voice in your head, whoever's voice it is, that voice is holding you back. It's slowing you down, it's damaging your self-esteem, and it's costing you money. By telling you not to ask for the things you want, that voice is cutting you off from dozens—maybe hundreds—of opportunities to improve your life and increase your happiness. It's also preventing you from learning how to negotiate for what you need with skill and confidence. It's preventing you from discovering the ways in which negotiating effectively can be an extraordinary tool for transforming your life.

WOMEN DON'T ASK

We know that this is true—that women don't ask for what they want and need, and suffer severe consequences as a result—because we've spent years studying the phenomenon. In the mid-1990s, Linda was serving as the director of the Ph.D. program at the Heinz School, the graduate school of public policy and management at Carnegie Mellon University, where she teaches. One day a group of female graduate students came to her office. "Why are most of the male students in the program teaching their own courses this fall," the women asked, "while all the female graduate students have been assigned to act as teaching assistants to regular faculty?" Not knowing the answer, Linda took the students' question to the associate dean in charge of making teaching assignments, who happened to be her husband. His reply was straightforward. "I'll try to find teaching opportunities for any student who approaches me with a good idea for a course, the ability to teach, and a reasonable offer about what it will cost," he said. "More men ask. The women just don't ask."

Could he be right? Linda recalled other situations in which a female student had protested because a male student had enjoyed some form of special treatment. One woman told Linda that she assumed she couldn't march in June graduation ceremonies the year she completed her dissertation because she wasn't scheduled to get her degree until August. She asked why Linda had allowed two men to march who also didn't finish until the end of the summer. Another woman asked why Linda had found funding for a male student to attend an important public policy conference and hadn't provided the same opportunity to her. A third woman observed a male student using department facilities to print up business stationery for himself and said she thought it was unfair that other students weren't allowed to do the same. In each case, the men had asked, and Linda, who saw it as a central part of her job to help students in any way she could, happily obliged.

Linda realized with chagrin that she'd been perpetuating discrimination—the last thing she wanted to do—simply by not noticing how much more often men asked for things that would help them get ahead. And the discrimination she'd perpetuated could have far-reaching consequences. Men with teaching experience would have meatier résumés and appear better qualified when they entered the job market than women who did not. The man who attended the public policy conference made valuable contacts that could be useful later in his career, and the woman who couldn't afford to go had missed out. The man who printed up his own stationery was able to present himself as a more polished and professional job candidate than the women who had not.

The social scientist in Linda perked up. She'd spent ten years teaching negotiation to students, salespeople, business executives, scientists, physicians, lawyers, and women's leadership groups. Did this difference in the rate of asking between her male and female students indicate that women weren't using negotiation to promote their careers as much as they could be? Was this a problem that contributed to the unequal treatment of women throughout their adult lives?

Linda turned to the existing research about gender differences in negotiation to find out. What she discovered surprised her: This large body of research looked almost exclusively at how men and women behave *when* they're negotiating. No one had taken a step back to look at what motivates people to negotiate in the first place, and—more significantly—whether men and women use negotiation to advance their goals at the same rate.

Eager to learn more, Linda and several colleagues launched a research program to explore these questions. She and her collaborators invited men and women into their research lab, asked them to play carefully designed games, and observed whether they used negotiation to improve their positions. They sent graduate students armed with questionnaires to airports and shopping malls. They designed experiments that explored the emotions people associate with negotiation. They created a huge Web survey to poll people of every age and economic group, from the lowest-skilled to the highest-paid professionals, about their attitudes toward negotiation. This survey asked participants about how and when they used negotiation and about the types of situations in which they felt they could negotiate. The bottom line: In every study, Linda's team found clear and consistent evidence that men initiate negotiations to advance their own interests about four times as frequently as women do.

THE COSTS OF NOT ASKING

Does this difference matter? Does the relative infrequency with which women assert what they want actually cost women, and if so, what are the costs? Since the wage differential between men and women still hovers around 77 percent—meaning women on average earn only 77 cents for every dollar earned by a man—Linda decided to look first at salaries. What she found shocked her: Not negotiating their salaries, it turns out, can be outrageously expensive for women. Here are a few examples of how costly it can be.

- At twenty-two, just out of college, you and a twenty-two-year-old man with the same qualifications are offered the same job for the same salary: $25,000. You accept the $25,000 while the man negotiates and raises his starting salary to $30,000. The man deposits the extra $5,000 in a low-earning account, an account that grows about 3 percent every year. Throughout your working lives, the two of you both average 3 percent annual salary increases but of course your salary can't keep pace with his because he started out higher. Every year, the man takes the difference between what he would have earned if he'd accepted the $25,000 (what you're earning) and what he's actually earning because he negotiated for more, and he adds that amount to the same low-yield account he opened when he was twenty-two. By the time he's ready to retire at sixty-five, that account contains $784,192—over three-quarters of a million dollars accumulated simply because he negotiated *that one time.* That's over three-quarters of a million dollars you *don't* have because you didn't negotiate. If the man puts the money in an account earning 5 or 6 percent, his gains would be even higher.
- At thirty, having just completed your MBA, you and a male peer receive job offers for $100,000. You take the $100,000—that's a lot of money, after all—but the man negotiates and gets his offer raised to $115,000. You both average 3 percent raises every year; he invests his extra money in an account earning 3 percent; and by the time you both reach sixty-five he's saved $1,519,486 (over $1.5 million) more than you have.

• You're forty, you're not in a high-flying profession, and you've already reached the middle of your career. You know you've been
chronically underpaid by market standards but you assume it's
too late to do anything about it. You and a male colleague in the
same position both launch a job search. You each receive offers
for $70,000 a year, which you know is at the low end of the range
for someone with your training and experience. Nevertheless,
you accept the $70,000 while your male colleague negotiates to
correct this imbalance and gets the offer raised to $77,000. Every
year until he retires, he invests the extra amount in a low-yield account and accumulates $381,067 more by the time you both
reach sixty-five—a nice addition to his retirement nest egg.

Those sums are high enough in themselves. When you add in
other forms of compensation that are often tied to salary, such as
bonuses, stock options, severance packages, and pension benefits (all
of which women are also less likely to negotiate), the financial losses a
woman can suffer from not negotiating become truly staggering.

But what if, like many of us, you don't measure your happiness by
the size of your paycheck? Even so, financial costs this steep can make
it hard to do many of the other things that matter to you more, such as
owning a safe and comfortable home, educating your children, taking
care of your family, and giving back to your community. The problem
extends beyond the financial realm, in any case. Think about all the
things you might negotiate besides your salary. Linda's research group
also found that women frequently don't ask to be promoted before a
promotion has been offered, don't request project assignments that
match their skills and interests, and don't propose taking on more responsibility as soon as they feel ready. Women don't ask if they can
work with people from whom they can learn and don't request additional training that could move them ahead faster. Women don't ask to
be recognized for their hard work, ideas, and contributions, and this
costs them dearly as well. Just as small income differences can rapidly

turn into huge disparities, small differences in how one's work is evaluated can start a process that snowballs throughout one's working life. The result is no surprise: Women earn less money, progress more slowly in their careers, and don't rise as high as similarly talented men.

SPREADING THE WORD

Convinced that these findings were too important to be confined to academic journals, Linda decided to write a book to help women understand and combat this force holding them back. She knew she needed a partner in this endeavor, however, and one who shared her passion for helping women achieve greater fulfillment in their lives. After a little searching, she found Sara.

Sara had spent much of her career exploring the barriers women face, especially in male-dominated professions, as they pursue life and career paths that differ dramatically from those of their mothers—and in many cases from those they'd originally planned to follow. She'd written extensively about women in literature and the arts, women in academia, and women in business—about their struggles and their remarkable accomplishments too.

Once the two of us joined forces, Sara set off traveling around the country, interviewing women about their experiences with negotiation. She talked to women from every walk of life; women of every age and race; women with different political views and religious beliefs; women with high school diplomas, vocational training experience, and advanced degrees from the most elite colleges in the nation. She talked to women who work full-time, women who work part-time, and women who devote all their time to caring for their children or elderly relatives. She heard story after story about women hesitating to negotiate on their own behalf and suffering the consequences.

Using these stories to help explain and illustrate Linda's data, the two of us wrote our first book, *Women Don't Ask*. In it, we looked closely

at the causes of this difference in negotiation behavior between men
and women, and showed the far-reaching impact of the phenomenon—on women, their families, their employers or employees, and society as a whole. We also established that it's not just older women who
hesitate to negotiate for themselves. Many of the younger women Sara
interviewed, especially the more successful ones, denied that they had
any trouble asking for what they want. They negotiated for themselves
just as much as their male colleagues did, they claimed. Unfortunately,
Linda's data revealed this to be untrue. Despite advances made by
women over the last few decades, the gap in the frequency with which
younger men and women negotiate is about the same as the gap between older men and women. That young women don't know this puts
them at an even greater disadvantage.

We found that the problem has a profound impact on the lives of
women outside the workplace too. Married women who work full-
time still perform two-thirds of the housework and childcare at home.
They enjoy far less leisure time than their male partners, and—unlike
men with families—experience a dramatic upward spike in their stress
levels at the end of the workday as they approach their "second shift."
Constant stress of this sort can produce sustained elevated levels of
stress hormones in one's blood, a significant risk factor for heart disease, diabetes, cancer, osteoporosis, and depression, some of the major
diseases that afflict women.

CHANGING WOMEN'S LIVES

Women Don't Ask created something of a sensation, with reviews of the
book and discussions of our ideas appearing in the *New York Times*, the
Wall Street Journal, Time, Fortune, the *Economist, BusinessWeek,* and
the *Harvard Business Review,* as well as *USA Today, Glamour, Self,
Cosmopolitan,* the *Times* (London), the *International Herald Tribune,*
and *French Cosmo.* The two of us were interviewed about the book on

local, national, and international radio and television shows, and U.S. Representatives John Dingell and Carolyn Maloney invited us to give a congressional briefing about our findings and their impact on the glass ceiling.

As thrilled as we were by this response, we enjoyed even more the hundreds of letters and e-mail messages we received from women telling us about the book's positive influence on their lives. Here are a few of the stories we heard:

- A young woman who read the book right before interviewing for her first job wrote to report that when she asked for more money the HR representative told her that she was impressed that she asked. "It's usually only the men that ask," she said.

- One woman who heard the two of us speak wrote, "I was so inspired by what you said that I went home that night and thought hard about what I wanted. I decided I wanted a raise and a better title. The next morning I went into my boss's office and asked for them. He stunned me by saying yes immediately."

- A woman who read the book wrote: "I have been a trial lawyer for nearly thirteen years and believe that I am a very good negotiator. But I have not once negotiated my salary and wouldn't have dreamed of negotiating my bonus—except for this year. I negotiated my year-end bonus and salary and was absolutely shocked when they *doubled* the bonus. And it was not a small bonus to begin with!"

- A man who'd attended one of our talks with his wife wrote: "*Women Don't Ask* has already had a profound impact on my life, as my wife was inspired to seek—and get—a significant raise from her employer."

- The mother of a college sophomore wrote that after hearing us on the radio her daughter "asked if there was bonus compensation for a job she was doing where she clearly was being asked to take on some leadership responsibilities. She would never have done it, she said, if she hadn't heard that interview! And she got the bonus."

- A woman who'd recently gotten married wrote that she interviewed several caterers for her wedding but couldn't afford the firm she liked best. Before reading our book, she said, she would have just gone with another company. Instead, she called the catering firm she really wanted and convinced them to lower their total cost enough so that she could afford it.

- A university professor who attended a talk we gave wrote to say that she'd been bothered throughout our talk by graffiti scratched into the lecture-room desk in front of her that said "Jennifer is a ho." Before, she said, she would have gone away and done nothing about it. Instead, she called the director of maintenance and asked him to have the desk repaired. "Racist graffiti scratched onto a desk would be removed immediately," she wrote. "Why are slurs against women acceptable? But until I heard you talk it wouldn't have occurred to me that I could ask for that to be fixed."

In addition to describing their successes, many women asked for our advice. "I know I need to negotiate more but I'm not sure how to start," one woman wrote. "I can't stand the idea of all the money I've left on the table during my career," wrote another, "but I still feel uncomfortable asking for what I *know* I've earned. Tell me what to do!" A third wrote, "I tried negotiating for more than I was offered a few times, but each time I panicked partway through and gave up." After every talk we give, women approach us and say the same thing: Tell us how to do it. We need to know more.

We've written *Ask For It* to answer their pleas for help. Our goal is to help them—and you—talk back to that nagging voice in your head. We want to help you feel confident and assured in saying,

"I'm not being pushy, I'm just asking for what I deserve."

"No, I'm really good at what I do. I've earned this."

And,

"This is not about how much I need, it's about how much I'm worth."

We start with that essential first step—showing you that you can ask for more than you're getting, more than you're offered, and perhaps even far more than you think it's possible to get. We describe the negotiation basics, discuss ways for you to have fun with the process, and detail strategies that have been shown to work especially well for women. By the end of the book, you'll be equipped to use the power of negotiation in sophisticated, flexible, and creative ways—and use it to achieve gains in your life that extend far beyond getting a raise or a promotion.

A Four-Phase Program

Although the main idea motivating the book—you can ask for more things than you think—is simple to comprehend, learning how to ask *well* requires some new tools. Our four-phase program will prepare you for every kind of negotiation, from the life-changing to the it-would-be-nice-if-it-happened-but-no-big-deal-if-it-doesn't. In each phase, we introduce a series of strategies and exercises that you can learn and use with great results. We describe each technique in turn, explore why it works, and suggest ways to tailor it to your particular needs or situation. We also direct you to the best sources for the information you'll need to be fully prepared.

Throughout the book, we also use stories from the lives of real women to illustrate the strategies we describe and the techniques we recommend. Many of these stories came from Sara's interviews or from the women who contacted us after the publication of *Women Don't Ask*. We also collected stories from friends and relatives, from the women who cut our hair, from women we sat next to on airplanes, from the mothers of our children's friends, and from women we met on volunteer projects. This subject strikes such a powerful chord that simply mentioning our work prompted many people to share their experiences. (In each case, we've protected their privacy by changing names and other identifying details.) We think you'll recognize yourself in many of these stories. We hope the experiences of the women whose stories we tell will help you envision putting this program into action in your own life. We hope they'll motivate you to aim high and feel entitled to reach for more than you ever thought you could get.

An early reader of the book said she thought the stories contained too many "Hollywood endings," and not all your negotiations will succeed, of course. But if you work through our program, plan ahead, and prepare thoroughly, you'll be surprised at how well you can do. You'll also learn how to glean important lessons from those negotiations that don't turn out as well as you hoped.

Phase One of our program, "Everything Is Negotiable," helps you take a step back and look at your life with a sense of expanded possibilities. Other books offer general advice about negotiating, focusing on what to do, what to expect, and how to behave during an actual negotiation. *Ask For It* starts earlier, first helping you to identify changes you'd like to make in your life, and then showing you how to make those changes happen. Where are you stuck or treading water? What do you think you deserve that you haven't been given? Are there big changes you'd love to make or a series of small ones, or both? You can improve many more aspects of your life than you think—but *only if you ask.* If you never even get to the bargaining table, whether that "table" is your boss's desk, a conference call, a community meeting hall, or your own living room couch (or in some circumstances an elevator, tennis court, luncheon buffet, or ladies' room), all the negotiating books in the world are useless. Even if you already have a specific goal in mind and just want a few tips about how to get it, Phase One is loaded with suggestions for how to aim a little higher, reach a little further, and enrich your life in ways you may not have imagined.

Phase Two, "Lay the Groundwork," shows you how to get ready for your negotiation by learning a few key skills and assembling the information you'll need to make a persuasive argument. We begin by introducing you to the basic concepts of negotiation strategy—what the pros know. We explain how to identify the information you need, and show you how and where you can easily collect that information. We help you assess the power of your bargaining position and take steps to improve that position.

In Phase Three, "Get Ready," we focus on fundamentals: how to set the right target, decide what to ask for, make the first offer (or avoid doing so if you can), and identify the best time to ask. We describe the advantages of taking a cooperative approach to bargaining—working together to find solutions that benefit both parties—rather than steeling yourself for battle and going in determined to "win." We suggest ways to manage the pace of the conversation so that you won't feel railroaded or cut off too soon. The pros and cons of bluffing, how much to concede on each "round" of a negotiation, and ways to get the process back on track if it feels as though it's headed in the wrong direction: It's all here. This phase ends with a "negotiation challenge," what we call our negotiation gym. The "gym" exercises will help you practice your new skills in a variety of situations, working up from easy ask-your-neighbor experiments to more difficult, higher-stakes challenges. Women who've worked through the negotiation gym report that by the end negotiating feels like a well-honed skill, a skill that they can call on routinely during the normal course of their days and weeks.

The final phase, "Put It All Together," helps you nail down your strategy and describes the benefits of getting together with a colleague or friend to role-play—practice—in advance. This part of the book includes advice to help alleviate the anxiety many women feel about negotiating. We give you tools to help you resist conceding too soon and show you how to prevent unexpected reactions from shaking your confidence. We also tell you how to create the best impression and avoid being branded by those time-honored epithets ("difficult," "high maintenance," "overbearing," "pushy," "not a team player") used to squelch women who come on "too strong." In the final chapter, we describe effective "endgame" tactics—how to avoid impasses, make your solution appear most attractive to the other side, and close the deal when the time is right.

DOES OUR PROGRAM WORK?

We know that our system works because Linda successfully used it to bring about dramatic changes where it all started, at the Heinz School. As part of her research program, she asked the Career Services Department at the Heinz School to add a question to the survey distributed to every student who completed a master's degree. The question was: "Did you negotiate your job offer?" In 2002, only 12.5 percent of the women had negotiated their offers while four times as many men, 51.5 percent, negotiated theirs. Linda did a quick back-of-the-envelope calculation, taking into account the students' average starting salaries, the career paths of most Heinz School graduates, and how much the students who did negotiate were able to raise their salaries. She concluded that the students who did not negotiate would lose about $1 million in income over their lifetimes.

Linda was pretty discouraged by these data—after all, she teaches the core negotiation courses at the Heinz School. She took it as a personal challenge to try to eliminate the gender gap in who negotiated their starting salaries. She offered workshops targeted specifically at women (although men were welcome and some did attend) to address the factors that hold women back from negotiating. At Linda's urging, the Heinz School also began offering a new course, Women and Public Policy, in which *Women Don't Ask* was required reading. Knowing that this was an issue close to Linda's heart, female students also began seeking her out for advice before their negotiations.

In July of 2005, three years after Linda launched this campaign, the Heinz School's career services office turned over the survey data from students who'd graduated that May. Linda was jubilant. In the 2005 graduating class, 68 percent of the women and 65 percent of the men (a difference with no statistical significance) had negotiated their job offers. Not only that, those who negotiated did so very successfully: The women were able to increase their starting salaries by 14 percent; the men increased theirs by 16 percent (again, no statistical difference).

Linda isn't finished. She continues to reach out to students, hoping that eventually everyone who graduates from the Heinz School will have learned the program laid out in this book. In addition, in 2006, Linda founded a center at Carnegie Mellon called PROGRESS (Program for Research and Outreach on Gender Equity and Society; www.heinz.cmu.edu/progress), whose mission is to teach girls and women to negotiate. Linda's first goal for PROGRESS involved developing a negotiation badge with the Girl Scouts Trillium Council, which serves 22,000 Girl Scouts in western Pennsylvania and parts of Ohio, West Virginia, and Maryland. Linda and her PROGRESS colleagues also partnered with the Entertainment Technology Center at Carnegie Mellon to develop "The Reign of Aquaria" (www.heinz.cmu.edu/progress/reignofaquaria), a computer game in which girls must use negotiation to reach the highest levels and win the game. "The Reign of Aquaria" incorporates many of the principles in this book—how to recognize opportunities to negotiate, use the basic skills of good negotiation practice, and communicate what you want. Both the badge program and the computer game have earned enthusiastic feedback from Girl Scout troop leaders, girls themselves, and parents.

Do You Need This Book?

What if you've seen other women treated unfairly but count yourself among the lucky ones whose brains and hard work have opened every door? You like your job, you're well paid, and your home life runs smoothly. You feel comfortable asking for what you want and you think you're pretty good at it. Even so, you may want to take a second look. You may not have been treated quite as well as you think. Or you may find a small change or two that would make your life easier and your job that much more rewarding. Even if you're already a good negotiator, there's plenty here to help you burnish your skills. You may discover hidden chances to move ahead even faster—or go further—than you thought it was possible to go.

If you're not quite that sure of yourself, becoming a confident and adept negotiator can enhance your sense of self-worth, expand your freedom to take chances, encourage you to try new things, and strengthen your relationships at work and at home. It can help you mediate the conflicting demands on your time and reconcile your multiple personal and professional goals—to have a fulfilling career and a rewarding personal life, advance the interests of your clients and contribute to your community, be a successful professional and a good spouse, partner, mother, and friend.

For centuries, the phrase "asking for it" has been used as an accusing finger to point at women. A woman who'd been sexually assaulted was "asking for it." A woman who'd been the victim of spousal abuse must have provoked her partner—she "asked for it."

Our goal is to help women ask for and get the things they—we—really want, to claim the phrase "asking for it" as our own and transform it into a dynamic tool for increasing our happiness and pursuing our dreams.

PHASE ONE

Everything Is Negotiable

2

WHAT DO YOU REALLY WANT?

"FROM THE TIME I was a little girl people were asking me what I wanted to be," said Vanessa, a woman in her early thirties who owns her own landscaping company. "It was kind of like the jump-rope song: 'Doctor, lawyer, banker, thief.' Pick one. But I didn't know what to pick. My mother was a teacher and my sister wanted to be a teacher so I thought I should be a teacher too. I got my teaching certificate right after college and taught sixth grade for five years. I only started to figure things out when a friend suggested I close my eyes and imagine myself doing something that made me happy. She asked me what I wanted to *do* instead of what I wanted to be. I immediately flashed on this image of myself in overalls out in the sun like a farmer. I realized that I wanted to work with plants and be outdoors. It's funny, because my mother loved gardening too, but it was just something she did, not who she was. My teaching schedule gave me the summers off, so I asked a local landscaping company to take me on as an apprentice. And that pretty much led to where I am today. Or what I am. I'm a gardener. But I never could have told anyone that's what I wanted to be. The question just stumped me."

One of the great challenges of growing up as a woman in our society is distinguishing your own desires and ambitions from the jumble
of stuff you've been told that you ought to want. If you're caught up in
the daily demands of your life, always trying to cross the next item off
an ever-lengthening to-do list, it can be hard to take a step back and
think long term. You may have become unaccustomed to looking at
the big picture and comparing where you are with where you'd like to
be. Or you may be so busy and successful that you think you've got
plenty—you've done enough, you should be happy.

The purpose of this book is to help you get more of what you want,
and the first step is to figure out what that is—what you *really* want.
Not what everyone else wants and not what you think you should
want. Not what you're willing to settle for in order to avoid conflict,
and not what you know you're pretty likely to get without asking. This
chapter provides you with a framework to help you review your current situation, revisit old goals and formulate new ones, and develop a
detailed picture of how you'd like your future to look. You may want
to change course, you may want to take several giant steps forward, or
you may just want to slip sideways. What's missing may not be anything huge, but significant nonetheless.

We start with a series of questions to help you think about your future in a systematic way. We know that your life may be complicated
and that certain changes could be difficult to achieve. To prime your
optimism, we tell the stories of several women who figured out what
was missing from their lives and found surprising ways to remove the
obstacles between them and their freshly conceived goals. You may
find yourself identifying strongly with one woman's story while feeling
less interested in the rest. Regardless of who or what mirrors your experience, the guiding principle in every case remains the same: Take
another look at your life. Make sure you're choosing the future you
want for yourself and not letting your circumstances decide for you.
Once you know what you truly want, you'll have already taken a big
step toward making it a reality.

IDENTIFY WHAT'S MISSING

To begin gauging the distance from where you are to where you want to be, work through the four sets of questions that follow.

What Do You Love?

Start by identifying the activities and conditions that have made you happy in the past and narrow in on those that you believe would make you happy in the future (sometimes they're the same).

- **What's your ideal job, the one you dream about?** What attracts you most about this job? What aspects of your dream job are missing from your current post?

- **When were you happiest at work?** Where were you working, what were you doing, and what were your expectations for what would come next? How do the circumstances of your current position differ from those when your work was most rewarding?

- **Is there something you love but stopped doing?** Did you abandon a hobby or a habit or a pastime or a personal tradition that you miss? When you were younger, did you love playing the guitar, water-skiing, or beating your dad's friends on the golf course? Reading biographies, vacationing by a particular lake every summer, or visiting your local minor league ballpark on Sunday afternoons? Or something else?

- **Are you good at something that you never get to do?** Do you pick up languages easily but never leave your hometown? Have great social skills but little contact with other people in your profession? Are you a creative problem solver but stuck in a "business as usual" environment?

- **When was your private life functioning most smoothly?** What's changed since then?

Michele—RECLAIMING AN OLD PASSION

Michele was the principal at a large suburban high school. Since taking the job, she'd spearheaded a curriculum overhaul that resulted in the school's test scores improving dramatically. Graduation rates had also increased by 6 percent during her tenure while rates at other schools in the district remained flat. In her home life, she was financially secure, married to a man she loved and admired, and the mother of two happy, healthy daughters. By all accounts, she had the perfect life—a great career, a good income, and a wonderful family—but she felt as though something was missing. She didn't know what would make her happier, however, and felt silly for wanting more when she was already so lucky.

One Saturday afternoon, she was cleaning out her basement and discovered a box of her old drawings. She'd been very artistic when she was young, and particularly loved sketching the faces of her friends, her younger siblings, and her aging grandparents. She knew she wanted a career in education, though, and as she got older drawing had dropped by the wayside. But on that Saturday, looking at her old work, she realized how much she missed expressing that side of her personality. Resolving to resurrect this hobby, she found a good drawing class at the continuing education center in her town. Unfortunately, the class met at 2:00 on Thursdays, but her school day didn't end until 2:30 and she usually stayed much later. At first, she thought she'd have to abandon the idea. Instead, she negotiated with her boss, the district superintendent, to leave school early on Thursdays with the proviso that she would stay if anything came up that required her attention.

She found that taking the drawing class not only made her happier but created what she called "a protected creative space" that was separate from both her job and her family. "It sounds like a little thing," she said, "but doing something completely different from what I do in the rest of my life—I can't tell you what it did for my sanity."

What Can You Do?

The next step is to assess your strengths and weaknesses. Make a list of each, indicating which of your strengths you most enjoy exercising and which of your weaknesses you think are most intractable—can't be changed or improved. Refine this list by separating what you see as your major strengths and weaknesses from those that are relatively minor.

Don't hesitate to ask other people to help with this process. Where do your colleagues or your supervisor see you making the biggest contribution? Do your friends think you have talents that are going to waste? Do members of your family feel that you're doing what you would enjoy the most or do they have a different perspective? Talk to your old teachers, tell them what you've done and what you've learned, and see if they have any advice. You may have become accustomed to playing a particular role in your life or seeing yourself in a certain way. Outside input can help shake up that picture or show you potential you don't realize you have.

Alison—FINDING THE RIGHT CAREER

Alison majored in biology in college, continued on to graduate school, and took a job researching skin aging at a cosmetics company. She was well paid and the work was interesting but after she'd been at the job for almost a decade she realized that she didn't want to do it anymore. She was tired of being a biologist and ready for a change.

Alison's old college roommate said Alison had never seemed particularly happy in biology. Alison's boyfriend didn't think she even enjoyed science that much. Her graduate school advisor was sympathetic but couldn't tell her what to do.

"You know what, though," he said. "Career services administers a couple of tests that show whether you have aptitude for one subject or another. I'm sure as an alum you could take them now."

Alison took three different tests at her alma mater's career services office. Afterward, she met with a counselor. "These tests show two things," the counselor said. "One, you're great with numbers. You have a real facility for applied mathematics. The other is that you process information very analytically. Have you ever thought of going into business?"

Alison never had, but the idea appealed to her. She asked her supervisor at the cosmetics company if it was possible to switch from the research side of the business to the management side. He arranged for her to get a job in the company's corporate offices with the condition that she begin studying for her MBA at night. Six years later, when we met her, she was the youngest vice president in the company's history. "Business and finance were totally unknown territory," she told us. "I was good at biology, but it wasn't especially fun for me. I'm good at this and I get a huge kick out of doing it."

What Do You Need?

Examine your life today. Which of the qualities on the following list must be present for you to feel happy with your circumstances?

- Stimulating, challenging work
- Likable colleagues
- Feeling that you're part of a team, not isolated
- Power and responsibility
- Autonomy
- Flexibility
- Clear evidence that your work is respected
- Freedom to be creative
- Feeling that you're making a contribution/doing something worthwhile
- Potential for you to earn more widespread recognition—in your field or perhaps among the public at large
- Opportunities to learn new things

- Rewarding friendships
- A stable, happy private life

Does your present situation contain enough of the qualities you need or is there room for improvement? Are some of these elements missing completely?

What Are Your Goals?

Considered honestly, how closely does your life today correspond with the life you'd like to have? Which of your early goals have you met or surpassed? Which ones are you still striving for? Are there any former goals that you've outgrown or no longer care about? Most important, what do you want now, in the immediate future? What do you want over the long term? To identify more concretely the changes you'd like to make in your life—how they may conflict or intersect, which ones have the most priority, which ones can wait—try separating your goals into the categories that matter most to you. Here are some to consider:

- **Personal goals.** Do you want to remain close to a group of childhood friends, stay in touch with the cultural traditions of your parents' generation, marry and become a mother?

- **Financial goals.** Are you resolved to avoid running up credit card bills you can't pay, set up a college fund for your kids, start saving for retirement early, earn your first million by the time you're twenty-five?

- **Athletic goals.** Would you like to run the Boston Marathon, conquer your fear of diving, learn to water-ski, improve your tennis game?

- **Goals involving hobbies and how you spend your free time.** Is it time to take tango lessons, learn to cook Indian food, make your own jewelry, teach yourself how to use a ham radio?

- **Self-improvement goals.** Are you ready to develop your leadership skills, learn French, get more organized, become a better negotiator?

- **Material goals.** Is it your dream to own your own home, a grand piano, diamond earrings, a summer cabin in the Rockies?

- **Philanthropic goals.** Are you committed to volunteering as a literacy tutor to help underprivileged children, donating time to a local arts organization, giving 5 percent of your income to charity every year?

- **Political goals.** Do you want to run for your local school board, volunteer for a presidential campaign, become a member of an organization that advances one of your core political issues?

Don't forget to include goals that might seem frivolous. As a girl Linda wanted to own a black Porsche (such are the risks of growing up in southern California, she says). When she was thirty-five, she bought herself one. Sara wanted to own a house with a yard big enough for her kids to play badminton in. Her current yard isn't quite flat enough but a friend down the street has a perfect field that she lets neighborhood children use. Linda wants to sail around the Caribbean on a catamaran. She and her husband plan to take sabbaticals at the same time a few years from now and she's researching materials to homeschool her daughter. Sara wants to see a live performance by the English comedian Eddie Izzard and she and her husband have made a pact that they'll fly anywhere in the country to see a show the next time he performs in the United States. So...do you secretly want to see how you'd look as a blonde? Attend a Trekkie convention? Get a job at HBO? Move to Colorado and work as a ski bum? Go to New York and see *The Daily Show*?

Many of your goals, of course, will not require negotiation, they'll involve commitment and follow-through on your part. But learning to negotiate effectively will make a lot of them easier to achieve.

IS IT REALLY ABOUT MORE?

Keep in mind that what you really want may not be about more—more responsibility, more money, more status. Changing your life for the better isn't always about being on the fast track or moving higher up the corporate ladder, sometimes it's about slowing down or moving sideways. So forget about the typical pathways to success in your profession. Take a fresh look at every aspect of your life and figure out what suits you. Consider hiring a personal coach to help you zero in on what would make you happier or help you strike the right balance among your many interests, goals, and commitments.

Evelyn—CAREER GREAT, PRIVATE LIFE NONEXISTENT

Evelyn worked as a commercial real estate broker in Los Angeles. In a field dominated by men, she was extraordinarily successful and widely respected by her colleagues. She earned over $800,000 a year in commissions and referrals, owned a beautiful house in the Hollywood hills, and was a vice president of her company. She traveled first class, stayed in the best hotels, and went everywhere—Europe, South America, the Far East.

At the beginning of her career, she'd had one goal and one goal only. "I wanted to be a hotshot," she says. "I wanted to be super-successful and make a lot of money. I wanted to show them what women can do and be better than all the boys." Evelyn had achieved all that and more, but for at least two years she'd felt restless. She was tired of all the traveling, she knew she was good at what she did but it no longer held much excitement for her. Plus, her social life consisted of a few close women friends in L.A. and dozens of friendly professional acquaintances around the world. Her relationships with men tended to go only so far because she was never around. Thinking about it, she realized that her goals had changed. She still wanted to be successful but she wanted to slow down a bit and achieve a better balance between her career and her private life.

After thinking about her choices and how they fit with her revised goals, Evelyn approached her boss about switching to the firm's much smaller and less lucrative residential division. At first he said no. There was no precedent in the company for people moving down to the residential division. Most people wanted to go the other way. The commercial division also had very few female VPs and he didn't want to lose one of the few women who'd risen that high in the organization. But Evelyn persisted, and after weeks of discussion she persuaded him to let her take a six-month leave from her current position to learn the residential business. Her boss was convinced that selling residential real estate wouldn't suit her and at the end of those six months she'd return to her original job. If she liked it, though, he agreed to let her go.

Those six months were "a revelation," Evelyn says. At home all the time, she finally decorated her expensive but largely empty house. She invited friends over, gave dinner parties, and went skiing in the mountains on weekends. She began seeing a man she really liked and eventually married. At the end of the six months, she told her boss that she wanted to make the switch permanent. Reluctantly, he agreed to let her go, and she never looked back.

UPDATE YOUR ROLE MODELS

When you were a girl perhaps you wanted to be a ballerina or a princess or a gymnast good enough to compete in the Olympics. Or maybe you wanted to be a movie star or play in a rock'n'roll band or become a starter on a professional women's basketball team. Maybe you wanted to be Oprah Winfrey or a female Bill Gates. When you started working, however, you probably chose role models a little closer to home: your mother, who started her own business when that was uncommon for a woman; your first boss, who always found time to mentor younger women; or the most visible woman in your field, whose job you hoped to hold someday. You had an idea about what you wanted to do and the shape you wanted your career to have, and you looked for people who represented the achievement of those goals. In many cases, those role models served two purposes—the ones who were close to home served as mentors, actively supporting your career and advising you on your progress, while those you didn't know inspired you by their example.

If you've been working for several years, however, many things may have changed. You've learned a lot, gained experience, and made a series of choices that led you to where you are today. Do your role models still provide you with useful ideas about what to do next? Has your career diverged from the path you laid out for yourself? Have you discovered that you want to do something entirely different from what you set out to do—and need new models to show you how to behave and proceed? Do the achievements of your old role models seem too modest now and do you want to aim higher? Or were the original role models you chose too remote in their success, and do their examples offer little guidance on how to get from here to there?

Step back and think about whom you admire today, or whose life you'd like to have. If female role models are scarce in your field, cast your net more widely. The lives of many successful men have a lot to teach us as well.

Samantha—MORE AMBITIOUS THAN SHE KNEW

Ever since she could remember, Samantha had wanted to be a lawyer. Her father was a lawyer, both her brothers were lawyers, and she never had any doubt that she wanted to be a lawyer too. She enrolled in law school right out of college, took a job with a midsize New York law firm as soon as she passed the bar, and made partner by the time she was thirty. She liked her work but felt restless. She was doing what she'd always wanted to do but it didn't feel like enough.

Talking with her colleagues, Samantha realized that she wanted more power and prestige. She wanted to serve as counsel to an important corporation. Someday, she might even want to serve on the board of directors of one of those companies. This would be a steep hill to climb, however, and she didn't have many female role models to choose from. Even today, very few women sit on the boards or serve as counsel to Fortune 500 firms. But one of the first female litigators to achieve national prominence was a trustee of Samantha's law school. She also learned that one of her father's classmates, a man, served as primary counsel to one of the oldest and most famous corporations in the United States. She contacted and met with both of them. They were happy to share their experiences and offer advice, and both promised to do what they could to open doors for Samantha. It took her several years, but with their help she changed the focus of her career and achieved her revised goals. She loves the high-stakes atmosphere in which she now works, and she still keeps in regular touch with those first two mentors who helped her get where she wanted to go.

Renée—CHANGING COURSE

Renée spent her summers during college working in the shop of a small company that made custom-designed furniture. Once she graduated, she planned to get her MBA and go into business. After four years of college, she was tired of school, though, and decided to continue working at the furniture maker for a year or two before going to business school. Four years passed, she'd become an expert finisher, and she still hadn't requested catalogues from any business schools. On her twenty-sixth birthday, her father called her on the phone. "So, honey," he said, "what are you going to do?"

"What do you mean?" Renée asked.

"With your career, professionally," he said. "Do you plan to stay in the stain shop forever?"

Renée was taken aback. "It's a really great company," she said. "I could do a lot worse."

"What about graduate school?" her father said.

"I don't know," Renée answered. After the phone call, she thought about her father's question and realized that she had no appetite for going to business school. What she wanted to do was design furniture. The firm where Renée worked was small and employed only one designer, a man with thirty years of experience and a national reputation. She decided to talk to him about the course of his career, hoping that she could follow a similar path.

The designer was flattered that she'd come to him for advice and invited her to apprentice with him. Renée loved the idea of an apprenticeship but she couldn't afford to spend several years without earning a salary. She assumed that the company's owner wouldn't want to pay her when she wasn't actually producing any work.

"You never know," said the designer, now her new mentor. "Why don't you ask him?"

The owner's response surprised her. He thought she'd make a great designer. The company was growing and pretty soon he expected to have more commissions than one designer could handle. Training Renée was the perfect solution. He agreed to keep paying Renée her same salary and told her to start shadowing the principal designer immediately. He also offered to pay her tuition so that she could study for her design certificate part-time at night. Renée had never expected so much, and she would never have known to ask if she hadn't identified the person whose life she wanted to emulate. After a year, she became the head designer's full-time assistant, and within five years she was designing her own line.

THINK BIG

Men are more likely than women to engage in risky behavior. This is true when it comes to physical risks (such as skydiving) and just as true when it comes to economic risks (such as investing in risky stocks). Men also tend to view most situations as inherently less risky than women do. Women's greater sense of caution has many benefits, enabling them to protect their children and themselves and preserve social stability in their communities. It even ensures that women who play the stock market perform better than men because men take too many risks and trade too much.

Women also tend to refrain from actions that put their relationships at risk. While this is a wonderful trait in many situations, it can be a handicap when it comes to negotiating. Afraid that asking for too much may make the other person angry and damage the relationship between them, women often decide that proceeding cautiously in a negotiation, or avoiding one altogether, will be a good strategy. In reality, it often means asking for less than they can get. So think big. A raise, a better title, a promotion: These are obvious next steps for many of us. But maybe what you want is more than just another step in the same direction. Let your imagination loose. Do you have any secret wishes or postponed hopes? Things you want but assume you can't get? What would surpass "good enough" and make your life feel wonderful? What do you want in your wildest dreams? Add your most extravagant wishes to your list of goals.

Angie—THE BEST PERSON FOR THE JOB

Angie worked in a manufacturing plant where less than 10 percent of the people with her capabilities and experience were women. Angie had gotten used to the expressions of surprise from every new supervisor (she'd had six in five years) when he discovered that she could keep up with any man in the place. What frustrated her was that she never felt as though the group was well run. She was sure it could be more productive with a little restructuring, but no supervisor ever stayed long enough to figure this out. For two years, she complained to her husband about the company's nearsightedness in never putting a supervisor in the job who wasn't using it as a stepping-stone to someplace else. She ticked off one after another missed opportunity to improve the group's output and control costs.

Finally, exasperated, her husband said, "Well, what do you want? Do you want to quit? Do you want to switch to another group? Do you want to go to some senior person and lay all this out?" At first, Angie was shocked by her husband's question. This wasn't about her, it was about the company and how badly managed it was. But the longer she thought about it, the clearer it became: There was something she wanted. She wanted to run the group. She wanted to be the supervisor. But since all her training was in production she assumed that the company would never promote her to a management position. She hadn't gone to business school and she didn't have management experience. Still, she felt sure that she could run the group better than anyone who'd held the job since she was hired.

Over the course of several weekends, Angie wrote up her ideas for restructuring the group and using an easy and inexpensive form of recycling to process raw materials more efficiently. She put her plan in her desk drawer at home and as soon as rumors began to circulate that her current supervisor was in line to be promoted, she took her plan to the division head and asked for the job. He was surprised, but he agreed to look at her notes. Three days later, he called her into his office. "Okay," he said, "I'll give you a shot at it. I'll make you acting supervisor for six months and we'll see what you can do." Within six months, Angie had increased the group's output by 7 percent and reduced materials costs by 6 percent. It was an amazing performance in such a short time. At the end of the trial period, the division head raised her salary by 20 percent and gave her the job permanently.

WHAT WILL YOU REGRET?

Researchers have found that people experience two different kinds of regret: regret about things they've done and regret about the things they didn't do. Overwhelmingly, people regret the things they didn't do far more. When asked to identify the biggest regret in their life, people are two to three times more likely to describe something they didn't do instead of something they did.

So try approaching the question of what will make you happy from a different angle altogether: What will you regret *not* doing?

- What one thing in your life do you most regret today? Is it too late or could you still do it?

- If there's something you wish you'd done in the past, can you do something similar that will make you feel better about passing up this old wish?

- Is there something you always planned to do but never got around to? How sorry will you feel if you never make it happen?

- What will you most regret at the end of your career if you never try it?

- What will you most regret at the end of your life if you never try it?

Beth—TOOK THE SCENIC ROUTE

As a teenager Beth did volunteer work for a presidential candidate and, she says, "caught the politics bug." In college she majored in political science and was active in campus politics. Right after graduation she began working on a congressional campaign for a hotly contested seat. She believed in her candidate, she felt like she was doing something important, and she loved the electric atmosphere of the campaign.

Unfortunately, her candidate lost, and at about the same time her father was diagnosed with prostate cancer. Her father owned a carpeting and flooring business and he didn't want to lose a lot of work to his competitors while he was sick. He asked Beth to come home and run the business until he recovered. Since Beth was out of a job, she agreed to keep the business on track until her father returned to work. Sadly, her father never recovered enough to go back to work full-time. He was in and out of the hospital for the next five years, until he died. By that time, Beth was married and had two children. Her life was too settled for her to go on the campaign trail, and she resigned herself to running a carpet business. She was good at it and made plenty of money but, she says, "Inside I felt like a failure. I hadn't abandoned my ideals, but I certainly wasn't acting on them."

When Beth's children were in their early teens, her state became embroiled in a fierce internal fight about the state's immigration policies. Beth thought her local state representative was on the wrong side of the issue and didn't represent the views of most people in the district. But he'd held his seat for twenty-four years and was running for reelection unopposed.

"You'll regret it if you don't do more to stop him," Beth's husband said to her. "You should run against him."

Beth was amused by the suggestion. She'd never even held a town office and she had no experience raising money for an election. But she decided to try. Her local popularity as a community-minded businessperson gave her a fighting chance.

She didn't win the election that year, but the campaign kicked off her career in local politics. Two years later, she successfully unseated the incumbent. Eight years later she ran for and won a seat representing her district in the U.S. Congress, a seat she still holds today. She laughs about it now. "I thought I'd be a carpet saleswoman for the rest of my life," she says. "I was not a happy person."

Leslie—LEFT SOMETHING BEHIND

Leslie lived in northern California, and throughout her early twenties she belonged to a mountain-biking club and participated in meets around the state every summer. When she was twenty-eight, she got married, and over the next four years she had three children. By then she was doing most of her biking in the local park pulling a kiddie trailer behind her.

The day after her youngest child turned eight, she had lunch with her best friend from her mountain-biking days. The two of them had dreamed about riding their bikes from one coast to the other, but her friend had also gotten married and dropped out of the biking scene. "I wish we'd gone on that cross-country ride when we had the chance," her friend said. "Boy, I miss long-distance biking."

Afterward, Leslie thought about how much she'd wanted to do that: ride from California to New York, camping along the way. In the midst of her regret, it occurred to her that it wasn't too late. She was forty but she was fit and healthy and with some training she could get back in shape. Her kids were old enough to last four weeks without her. They could spend two of those weeks with Leslie's mother at her beach house, fly out with their father and meet Leslie somewhere along the route, and then drive the rest of the way and wait for her at the end. It could be an adventure for her family too.

She talked about it with her husband, talked about it with the kids and her mother, and finally called her friend and proposed doing the trip together. "If we wait until our kids go to college we won't be strong enough," she said. "Why regret it later when we could do it now?" The two of them trained for six months before making the trip, which took them five weeks instead of four but was, in Leslie's words, "a peak experience. I can't believe I almost missed it!"

IF YOU COULD HAVE ANYTHING

As a final exercise in identifying what you really want, try asking yourself what you would want if you knew for sure that you could get it. If you could be assured that no one you know would react negatively, that there would be no political costs within your organization, no loss of prestige, no financial downside, and no sacrifice required by your family and friends. Then what would you want? In many cases, you can pursue goals that you thought were out of reach without provoking conflict, straining any of your relationships, or hurting anyone you love.

But first you need to know what you want.

3

RUN YOUR OWN LIFE

JOELEEN'S JOB required her to make four or five coast-to-coast trips a month. After two years of exhausting cross-country flights, an airline bumped her up to first class on a flight from New York to San Francisco. The extra leg room and wider seats made the flight much more comfortable, the food was better (there was food!), she got more work done, and she arrived in California feeling much less tired. Back at the office, she mentioned to a colleague how much she'd liked the first-class trip. "You mean you've been traveling cross-country in coach all this time?" he said. "The travel office will always bump you up to first class for a long flight if you ask."

Penny, a successful businesswoman who owned her own company, thought she never missed an opportunity to negotiate. If she wanted something, she didn't hesitate to go after it. Then, on a business trip to Dallas, she and her business partner stayed in a new five-star hotel that had just opened. The first morning at breakfast, Penny's partner talked about how impressed he was with the hotel: the beautiful furnishings, the gorgeous view of the city, and the quality of the room service food he'd eaten for dinner. He said his bathroom was bigger than his kitchen in New York. He asked Penny what she thought. Penny agreed that the rooms were lovely and the views were great, but she was disappointed that there wasn't a big spa-type robe in the closet, which is pretty standard at luxury hotels. Her partner laughed. "Of course they have robes," he said. "In a place like this? You just have to call down and ask."

A few months later, Penny had a second enlightening hotel robe experience. She and her family were staying at a Ritz-Carlton on vacation. There were robes in the closet for her and her husband but none for the kids. She told them that the hotel only had robes for adults but they wouldn't let it go, they wanted robes too. Rather than argue, she told her daughter to call the front desk—let them explain, she thought. So her daughter called down and within five minutes two kid-size robes were delivered to the room. She was astonished. Both incidents made her wonder: *What else have I been missing out on because it didn't occur to me to ask?*

Probably a lot.

We all know that we should negotiate the price of a house or the price of a car. We may not like it, and we may even avoid it if we can, but we recognize that negotiation is necessary in transactions of this type. But what else is negotiable? If you're like many women, the list of situations in which you believe you can negotiate is pretty short. You think that in most cases if attractive alternatives were available, you would know about them. At work, you expect that the people in power will advertise job openings, announce the existence of funds for training, and invite people to signal their interest in new projects. Outside work, you assume that the posted prices—for clothing, furniture, jewelry, snow removal, catering, vacation travel—are fixed and nonnegotiable. But many aspects of your life that you may accept as givens can probably be changed for the better.

WHO'S IN CONTROL?

Using what they call a locus-of-control scale, psychologists measure whether people believe that the controlling force in their lives is internal (they're in control) or external (outside forces determine their fate). Men for the most part believe that the locus of control in their lives is internal, that they "make life happen." Women are far more likely to believe that "life happens to them"—that they don't have much control. This is what we call the oyster-versus-turnip view of the world. Men see the world as their oyster (they're surrounded by opportunities, and they just need to choose which ones they want), while women are more likely to think "you can't get blood from a turnip" (what they see is what they get and they need to make the best of it). Although you may know some turnip men and oyster women, the underlying truth of the distinction has been conclusively demonstrated, and not just in the United States but also in countries with cultures as diverse as those in Britain, Belgium, the Netherlands, Sweden, Bulgaria, Czechoslovakia, Hungary, Poland, Romania, the former U.S.S.R., India, China, Mexico, and Brazil. These studies also showed that even senior female managers, women whose jobs involve high levels of responsibility and authority, still—far more than men in the same jobs—believe that their lives are subject to the control of external forces.

DO YOU BELIEVE IN CHANGE?

Linda and three colleagues developed a rating scale to see whether or not people view situations in their life as being amenable to change via negotiation. Women were 45 percent more likely than men to score low on this scale, meaning they saw far fewer opportunities to negotiate in their personal circumstances. Significantly, a difference of as little as 10 percent on this scale—that is, a score that was only 10 percent higher—translated into about 30 percent more attempts to negotiate.

WHO MAKES SURE YOU'RE PAID WHAT YOU'RE WORTH?

Organizational psychologist Lisa Barron asked both men and women to indicate whether or not they agreed with the following statement: "I determine my own worth and it is up to me to make sure that my company pays me what I'm worth." While 85 percent of the men in the study agreed with this statement, only 17 percent of the women agreed. But when Barron changed the statement to read, "My worth is determined by what my company pays me," the results were reversed: 83 percent of the women but only 15 percent of the men agreed. This study highlights an assumption that many women need to combat— the assumption that someone else gets to decide what their work is worth and what they should be paid. Not only does this give far too much control to other people, it's predicated on the notion that this "someone else" will be fair and that his or her judgments about the value of our work will be accurate. That's a lot of trust to put in other people.

Sandra—BADLY UNDERPAID BY INDUSTRY STANDARDS

Sandra was the vice president of a small architecture firm with seven employees. The man who owned the firm was extremely charming and worldly, qualities that were a major factor in bringing in business. But he also didn't separate his own finances from those of the firm. He went to the till whenever he needed money. Since he lived extravagantly, cash flow was always a problem. Rather than curb his own spending, he kept staff salaries as low as possible to make sure that his monthly commitments, the payments he couldn't put off, remained small.

Sandra put in many more hours than her boss and she'd designed two of the firm's most prominent and admired projects. She effectively ran the office and knew the firm would fall apart if she left. She liked her boss and liked working in a small firm. But her salary hadn't changed in three years and she knew she was badly underpaid compared to her peers at other firms. She kept waiting for her boss to give her a raise, but it never happened. Finally, she reached the point where she knew she had to get a salary increase or leave.

Arming herself with industry figures about salary ranges for her position in her region (she lived in Chicago), Sandra identified what she thought she deserved and went into her boss's office and asked for it. Her boss responded by shouting about the firm being on the verge of bankruptcy and her wanting to push it over the edge.

Instead of losing her composure or backing down, Sandra said in an even tone, "What would push this firm into bankruptcy would be my leaving. I love it here and I don't want to leave, but it's not just a matter of simple fairness. I have my professional self-respect and my future to think of too. I can't continue to work for so much less than I'm worth."

Sandra's calm response stopped her boss in the middle of his harangue. "He seemed so surprised that I hadn't backed down," she says.

"Well, how much did you say you want?" he asked.

Sandra named her figure. Without even trying to bargain, her boss said yes. A few weeks later, apparently terrified that she would leave, he raised her salary again.

Afterward, Sandra said, "I don't know why I waited so long. I just left it all up to him when I knew he'd continue to pay me as little as I let him." She'd let her boss limit what she earned instead of taking control of the situation and making sure she was paid what she was worth.

WHO CHOOSES THE WORK YOU GET TO DO?

It's a hard fact of business life today that to move ahead briskly and get paid a fair salary you need to hustle. You may expect your supervisors to take a proactive approach to management and reward good work, promote people as soon as they're ready, and cultivate the talents of everyone who reports to them. Clearly, these are things good managers should do. Unfortunately, in today's business climate, a lot of managers are too busy focusing on their own performance targets. Their management style is more reactive—they respond to crises and hand out rewards and opportunities to the people who interrupt their busy schedules and ask. This gives men a huge advantage since they're the ones who typically do the interrupting. They announce what they want to do next, make it plain that they're in a hurry, and push to move to the next level.

To determine whether you're leaving too much power in the hands of others, ask yourself the following questions:

- Do you usually wait to see what kind of raise you get or do you try to negotiate in advance for the raise you think you deserve?
- Do you wait to be promoted or to be assigned more responsibilities or do you ask for those things when you think you're ready?

- Do you think you're qualified to move up to the next level at work but assume your boss doesn't agree because he or she hasn't promoted you yet?

- Have you accepted being given the same sort of work to do over and over again even though you'd like to learn new skills and try different types of assignments?

- Do you think that if you work hard and produce outstanding results your superiors will recognize your contributions and reward you with the salary you deserve?

- Do you typically ask for changes at work that would make your life more convenient or do you tolerate small inconveniences even when you can see a simple fix?

- Have you identified the next step you want to take in your career? Does your supervisor know what you want to do?

- Do most of your colleagues perceive you as someone who's interested in moving ahead and rising in your organization or are most of your coworkers unaware of your ambitions?

If your answers suggest that you've ceded too much control to others, start volunteering for the projects on which you want to work (or projects that will earn you brownie points), don't wait to see whether you're assigned to them or not. Tell your boss, "I want to take this training course," or "I'd like exposure to another side of the business," or "I need some field (or sales, or line) experience." Don't expect people to keep you on their radar screens or to let you know whenever a new opportunity arises.

Above all, don't assume that because your boss likes you he's thinking about your professional development and the next step you need to take. He may just be happy that you're doing the job he needs done right now. He may be thrilled and relieved to have someone he can trust in an important position, and it may not occur to him that you're capable of doing a lot more. Or he may be grateful that you're not asking for more because he's getting top-quality work at bargain prices. Don't leave it up to someone else to determine the shape of your career. Identify your professional goals and figure out how to achieve them. Tell yourself, "*This* is what I want to do," "*This* is where I think I can make the biggest contribution," and "*This* is what I want to be doing in five years." And then take the necessary steps to make those things happen.

Nora—DO WHAT YOU WANT TO DO, NOT JUST WHAT YOU'RE GOOD AT

Nora, a journalist, spent a decade covering science and technology for a large metropolitan newspaper. When her son was born she needed a job with more regular hours, and she found one in the communications department of a large university.

During her first year on the job, several newsworthy but tragic events occurred at the university. These included the death of a freshman from alcohol poisoning at a fraternity party, the suicide of a depressed student, and a terrible accident during a clinical trial at the medical school. Because Nora knew how to talk to reporters from her years as a journalist her boss made her the media contact for each of these events. Nora recognized that she was good at balancing honesty with damage control, but she was frustrated too. The university's science and technology departments were producing mountains of interesting work. Whenever the university announced a newsworthy discovery, her office coordinated the publicity, writing press releases and talking to outside science writers. Nora's interest in science and technology had led her to choose the job in the first place, but rather than writing about scientific breakthroughs she was spending most of her time trying to protect the university's reputation.

At a dinner party one night, her hosts asked about her job and she described her disappointment about the kinds of work she was being given to do. "Have you talked to your boss about it?" one of the other guests asked her. "Why don't you tell him you want to do more writing?"

Nora turned this idea over in her mind for a few weeks and then went to her boss and explained her feelings. He promised to reduce her public relations burden and actually apologized for not letting her do the job he'd hired her to do. He still asked her to talk to the media on occasion but also made sure that she had plenty of time to write. "I was just doing what I was told," she says. "I don't think of myself as a passive person but I thought that if I said I was unhappy I'd be perceived as complaining."

What Can You Change?

Deepak Malhotra, now a professor of business administration at Harvard Business School, gave his students an unusual assignment when he was teaching negotiation at Northwestern University. He asked a class of adults working toward their MBAs at night to "go negotiate something in the real world." Of the forty-five students in the class, thirty-five negotiated something for themselves and ten negotiated something for an employer. The students negotiated for everything from the cost of a cup of coffee at Starbucks, the price of a wedding band, and a housepainter's bill to the terms of a performance evaluation, commitment from an employer to pay tuition and housing expenses, and increased compensation for taking on added responsibilities. The median amount of money saved by the students who negotiated something for themselves was $2,200. The median amount saved by those who negotiated something for their employers was $390,000 (and these were just the medians; some saved more).

Afterward, Malhotra asked his students to name the most important tactic that had helped them achieve these extraordinary results. Almost unanimously, they said, "Choosing to negotiate at all." The biggest benefit of completing the assignment, they reported, was learning that they could negotiate for things that they'd never thought were negotiable.

With this in mind, start thinking in a bolder way about what's available and about the possibilities for change. If you're unhappy with the status quo or there are certain aspects of your life that cause you constant frustration, start with the premise that they can be changed, and set about figuring out how to do so. Instead of wondering "Is that negotiable?" assume that it is.

Luisa—WAITING INSTEAD OF ASKING

Luisa worked at a small regional art museum that mounted two original shows a year in addition to hosting two or three traveling shows organized by other museums. Although she'd majored in art history in college, Luisa didn't have an advanced degree and had started at the museum as an administrative assistant to one of the principal curators. Since she was smart and hardworking, her boss quickly shifted more and more responsibility onto her shoulders. After ten years, she was working closely with the curators and assistant curators to develop the conceptual approach for each show. On her boss's behalf she made initial contact with curators at other museums all over the world when her museum wanted to borrow pieces for a show. She drafted catalogue copy and collaborated with curators in scripting the recorded guides for museum patrons to use as they browsed through an exhibit. She received regular raises and felt she was fairly compensated for her work, but in ten years her title had never changed. She was still an administrative assistant. She chafed at the inaccurate impression this title conveyed about her actual function, but she assumed her boss didn't change her title because she lacked that advanced degree.

One day an assistant curator who'd just been hired from a larger museum spotted her name among a list of contributors to the catalogue for an important exhibition.

"That's a bit grand for an administrative assistant, don't you think?" he said to Luisa. "Putting your name in the catalogue."

Luisa was incensed. The man's tone had been insulting and he clearly didn't know how much she'd contributed to conceptualizing and organizing the show. She went straight to her boss and protested. He apologized profusely and immediately changed her title to "senior project manager," saying, "We should have done this years ago." He also raised her salary 10 percent. "This place couldn't function without you," he said.

Afterward, Luisa wondered why she hadn't asked for the better, more accurate title earlier. Everyone who'd been at the museum for any length of time recognized how much she contributed. Her boss clearly did.

"I just assumed it was up to him," she says. "Since he hadn't changed it, I figured he had a good reason."

Instead, tied up in his own work, her boss never thought about it. The new assistant curator had motivated Luisa to do something she could have done years earlier: exert more control over her career by asking for what she wanted and what she'd earned. Instead she waited for something to change—and she waited a long time.

What Drives You Crazy?

In addition to fixing sizable problems, don't forget that you can probably improve many of the smaller, less-than-ideal aspects of your life too. Pay attention to daily irritants, those inconsequential things that happen all the time and consistently make you frustrated or annoyed. Does the man in the office next to yours regularly poach your office supplies instead of going to the supply closet to fetch his own? Talk to him about it. Are the women's bathrooms at work always grubby and unclean smelling? Ask the office manager to discuss the problem with your firm's janitorial service. Does your boss frequently throw you an extra project at 4:00 on Friday afternoon? Go into his office at noon on Friday and ask him to spell out what he needs from you by the end of the day. Does the coffee at work taste dreadful? See if your company will invest in a better coffeemaker and better-quality coffee. Would you like to listen to music through headphones while you work, and actually think this would boost your productivity, but assume it's not acceptable since no one else does it? Explain this to your manager and see how he or she responds. Does the person who cleans your house always unplug your VCR to use the outlet, forcing you to reset the clock every week? Ask him or her to use another outlet in the room that only has a lamp and a CD player plugged into it. Sometimes small changes can make a world of difference.

Melanchtha—CAN EXCEPTIONS BE MADE?

Melanchtha worked for a downtown advertising firm in accounts payable. Until her oldest child moved up to middle school, she took a commuter train into the city from her house in the suburbs. The middle-school bus came fifteen minutes later than the elementary-school bus, however, and waiting for the bus with her daughter made Melanchtha miss her regular express train. If she took the local that followed, she arrived at work thirty minutes late. She started driving downtown instead. Only management-level employees were given parking spots in the company's garage, however, forcing Melanchtha to park on the street and feed her meter every hour or two. She worried constantly, with a feeling of mounting panic, that she'd get out there too late, and even so she began accumulating expensive parking tickets.

One day her boss stopped by Melanchtha's desk. "What's going on with you, Melanchtha?" she asked. "For the past few months you've seemed like you have a cloud over your head." Melanchtha explained her parking situation and how distracting it was. "I can fix that," her boss said. Two days later, she returned with a sticker for Melanchtha's car and a pass card that would let her use the company garage.

WHO CAN YOU ASK FOR HELP?

Like Melanchtha, a lot of women try to make the best of things, often at great personal cost, even when it becomes obvious that a situation is careering out of control. If you need help because your responsibilities or the demands on you or your personal circumstances have changed, try pointing this out. Ask for help in the spirit of "here's a problem we need to solve" rather than "I'm overwhelmed and can't handle my job."

Victoria—CAN'T DO IT ALL

Victoria was a social worker at a large home for the elderly. When she started at the job, she had a reasonable caseload and no trouble keeping up with her paperwork. Five years after she started, she was promoted to supervisor of the social-work team, which included six full-time social workers and two part-time grief counselors. At the same time, the state instituted more rigorous reporting requirements for nursing homes and began biannual inspections. Victoria wanted to continue working with patients—that was why she became a social worker in the first place—but the responsibilities of managing her team and the paperwork she had to fill out for the state left her very little time. She grew increasingly unhappy about the quality of care she was able to provide to her patients and their families.

At her first performance review as supervisor, a year after she was promoted, Victoria told her boss that she needed an administrative assistant to help with her paperwork because patient care was suffering. She was worried that her boss would think the supervisor's job was too much for her, and the nursing home's management had always been resistant to change, but she was frustrated and worn out and decided to ask anyway. To her surprise, two months later Victoria's boss called her into her office to talk about the situation. Together, they figured out that even half-time clerical help would free up a lot of Victoria's time, and that the nursing supervisor could probably use help too. When her boss proposed to the nursing supervisor that she and Victoria share the services of a full-time assistant, the nursing supervisor's eyes filled with tears. "I can't tell you what a huge difference that would make," she said. "I feel like I'm always behind, always letting people down. But I didn't have the nerve to ask." Working quickly, Victoria's boss hired someone for the assistant's position within six weeks. Afterward, Victoria said, "Now I don't know how I did it all. I was exhausted all the time. My husband was pressuring me to quit. And I would have too, if I hadn't made up my mind to just see if the situation could be fixed."

How Do You Make Decisions at Home?

Negotiation can be a valuable tool outside of work as well. Although many women today think of their primary relationships (their relationships with spouses or life partners) *as* partnerships—partnerships in which they share both responsibilities and dreams—in practice working women continue to take on far more than an equal share of the household chores. Although your family may depend on two incomes and you couldn't stay home full-time if you wanted to, you may still feel as though you should be able to do everything a full-time mother and housewife can do. We've already talked about the stress and health damage this can cause. With that in mind, start asking for help with some of the chores that wear you down.

Sara—A BETTER BALANCE

Even after writing *Women Don't Ask* and encouraging women everywhere to ask for more of what they needed, Sara was stuck in an unbal-
anced household routine that she hadn't thought to change.

Sara and her husband are both full-time writers and work at home.
For a long time, although they were both committed to a fifty-fifty
split of chores and childcare, they weren't completely successful. Since
her husband can't cook, Sara did all the cooking and the grocery shopping. Her husband hates yard work, so Sara took care of the garden.
Sara's better at managing their finances and paid the bills. She'd sign
the kids up for after-school sports and lessons, buy presents for them
to take to birthday parties, and choose camps for them to attend in the
summer. It wasn't that Sara's husband did nothing: He washed all the
dishes, mowed the lawn, took out the garbage, and participated fully
in taking care of their two boys before and after school and on the
weekends. He took the car to be fixed when it needed servicing.

This arrangement worked pretty well. The kids' lunches got
packed, the refrigerator was usually well stocked, and most of the time
the toilets (at least) were clean. The one thing Sara couldn't seem to
keep under control was the laundry. Morning after morning, she'd
find herself running around looking for soccer socks for one child, a
T-shirt for the other, and underwear for herself. Sheepishly, she sent
her kids to school more than once with spaghetti sauce on their jeans
and mud on their jackets.

One Monday morning Sara was dashing up and down stairs looking for her younger son's favorite shirt when she spotted her husband
reading the newspaper at the kitchen table. She stopped. "Honey," she
said, "I have a proposal for you. How would you feel about taking over
the laundry? I just can't keep up with it. Could you take it on as your
responsibility? Could that be one of your family jobs?" Her husband
thought about it for a minute, and said, "Sure. I can do that. I'll be the
laundry guy."

Now, although the kids' laundry isn't always in their drawers when they need it, it's usually washed and folded in a laundry basket, and that's a huge improvement as far as Sara is concerned. It was a small change, but it took a long time for her to realize that she didn't need to feel stuck with a situation that clearly wasn't working, and she didn't need to assume that the problem was hers alone to solve.

Anne—ASK FOR CHANGES AS SOON AS THE SITUATION GOES OFF-TRACK

The fall after they were married, Anne entered law school and her husband, Robert, started business school. In addition to her class work, Anne also managed their household—paying the bills, shopping for groceries, cooking meals, cleaning the house, doing laundry, running errands, and taking care of the yard. She'd done most of these things before they were married because she worked fewer hours than Robert. Now that they were both students with comparable demands on their time, it didn't occur to Anne that this could change. By Christmastime, she was overwhelmed and exhausted. She was disappointed in her grades and wished she had more time to study. The second semester wasn't any better. After only three weeks, she'd fallen so far behind that she thought she'd have to drop a class.

Then something unexpected happened. Anne fell walking down a flight of stairs and broke her leg. While she could still get to her classes on crutches and do her schoolwork, she could no longer handle most of the household chores. As a result, she and Robert essentially switched roles. Anne quickly caught up with her schoolwork and began to excel in her classes. Robert, on the other hand, started falling behind. He couldn't believe how much time it took to manage their household. He admitted to Anne that he'd thought she spent perhaps five hours a week on housework when it turned out to be more like sixteen or eighteen. He apologized for taking what she'd done for granted.

When Anne's leg healed, she and Robert sat down to reassess who did what. After a few months of trial and error, they worked out a system that kept the house running smoothly and gave both of them enough time to do their schoolwork. "It never would have occurred to me to ask Robert for help if I hadn't broken my leg—truly, it never crossed my mind," Anne said. "Robert's not unreasonable. He wants me to succeed in school. But it took breaking one of my bones for me to realize that he could take on some extra chores now that I was busier."

The importance of negotiating outside work can extend well beyond the distribution of chores, however. Sometimes we're so busy we forget to ask ourselves whether we're really happy, if perhaps something is missing. Many of us also bring unexamined expectations about mutual decision making to our relationships. We take it for granted that we'll make important decisions together, as a team, or we assume that we're in agreement with our partners about shared goals even though we've never actually discussed them. Will you be ready to negotiate your new situation when your husband loses his job, or gets a great opportunity in another city, or you have twins, or your father gets Alzheimer's disease? You need to know how to recognize and speak up for your needs, and even negotiate hard to get them met.

Stella—DON'T LET YOUR LIFE RUN YOU

Stella was the managing editor of an arts and antiques magazine. Her husband Don was a sportswriter at their city's daily paper and traveled frequently to cover sporting events around the country (and sometimes around the world). They both made good salaries, they owned a beautiful apartment, and they dined at the best restaurants in every city. They traveled a lot and lived an exciting, cosmopolitan life.

Stella had always assumed that she'd become a mother at some point, and she even occasionally dreamed about the daughter she expected to have. But Don never signaled that he cared much whether they had children or not, and Stella turned forty without ever sitting down with Don to make a conscious decision one way or the other. Then, when she was forty-one, Stella accidentally became pregnant. She and Don were surprised by how excited they were at the prospect of becoming parents. At ten weeks, sadly, Stella miscarried. She tried again and miscarried a second time. She and Don consulted fertility specialists, but she was forty-two by that time and the doctors told her it would be an uphill and expensive battle, and the odds that she'd conceive a viable pregnancy were small.

Stella was heartbroken. She hadn't stopped to say, life is crazy and good in so many ways, but maybe it's a little out of control and I need to take a step back. I need to assess where I am and what else I want. After several months of grieving, Stella realized that the game wasn't over. She could still become a mother if she really wanted to. A month before her forty-fifth birthday she and Don adopted a little girl from Guatemala.

Luann—WE NEED TO TALK ABOUT THIS FIRST

Luann was a successful clothing entrepreneur with her own line of high-quality athletic apparel for women. She'd started her business when she was twenty-five and fresh out of business school; by her thirtieth birthday, the company had annual sales of $150 million. When she was thirty-two she opened her first retail store, and within three years she'd opened eighteen stores nationwide. Unlike many women, she'd never really imagined herself as a mother and felt no strong desire to have children. She'd seen the demands that parenthood made on some of her friends, and she couldn't see any way that having a child wouldn't force her to scale back her career.

Luann's husband, Jason, had a successful career as a hospital administrator, but he also very much wanted to be a father. And he felt strongly, knowing Luann as well as he did, that Luann would be glad she'd had a child if she did it. Luann loved Jason and wanted him to be happy, so the two of them worked out—negotiated—a solution. They agreed that they would have only one child, that Jason would take a leave from his job to be home with the baby for the first year of the child's life, and that when he returned to work they would hire a full-time nanny. Jason would do at least half the childcare when the nanny wasn't working and Luann would continue to travel as much as she needed to as her business grew. Once they decided to go ahead, Luann quickly became pregnant. When the baby was born, she found, just as Jason had predicted, that she immediately fell in love with her son. She's still just as invested in her career, though, and glad that she and Jason were able to think through the implications of their decision together.

So it's up to you. If you want more (more money, more responsibility, more interesting work, more opportunities, more anything) or you want something else (a new house, another child, a pet, a different boyfriend, a break in your routine, another degree, someone to mow your lawn) you need to resolve to get it for yourself. This is your only life. You might as well make the most of it.

4

FAIRNESS—YOU BE THE JUDGE

MOST WOMEN do not think that they've been unfairly treated. Although the vast majority of American women believe that women in general suffer discrimination in this country, in study after study researchers can find very few women who say that they themselves have experienced discrimination. If you're one of those women, you might want to check again. You may be the victim of a phenomenon that the social psychologist Faye Crosby calls "the denial of personal disadvantage," in which members of a particular group recognize that other members of their group have suffered discrimination but believe that they themselves have escaped unfair treatment.

What could cause such a strange discrepancy between women's beliefs and their experiences? One explanation could be that it's hard to confirm discrimination in any particular case but easy to detect at an organizational or societal level.

This is how it works: Suppose that a man receives a promotion over a woman and the man has more experience but the woman has more education. The woman might conclude that her employer values experience over education, which is why the man was promoted ahead of her.

If this same woman were to have access to personnel data for the company as a whole and look at the larger picture—the percentages of men and women promoted throughout the organization—she might clearly see a systematic pattern of discrimination. Very few of us get to see that larger picture, however, and it's often not obvious at all that we've been treated unfairly even when we have.

You may think that this is old news and no longer a problem today. We've met many young women who say this type of discrimination is a thing of the past. All those old battles have been won, they tell us confidently. Women are everywhere in the workplace, where's the problem? Regretfully, we have to warn them: It's illogical, bad for business, disappointing, and hard to accept, but negative attitudes about women's abilities persist in today's society and in subtle but pernicious ways they prevent women's work from being evaluated on its own merits.

RECOGNIZE THE POWER OF SUBCONSCIOUS BIASES

None of us wants to think that our coworkers and supervisors, people we like and respect, treat us differently because we're women. We respond to each event in our lives as it happens, ascribe positive motives to the people around us, and assume that they have good reasons for making the decisions they make, even if we're not completely sure what those reasons may be. The kicker is, they may not fully understand their reasons either, because their decision making may be influenced by subconscious biases of which they're not aware.

Research has shown that subconscious biases exert a powerful influence over people's behavior, and that most of us hold these biases without realizing how they influence our judgments. This same research confirms that subconscious biases about women's abilities often cause well-intentioned people to devalue the work of women simply because they're women. People feel more reluctant to promote an un-tried woman into a position of greater responsibility than they feel promoting an equally untried man, for example. And they may not understand or stop to examine the sources of their reluctance.

A group of prominent psychologists, Mahzarin Banaji, Anthony Greenwald, and Brian Nosek, have found a way to get inside people's heads and measure what they really think about women in the work-place. (They use this tool to measure the power of many other types of bias as well.) The researchers asked participants in the study to log on to a Web site and watch as a series of words appeared on the screen one at a time. The researchers chose a series of men's names, a series of women's names, words associated with work, such as *salary, office, business,* and *career,* and words associated with home, such as *parents, children,* and *family.* They asked participants to place a left finger on the *e* key on the left side of the keyboard and a right finger on the *i,* on the right side of the keyboard. If a word appeared on the screen that participants associ-ated with either men or work they were told to press the *e* key with their left finger. If a word that they associated with either women or family ap-peared, they were told to press the *i* key with their right finger. Each par-ticipant worked through a list of words and the researchers timed them to see how long it took them to complete the task. The participants were then asked to repeat the task but this time they were told to switch: to press the left key (the *e*) if they associated a word with either men or *home* and to press the right key (the *i*) if they associated a word with women or *work.* The researchers found that it took the vast majority of the participants, both men and women, significantly longer to com-plete the second round because people find it harder to associate women with work (and presumably men with home) than to associate men with work and women with home. When we last looked, over 83,000 people had taken this particular test with similar results.

You may think that you're not one of those people but you can find out. Log on to www.implicit.harvard.edu and take the gender/career test yourself. At a conscious level you don't find it difficult to associate women with work. Nonetheless, like pretty much everyone else who has taken this test, it will probably take you twice as long to pair women with work as it would for you to pair women with home. We've both taken it, and our experience was identical to that of the original participants in the study. This doesn't mean that we believe women shouldn't be in the workplace, it merely shows the power of cultural socialization on the subconscious workings of our minds. Unfortunately, psychologists believe that these subconscious biases influence our behavior in ways we don't realize and can lead us to make subconscious associations and judgments that directly oppose our consciously held opinions. This can lead to a manager undervaluing a woman's work performance without knowing that he or she is doing so. Since most people don't understand how subconscious biases can influence their judgment, they don't adjust for these biases, and can inadvertently end up discriminating against women.

PLAYING LIKE A GIRL

Judging the musical ability of a top-ranked musician auditioning for a symphony orchestra might seem pretty straightforward. Some people are clearly superior musicians and presumably any expert can tell the difference. As it turns out, this is far from the case. Two economists found that the use of a screen to hide the identity, and thus the gender, of auditioning musicians increased by a full 50 percent the probability that a woman would advance in the audition process. Using a screen increased the likelihood that a woman would win an orchestra seat by 250 percent.

Other studies have also revealed the power and persistence of subconscious biases. Using what came to be known as the Schein

Descriptive Index, the psychologist Virginia Schein assembled ninety-two words and phrases commonly used to describe people's characteristics. She then asked people to choose words that they associated with men, words they associated with managers, and words they associated with women. She found that participants chose many more of the same words to describe both men and managers, and very few of the same words to describe both women and managers.

MEN ARE LEADERS, WOMEN ARE BOSSY

To study whether people respond differently to men and women who exhibit "leadership behavior," researchers assigned male and female actors to small groups whose members didn't know they were actors. The actors had been coached to remain cooperative and pleasantly assertive while the group worked together to make a series of decisions. Researchers observed that the participants responded much more positively to the male actors playing these leadership roles than to female actors behaving in identical ways. Afterward, participants described the men as having "more ability, skill, and intelligence" while they saw the women as "emotional, bossy, and domineering." Asked directly about their attitudes toward men and women in leadership roles, the participants reported no sex biases and believed that they held none.

On the job, these unrecognized prejudices can play out in a number of ways, particularly if an organization hasn't developed a detailed and specific system for evaluating the work of individual employees. Managers may decide not to promote women for vague and largely subjective reasons—they "need more experience," "lack leadership potential," or just "aren't ready yet." If women in these organizations participate in the work of a team and the team turns out excellent work, the women typically receive the least credit for the team's success.

Evaluations of a woman's work may also be skewed if she's working in an area in which there are very few other women, which is common in certain professions, in specialties heavily identified as "masculine,"and at senior management levels in most organizations. Compounding the problem, the more power and status associated with a job, the more "masculine" it's perceived to be. When women rise to the highest levels of senior management where there are few other women—when they're perceived as tokens or as trespassers in a male domain—they're more subject to stereotypical judgments about their work. Since subjective judgments can have a huge impact on the evaluation of a senior executive's performance, women who reach these heights of success often find their work slammed for reasons that they can't clearly identify as sexist or discriminatory.

Jacie—"HE TOTALLY OVERLOOKED ME!"

Jacie worked for a home heating-oil company in New England doing cold calls: calling up new home buyers and trying to sign them up as customers. She had an appealing voice and she never pushed a hard sell, and her "hit rate"—the percentage of contacts she was able to turn into customers—was the highest in her office. After Jacie had been with the company for two years, her boss, Raymond, was promoted and moved to corporate headquarters. He gave his old job, regional sales manager, to Jerry, the only male in the office, who'd started at the company six months before Jacie.

Eighteen months later, Jerry was abruptly fired. The following week Raymond took Jacie out to lunch. He said he wanted to explain why he'd let Jerry go because he knew Jacie liked Jerry.

"The thing is," Raymond said when they sat down, "Jerry was a disaster at managing his budget. The amounts he posted for overhead costs swung wildly from quarter to quarter. None of his numbers tracked. He was a great guy but he just didn't have the skills. We've already started a search and hope to have someone in place in six to eight weeks."

Jacie was a little confused. "You're going to hire someone from the outside to fill Jerry's job?" she asked.

"Why, yes, of course," Raymond said. "We don't have anyone—" He stopped. "I assume you're not interested?"

"Why would you assume that?" Jacie said.

"Well, I don't know." He seemed confused. "Would you be comfortable with the financial management end of things?"

"Raymond!" she said. "You hired me! Do you even remember my résumé? I majored in marketing in college but I minored in finance. I'm not afraid of numbers. I could do a hell of a lot better job managing the office than Jerry did, and certainly better than anyone you could bring in from outside. I know the company. I know the territory. And I know what things around here cost." A few days later, Raymond offered Jacie the job.

Raymond hadn't considered her for the job, Jacie was sure, not because he consciously believed that women don't make good managers but because it never occurred to him. "He totally overlooked me," she said. Despite her abilities, Jacie wasn't even on Raymond's radar screen.

Back when Raymond promoted Jerry, Jacie didn't think she'd been treated unfairly. She liked Raymond, she knew he liked her, and she assumed he had good reasons for his decision. When she finally took over the regional manager's job she realized that even eighteen months earlier she'd been a far better candidate than Jerry. Jerry had majored in communications. He had no financial management background at all.

BIAS WITHOUT MALICE

We tend to assume that most people wouldn't consciously cheat us, and most probably wouldn't. But there's a world of difference between not consciously cheating someone and checking regularly for inadvertent inequities. And of course people also differ about what they consider to be fair. Many people think "She didn't ask so I didn't give her more" is perfectly fair. You had a chance to negotiate, you didn't take it, and that's your problem, not his (or hers). Even people who believe that they're committed to equal opportunity and opposed to gender bias can fail to adjust the scales if a woman doesn't ask for more than she's offered. We think this is wrongheaded and penalizes women for a social problem foisted upon them by society. But it's the reality in many situations.

Mary—TIME TO BE PAID WHAT YOU'RE WORTH

Mary was a successful plant biologist at a large state university. She was highly sought after to speak about her research at scientific meetings and was one of the few women who'd reached the top ranks of her profession. As far as she could tell, she'd encountered few obstacles in her rise to prominence in her field. She didn't think she'd ever been treated unfairly because she was a woman.

Like many scientists, Mary had to apply for grants to fund her research. The grant money she brought in went directly to her department, which used some of it for overhead, paid Mary and her research assistants, and covered her lab costs. Since her research was very specialized, for most of her career Mary didn't collaborate with other researchers at her institution.

When Mary was in her fifties, she and six of her colleagues put together a grant proposal to conduct a long-term joint study. As part of the proposal, all seven scientists had to submit their salary requirements. When Mary saw the other six scientists' salary requests, she realized that they were all earning more than she was, even three scientists who were much more junior than she was.

Mary was furious. "I was ready to quit on the spot," she said. "I'd had plenty of offers from other universities. I knew I'd have no problem getting another job." As she was typing up her resignation letter (with "steam coming out of my ears," she said), a male colleague came into her lab. "I told him what I was doing and he asked if I'd ever negotiated my salary with the department head. When I said no, he told me he negotiated his salary every year and made it his goal to get at least 3 percent more than he was offered."

Mary had always just accepted the raises she'd been given. Since most of her colleagues routinely negotiated for more, the gap between her salary and theirs had widened every year. "I was truly shocked," she said. "I thought the university had some sort of scale and paid everyone at the same level equally," she told us. "I was incredibly naïve! I'd worked hard all those years and never thought once about whether I was being paid fairly." Mary never asked for more so her department head hadn't offered her more. As far as he was concerned that was one piece of paperwork, one administrative matter, that didn't require further attention.

Once Mary realized how things worked, she went directly to her department head and asked to have her salary raised to $10,000 more than the salary of her best-paid colleague. "I'm better known in the field, I've published more papers, and I've been underpaid for years," she said. "I've always been loyal to this place. Don't convince me that I was wrong."

Her department head initially seemed confused. "I thought you were comfortable with what you were getting," he said. "I figured—I don't know—that you weren't especially materialistic."

"Materialistic!" Mary said. "I have two kids in college! Materialism has nothing to do with it. Besides, I bring in more grant money than anyone else here. I should get paid what I'm worth to the department. And I'm worth a lot."

Her department head agreed, apologized for what he called "the misunderstanding," and gave her the raise. As soon as she left his office, Mary went straight to the labs of the other women in the department and made sure they all knew that they needed to negotiate their salaries too.

People in power may not mean to favor men, but if they don't recognize this problem and take steps to correct it, by default they're going to be handing out resources and opportunities inequitably. The people who ask for more get more than the people who don't. Talent and hard work only take us so far.

Jeanne—PARTICULARLY OUTRAGEOUS

Jeanne, a prominent legal scholar, worked at a private think tank analyzing the impact of legal rulings on wage discrimination in the United States. Concerned about diversity in the workplace, a large government agency commissioned her and two of her male colleagues to investigate whether there was wage discrimination at the agency. Halfway through the project, one of the people she'd gotten to know pretty well at the agency told her that her two male colleagues were earning twice as much as she was for doing the same job. It turned out that the agency had offered all three the same fee. Jeanne, assuming that there was a set fee for the job since it was a government contract, accepted what she was offered. Her two colleagues had negotiated and doubled their fee. She found this particularly infuriating since the three of them had been hired to assess gender discrimination in the very agency that was paying them unequally for the same work.

CULTIVATE THE RIGHT NETWORKS

Women may not know they're being treated unfairly for another reason as well: They're typically excluded from men's social and professional networks—networks through which men exchange information, build alliances, and help each other position themselves for advancement. Women are also less likely than men to participate in social activities with their colleagues, sometimes because of family demands and sometimes simply because they haven't been invited. As a result, they often don't know as much about office politics. They don't know what to ask for, or who, when, and how to ask.

Ainsley—ACCESS TO INSIDER INFORMATION

Ainsley was a surgeon at a major teaching hospital in southern California. Eight years after she started at the hospital, Ainsley discovered that the male surgeons in the department held an annual round-robin tennis competition, with matches every week from May to September. Ainsley had been on her varsity tennis team in college and knew she could probably beat half the guys in her department. But it had never occurred to them to invite her or any of the female surgeons to play, and none of the women had known about the tennis group. Ainsley immediately asked to join.

She quickly discovered that there was a lot more going on besides a friendly game of tennis. She was shocked by how much information was exchanged on the courts. The other surgeons discussed hospital politics, gave each other advice about getting onto powerful hospital committees, and shared gossip about which older surgeons were thinking of retiring, who the department head was trying to bring in from a snooty East Coast medical school, et cetera. At the end of the summer, a seat opened up on an important management committee at the hospital, and this was not widely known. But Ainsley learned about it from her tennis pals. She proposed herself as a replacement for the retiring doctor whose seat had become available. Ainsley was well qualified, had the support of her tennis-playing pals on the surgical staff, and was elected to fill the seat. No female surgeon had ever sat on the committee. This experience showed her the power of "insider knowledge" and woke her up to the value of building important networks.

EVALUATING FAIRNESS

How do you know if you're being treated fairly? To many of you, it may be obvious that you're not; some of you may be unsure; and others will be convinced that you've been treated just like everyone else (this may be especially true if you're under thirty). Since many explicit forms of unfairness, such as rules preventing women from applying for particular kinds of jobs, have largely been abolished, you may assume that there are few remaining barriers to women. You may conclude that you've received a pretty fair shake all in all. At the risk of sounding like your mothers, we urge you to take a step back and consider whether this view truly reflects reality. Use the questions below to achieve a more accurate picture of your situation.

- **Gender equity**
  - Has your organization made an open commitment to gender equity?
  - Does your organization track promotion and hiring decisions to ensure gender equity?
  - Does your organization conduct regular compensation analyses to ensure that men and women are paid equally for equal work?
  - Has your organization made managers responsible for ensuring that the women they supervise advance at the same rate as the men?

- **Evaluation systems**
  - Does your organization use evaluation systems that are de-

tailed, precise, and consistently applied, so that everyone performing the same function at the same level must meet the same standards and performance targets?

– Are your organization's evaluation systems transparent and widely understood?

– Does your organization tie promotion decisions directly to performance or can these decisions be influenced by vague or subjective criteria, such as management ability or leadership potential?

– Is information about your performance collected from a wide variety of sources or does it rest on the judgment of one person?

• **Compensation**

– Does your organization tie salary decisions to performance and use objective criteria such as sales figures, billable hours, department productivity, or employee, student, or customer evaluations?

– Does your organization give all employees a cost-of-living increase every year and award merit increases on top of that? If so, do you understand the process for deciding who gets merit increases? Do you know whether your organization gives merit increases frequently or if this is rare?

– Are there levels, categories, or ranks in your organization and is compensation limited by level?

– Does your organization award bonuses? If so, do you understand how bonuses are determined?

– Does your organization offer any nonmonetary forms of compensation, such as housing assistance, company cars, stock options, college tuition for your kids, access to company-owned vacation properties, sweetened retirement packages? If so, do you understand the system for awarding these alternative forms of compensation?

– Does your company offer managers and/or personnel executives

incentives to keep salaries as low as possible? Does the person
you must ask for a raise have a personal stake in not giving you
more?

— Does your organization prohibit employees from discussing
their salaries, signaling that it may want to restrict access to information in order to keep compensation as low as possible?

• **Advancement**

— Does your organization make promotion decisions (not just
salary decisions) based on vague or subjective criteria such as
management ability or leadership potential rather than on
more objective factors such as sales figures, billable hours, department productivity, or employee, student, or customer evaluations?

— Does your organization rely on a ranking system to identify
functional areas or levels of seniority within the organizational
hierarchy? If so, is it possible to skip a level or adjust your ranking if you're qualified, you've expanded the scope of your job, or
you've been asked to do more than you were originally hired
to do?

— Are the lines of advancement at your organization very structured and rigid or is there more than one way to progress in the
direction you want to go?

— Are all employees reviewed for advancement at the same time
(biannually? annually?) or is the process more unstructured,
leaving room for managers to overlook qualified employees or
make decisions arbitrarily?

— Do one's personal connections influence advancement decisions? Is it what you know or whom you know that determines
whether you're promoted?

— Have you ever discovered that you missed an opportunity to
advance because you didn't know an assignment or job was
available?

- **Hiring**
  - Does your future employer announce salary ranges for particular jobs or functions or does it pay on a case-by-case basis, making negotiation particularly crucial in getting what you're worth?
  - Does the company for which you want to work make "I-deals" (idiosyncratic deals), tailoring hiring contracts to suit the qualifications and needs of particularly desirable employees?
  - Before making you an offer, has a potential employer asked you to reveal your previous salary or state your salary requirements—forcing you, essentially, to make the first move in the negotiation?

If you discover that you're not being treated fairly or you're not sure and want to find out (which is a good idea), the chapters that follow will give you the specific tools you'll need to right the balance.

You may think you have enough. Or you may think that if you're talented and work hard it doesn't matter who you are, where you come from, or whether you're male or female, you can rise as far as your abilities will take you. That's the American way, isn't it? In addition, if you're very successful you may assume that you've experienced fair treatment along the way, otherwise you wouldn't have done so well or risen so high. Unfortunately, no. Even very successful women often discover that equally qualified men have been rewarded far more extravagantly or allowed to jump steps as they ascend the corporate ladder or enjoyed special treatment not offered to their female peers. This is increasingly true with the rise of "I-deals," which allow employees to negotiate customized contracts that guarantee them special authority, perks, and benefits—arrangements others miss out on if they don't negotiate for them. The special arrangements guaranteed by an I-deal can include anything from "diva" treatment, such as a contract provision required by Jennifer Lopez that her dressing rooms will be decorated

only with white furniture, drapes, candles, and flowers, to more standard requests such as a timed series of raises, bonus guarantees, more
vacation time, a promise to underwrite a future training program, or—
you get the idea. You don't know what the people around you may be
asking for, and getting, that hasn't been offered to you. You deserve to
be treated fairly, and it's up to you to make sure that you are.

PHASE TWO

Lay the Groundwork

5

NEGOTIATION 101:
BASIC CONCEPTS

FOR MANY PEOPLE, the word *negotiation* summons up images of something formal and structured: world leaders trying to end a regional conflict, corporate boards agreeing to the details of a severance package with a departing CEO, someone in a procurement office working out the terms of a contract with a supplier. They may also think of hardball tactics: feigning anger to intimidate the other side, snapping a briefcase shut and walking out. Many of them see negotiation as a form of combat, a competitive, often hostile interaction in which each side tries to beat the other or wear them down by haggling. In movies and on television, ruthless characters shake their fists and threaten their rivals. On the evening news, labor leaders and management representatives deliver ultimatums. Foreign diplomats sit unmoving behind long tables, the antagonism among them palpable in their silence. No wonder so many women avoid negotiating. Everything about it seems unpleasant, and we're smart enough to know that it would be nuts to behave in this way with someone we know, especially someone with whom we have an ongoing relationship.

Fortunately, negotiation rarely takes place in such formal circumstances. It's least effective when conducted as a battle or a contest, and in most cases out-and-out conflict can be avoided. Negotiation is not the exclusive territory of labor leaders and diplomats, and it's not an advanced business skill used only in executive boardrooms. The ability to negotiate well is not an inborn gift or a rare and special talent.

Put simply, negotiation is a tool to help change the status quo when change requires the agreement of another person. Changing the status quo can mean asking a waitress if the kitchen can leave the croutons off your salad or it can mean asking your boss if you can work four days a week instead of five. It can mean asking the dry cleaner to have your suit ready this afternoon or it can mean asking for a transfer to a different regional office so you can follow your partner to a new job. The little negotiations involve the same processes as the big ones, and in all cases employing hardball tactics is usually the worst way to get good results. The most successful negotiators, the ones who reach agreements that benefit both sides, don't bully each other or raise their voices. They ask a lot of questions, listen carefully, share information, and try to understand both points of view. They enjoy the challenge of finding ways to satisfy everyone's interests and try to tease out solutions that leave no one feeling aggrieved, misused, or unhappy.

Seen this way, negotiation is probably something you already do every day (if you have kids, you're an old hand). You talk to your boss about promoting a talented junior worker whom you supervise. You discuss with a client how to customize a product in order to best serve his or her needs. You ask a colleague to help out on a challenging project. You decide with another volunteer how to split up the tasks on a community service initiative. You work out a plan with your siblings to celebrate your parents' fiftieth wedding anniversary. Talking, discussing, deciding, working things out—these are all parts of negotiating, and they're all skills that many women already possess.

Every negotiation also takes place within the context of a relationship, a relationship in which each party has something of value to offer. Negotiating well involves understanding the nature of the relationship between you and the other negotiators and accurately estimating the value on each side—what you both "bring to the table." It may take some research to obtain this information (research we're going to show you how to do), but if you learn a few basic principles, plan carefully, and *practice,* you can become an effective negotiator pretty quickly. We've designed this book to guide you through that process.

MEASURE THE PLAYING FIELD

Once you know what you want and have resolved to negotiate to get it, you need to do a little preliminary legwork. You need to familiarize yourself with the basics of good negotiation practice, the working concepts on which professional negotiators rely. Then you need to do some research: How much are you worth? How much bargaining power do you really have? And how do things stand on the other side of the table? Numerous external factors may influence the course of your negotiation, such as your employer's financial stability or long-range plans, your organization's system for evaluating individual work or making exceptions to standard operating procedure, and the pet peeves and priorities of the person you need to ask. The more you can learn about the context within which you'll be making your request and the personalities of the major players, the better equipped you'll be to improve your negotiating position and argue persuasively for your point of view.

The first step is to identify any relevant circumstances and relationship factors that may influence the outcome (experts call this assessing the negotiation environment). You wouldn't want to negotiate the same way with your partner as you would with a stranger (or you won't be together very long) and you shouldn't negotiate the same way with a beleaguered boss as you would with a recruiter who's offering you a job. To gauge your situation accurately, ask yourself the following questions:

How Many Parties Are Involved?

The number of parties is the number of "sides" in the negotiation. For example, when the United States is negotiating with another country over trade issues, there are only two "sides" (two signatories) to the agreement, even though each side will be represented by many people. The situation becomes more complex if other countries join the negotiation, increasing the number of sides. The complexity comes not simply from the fact that each country may bring different goals to the negotiation but also from the fact that certain countries may form coalitions or alliances in order to increase their leverage at the negotiating table. The same is true in more small-scale negotiations. If you and your three sisters, all of whom live in different cities, are trying to decide who will host the whole family for Christmas or Chanukah or Kwanzaa, your negotiation will probably be more complex than if you were simply negotiating with one sibling. Similarly, if you're a small-business owner negotiating for a new contract and other subvendors will be participating in the project, reaching an agreement will be more complicated. Everyone involved may bring different expectations to the negotiation and other subvendors may band together to try to push through their own agendas, which may differ from yours.

One Issue or Many?

Negotiations in which there is only one issue to be decided, called *distributive negotiations,* have a fundamentally different character than negotiations with more elements in play, which are called *integrative negotiations.* If you're buying a used car, chances are you'll be negotiating over a single issue, the price. If you're buying a new car instead, you'll also want to agree on a color, the trade-in value of your current car, and the price for any extras you want, such as an upgraded audio system, GPS navigator, trunk cover, roof rack, or splash guards. Unless you're paying cash you'll need to discuss financing arrangements. In a job negotiation, the issues to be decided in addition to salary could include title, scope of responsibilities, starting date, number of vacation days, features of your benefits package, a timetable for reviews and promotions, and potentially many more. In a negotiation for a promotion, the issues could include the date the promotion will take effect, the number of people you'll supervise, your new salary, whether or not you'll have an assistant, and so on.

What's the Nature of Your Relationship?

Think of the relationship dimension of negotiations as a continuum. At one end envision a negotiating partner whom you'll never see again, such as the seller of a house. At the other end put your mother. Most negotiations take place closer to your mother's end of this continuum, with someone whom you can expect to see again, someone with whom you have a continuing relationship.

The nature of your relationship with the other negotiators will have a huge impact on your negotiation because it will determine the amount of information you have about the other side, the level of trust you share, and the potential for cooperation. In addition, the outcome of a negotiation with someone you know will influence your future interactions with this person and his or her friends and colleagues; it may enhance or damage your reputation, and can potentially set a precedent for later events.

How Formal or Binding Is the Proposed Agreement?

Will the agreement you reach *require* both sides to follow through? Will it conclude with a legally binding contract, for example, or will you be making a handshake agreement, one that each side promises to carry out? These two agreements differ in several ways. First, they differ in their level of transparency. Written contracts detail the terms of an agreement. Verbal agreements leave the door open for each side to walk away with different ideas about what's been decided (and this can happen without malice on either side). Sometimes verbal agreements lead to simple misunderstandings or participants remember the sequence of events differently. In other cases, the terms of the agreement are so vague that the parties have different expectations for what will happen and when. Consider, for example, what happened when a friend of Sara's, who works in advertising, asked her boss for a raise. After some discussion, he agreed to increase her salary by 4 percent. She assumed the raise would take effect immediately but several months passed and her paycheck never changed. She hadn't asked about the timing of the raise or gotten his commitment in writing. After a couple of months of waiting, she had to work up her nerve to ask her boss to name a specific date when her raise would go through.

The two types of agreements also differ in their degree of enforceability. A written contract can usually be enforced in a court of law. A verbal agreement relies on continuing commitment by both sides. In a negotiation that will not produce a written agreement, if the people on the other side don't feel as though they've gotten a good deal, they may be less likely to follow through. For this reason, make sure that what you agree to will give the other negotiators sufficient incentive to carry out their side of the bargain.

How Will this Negotiation Affect Other People?

A negotiation is said to be linked if it affects a future negotiation with someone else. For example, if you're a manager hiring a new employee, that negotiation may influence future negotiations with other employees (especially if you give the new person something other employees will want). Linkage ratchets up the stakes in a negotiation because whatever the parties agree to today may set a precedent for the future. Other negotiators may be reluctant to give you something not because they don't think you deserve it but because giving it to you may cause them problems later on. Say you own a unit in a cooperative apartment building where the rules prohibit subletting for more than a year. You're being transferred overseas for two years and ask if an exception can be made because you know you're coming back. The co-op board may resist making an exception for you because then other people will ask for exceptions too. Your awareness of the presence of linkage can help you prepare a persuasive counterargument or adjust your strategy—by proposing strict guidelines for making exceptions in the co-op example, or by asking for something different that won't cause as many problems in other situations.

How Does Timing Affect the Agreement, and What Are the Costs or Benefits of a Delay?

If you do not get what you want now, will circumstances change in ways that will make it harder or easier for you to reach your goal later? For example, if you're trying to buy a house and the negotiation is proceeding slowly, is that a benefit (giving you time to sell your own house or for the market to change to your advantage) or is that a cost (you've sold your house already and you'll need to find temporary living arrangements until you buy a new one)? What are the consequences of delaying for the other side? Knowing how these consequences change for both of you will be a critical ingredient in your negotiation strategy.

How Much Do You Know About the Other Side's Position?

In any negotiation there may be many unknowns, most of which will involve the information you lack about the other side. Do they think what you're trying to achieve in the negotiation is reasonable, easily doable, or completely out of the question? How far are they willing to compromise? What do they really want? As we'll discuss in Chapter 7, learning as much as you can about the other side will greatly increase your chances of getting what you want. At this stage, however, it's simply important to catalogue what you know about them and what you don't know but would like to find out.

Who Are the Decision Makers on the Other Side?

Will you be negotiating with just one other person or many? If many, then you need to understand each negotiator's full range of interests. If you're negotiating for a promotion and your new position will involve working for more than one boss, what are each boss's priorities and goals? Another factor to consider is whether the people you're negoti-ating with have final say over the matter or if other stakeholders need to sign off on the agreement.

Will the Results of the Negotiation Be Private or Public?

Will the negotiation take place in a private setting or will the negotia-tion process (and outcome) be made public? For example, will you be negotiating for your compensation behind closed doors or will your compensation be revealed to others (as is the case in the public sector)? Not only will you probably need to choose different tactics in the two situations but whether the negotiation is public or private will also in-fluence the impact of linkages (see above) on the negotiation.

Will the Agreement Set a Precedent?

Are you asking for something that has never been done before? Will you be breaking new ground or are you asking for something that should be coming to you anyway, because people at your level who have achieved your performance targets routinely get rewarded in this way? As we'll discuss in Chapter 8, understanding the precedents can help you to improve your bargaining power in the negotiation. If you're negotiating to get flextime at work, for example, you may be more successful if you can point to other workers who've been granted the same benefit.

What Are the Accepted Norms for Negotiation Behavior in This Situation?

At an open-air market in Mexico, buyers and sellers are expected to haggle and it's generally assumed that the exchange will be lively and protracted. At the Giant Eagle supermarket in Pittsburgh, however, the cashier will not negotiate with you over the price of tomatoes. Most antique sellers in this country expect to grant slightly lower prices to customers who negotiate but they don't expect (or react well to) persistent prodding to cut their prices in half or more. Expectations regarding appropriate negotiation behavior (or what experts call the "context" of a negotiation) differ from one profession to another, between people of different ethnic or cultural backgrounds, between men and women, between people of different ages, and even between people from different regions of the same country. (New Yorkers may respond to and respect certain types of aggressive behavior that might be considered impolite among southerners, for example.) If you know what is expected or considered appropriate in a particular context you can adjust your style and approach accordingly.

INSIGHT FROM THE PROS

Professional negotiators have discovered the benefits of sketching out both the lower and upper limits—the least you can realistically accept and the most you're likely to achieve—in advance of your negotiation. These basic building blocks of negotiation strategy will help you decide what to aim for, what to accept, and when to walk away. They'll give you a clear picture of the path before you and help you make a few crucial decisions upfront.

BATNA: Best Alternative to a Negotiated Agreement. Before you enter into any type of negotiation, it's essential that you fully understand your alternatives. If you don't get what you want, what will you do? What's the best choice you can make for yourself if the negotiation ends in disagreement? If you can't persuade the other negotiator to give you what you want, what's your fallback position?

The better your options if you don't get what you want, the more power you have. If someone who's offered you a job knows that you have another attractive offer, you're in a better position to negotiate for the salary you want because he needs to make it worth your while to accept his offer. If someone who wants to sell you her house knows that you like another house too, she'll realize that she needs to give you a good price or lose the sale.

Sometimes your BATNA is the status quo and sometimes your BATNA is another option you can pursue. Here are some examples.

BATNA

BEST ALTERNATIVE TO A NEGOTIATED AGREEMENT

- You're negotiating with a salesperson at a dealership to buy a particular car. If you can't reach an agreement with him or her, your BATNA is:
  - Status quo

    Keep driving your old car or use public transportation if you don't have a car
  - Other option

    Buy the car from a different dealer or buy a different car

- You've been offered a job and you're negotiating the salary with your prospective employer. Your BATNA if you don't get the salary you want is:
  - Status quo

    Stay with your current employer or keep looking for a job if you're unemployed
  - Other option

    Find a different job or start your own business

- You're negotiating for a promotion with your current boss. If he turns you down, your BATNA is:
  - Status quo

    Stay in your current position

— Other option

Find another job or start your own business

- A headhunter is trying to recruit you. If the job isn't attractive enough, your BATNA is:
- Status quo

Stay in your current position
- Other option

Put out feelers to see what else is out there

- You want your partner to help with more of the housework. If he or she refuses, your BATNA is:
- Status quo

Continue doing most of it
- Other option

Hire a housekeeping service to clean once a week, lower your standards, or get another partner

In order to accurately assess the strength of your negotiating position (which we'll focus on in greater detail in the next chapter), you first need to understand the strength or weakness of your BATNA.

Reservation value (RV). What is your bottom line or cutoff point—the maximum amount you'd be willing to pay or the minimum amount you'd be willing to accept? In essence, this is the worst deal you'd accept before choosing your BATNA instead. In negotiating the salary for a new job, your reservation value would be the minimum you'd accept to take the job; any lower and you would turn it down. If you were on the other side of the negotiating table, your reservation value would be the highest salary that you'd pay to hire this particular candidate.

In practice, you may find it tricky to narrow down your reservation value to a precise figure. Students who consult Linda before negotiating their job offers frequently struggle with this. "If my reservation value for the job is $70,000 does that mean that I should really say no to $69,999 if that's their final offer?" one student asked. In this type of situation, having a range for your reservation value makes more sense—in this case, in the high 60s to low 70s. But the key is not to make the range too broad and to identify that range—your reservation value—*before* your negotiation begins. Otherwise, you risk accepting too little during the actual process.

Contract zone. This is the difference between each negotiator's reservation value or bottom line. Continuing with the job negotiation example, suppose that a recruiter is willing to pay a candidate up to $75,000 and the candidate is prepared to accept anything over $70,000. In that case, the contract zone would be between $70,000 and $75,000. An agreement could be made anywhere between those values but not outside because the recruiter won't pay more than $75,000 and the candidate won't accept less than $70,000. As a negotiator, you usually won't know the actual limits of the contract zone because you will know only your own reservation value, not the other side's.

Target value (TV). Your target value (also called your aspiration value) for a negotiation is your goal: what you'd really *love* to achieve in the negotiation. This is different from your reservation value (which is the worst deal you'd accept), and it's different from what you think you're pretty sure to get. In the salary negotiation example, if you're a job candidate and your reservation value is $70,000, your target value should be something higher and more ambitious, such as $80,000. Later chapters will provide you with the tools to determine the right targets for your negotiations. For now, think of your target value as whatever you'd be thrilled to get. Linda tells her students that their target should be the deal that would make them jump up and down and call their mothers or partners, or both, right away.

TARGET VALUES

The target you set for your negotiation should be:
- Better than your BATNA
- Ambitious (pushing the limits of what's possible)
- Realistic—something the other side might potentially agree to (an impossible goal won't get you very far)

Understanding these basic concepts will help you structure your negotiation plan and develop an effective strategy. The next step is to gather the information you're going to need—about the strength of your bargaining position and about the situation on the other side of the table. This will enable you to craft a proposal that will not just work well for you but will also appeal to the other side.

6

HOW MUCH ARE YOU WORTH?

INFORMATION IS POWER in a negotiation. The more information you have, the better equipped you'll be to set an aggressive but realistic target and defend your position confidently and persuasively. Imagine that you've asked for a 15 percent increase in your salary and your boss says you're asking for way too much. What if you could show that people with your qualifications are compensated at that higher level throughout your industry? What if you had data confirming that your company's major competitor pays higher wages across the board? What if you'd collected information about the local market for your skills and discovered a regional shortage of people who can do your job? If your boss says the company can't afford to give you such a big increase and you know that profits in the last quarter were up 20 percent over the same quarter a year ago, wouldn't you feel less inclined to back down immediately?

Assembling a reserve of relevant information about your value in the market will give your strategy a strong foundation. All this information will help you identify your BATNA (best alternative to a negotiated agreement) so that you know when to walk away—when what you're being offered is objectively inferior to your other alternatives.

Most of all, it will bolster your argument and help you convince your boss to make a favorable counteroffer.

Patricia—PROVED HER STUFF

Patricia, one of Linda's students, wanted to work in a nonprofit agency devoted to increasing teenage literacy. She also got married right after completing her degree and followed her husband to his new job in the southern city where he'd grown up. Job opportunities doing what she wanted were scarce and after four months of searching she received only one offer. The job didn't pay much and the position didn't take full advantage of her talents. But having no other options she took the job with the understanding that she and her boss would revisit her responsibilities and salary in six months. During that time, she gathered information (from Web sites, her student friends, career services at the Heinz School) about salary ranges for the work she was doing. When she met with her boss after six months, he was impressed by her work and ready to promote her. But he only wanted to pay her 10 percent more. Using the information she'd gathered, she was able to demonstrate that her market value was actually 23 percent more than she was earning. Having this information helped her set an appropriate target (she decided she wanted 20 percent), resist backing down when her boss said 10 percent, and finally convince him that what she was asking for was reasonable and fair.

DON'T UNDERSELL YOURSELF

In Phase One, you figured out what you want—your big-picture goals. Now you need to zero in on what you can ask for in the specific negotiation at hand. If you think you deserve a better title, what title should you propose? If you've decided you want a raise, how much should you aim for? That's easy, you may think. I want the next title above my own, and I want 5 percent more than I'm making now. Although a promotion to the next level may be an obvious goal, perhaps you can do better. Maybe you can skip a step or a level. A 5 percent increase might be a reasonable target for a salary negotiation, but then again it may be too low. In the absence of reliable data, women often underestimate the value of their work, their skills, and their potential. Women also frequently underestimate how much is available—not just how much money but how many opportunities. As a result, they ask for much less than they can get.

Women do much better with more information. One of Linda's studies demonstrated this vividly. With two colleagues, Linda analyzed the starting salaries negotiated by men and women who were entering the workforce after earning their master's degrees from a top-rated business school. They found out that women had accepted salaries that were 6 percent lower on average than those negotiated by the men. This may seem like a pretty wide spread (it is) but the annual bonuses negotiated by men and women differed even more dramatically: Women's were *19 percent lower* than men's on average. Linda discovered that guidelines about starting salary ranges are readily available for many industries and jobs but it's hard to find information about standard bonus amounts. With less information, the women priced themselves far too low.

POINTS OF REFERENCE

Researchers asked people to review college application folders and predict the success of incoming college freshmen. At the end of the experiment, the researchers asked the subjects to pay themselves what they thought their work was worth. In the absence of any external guidance, men paid themselves *63 percent more* on average than women did. This changed when the researchers left a list on participants' desks containing eight names (four male and four female) as well as (fictional) amounts that each subject had paid him or herself. With this list as a reference, male and female subjects paid themselves similar amounts—amounts that corresponded to the average on the lists. This was true whether the phony list showed men paying themselves more than women or women paying themselves more than men. In other words, women didn't pay themselves less in the first version of the experiment, with no lists on the tables, because they thought they deserved less or believed that their work was inferior to men's. They just had difficulty accurately assessing the value of the work without any external reference points. They needed more information.

Setting the right target, in other words, a target that's high but fair, ambitious but appropriate, well founded but also realistic, requires research. You need to know the current market for your skills. You need to know not only what your own organization pays people doing the same job but what competing organizations pay people who do that job. The same is true when you want to buy something. If you want to negotiate the price of a product or service, vacation itinerary, mortgage refinancing, or consignment agreement, you need to know the best rates and prices available—where to find the best discounts, who's offering combination packages or buyer's incentives, whether you'll be sacrificing quality if you push for a lower price (and where that threshold lies), and how to find the most reliable vendors, providers, or partners.

Not so long ago, you had to be an industry insider to get much of this information. Today we have easy access to a wealth of information from a vast array of sources. These include trade journals, company newsletters, annual reports, business magazines (and their Web sites and links), government publications and Web sites, career counseling Web sites (including thousands aimed specifically at women), the Web sites of professional and industry associations, the blogs of people who work in particular industries, and—last but not least—your personal and professional networks. A vast array of consumer publications and Web sites provide information about prices for retail products as well as both expert and consumer ratings of product and service quality. A lot of information is out there, you just need to know where to look.

ONE-STOP SHOPPING

The Web is an amazing information resource, and you may be able to locate everything you need to know in a few hours of searching and scrolling (if you don't have Web access, use the computers at your local library). The Web is particularly useful for establishing the market value of your skills. Searching for "information about salary" using general-subject search engines such as Google, Yahoo!, or MSNSearch yields over 200 million hits. Searching for "lawyers salaries" yields over 6 million hits, "social workers salaries," 41 million hits, "retail clerks salaries," almost 800,000 hits. You get the idea. Of course, you don't need to comb through millions of sites to find what you're looking for. Refine your search to suit your needs.

Try "Wisconsin nurses salaries." This will take you to www.wisconsin nurses.org, which contains data about nurses' salaries in the state. It also provides information about important issues facing the nursing profession in Wisconsin, reports on public policy changes that affect nurses, lists of job openings, and links to chat rooms or online discussion forums in which nurses talk about their experiences and share advice. You'll also find links to press releases and newspaper articles of special interest to nurses in Wisconsin. If you're interested in moving into administration and want to know how much more training and experience you'll need, try "qualifications nursing supervisors Wisconsin." In addition to information about the qualifications needed for the job you want, you'll pull up listings for administrative openings at organizations around the state.

If you're a teacher or interested in becoming a teacher, go to www. govspot.com/lists/teachersalaries.htm for state-by-state information about salary levels. Or you can go to a site like www.salary.com and type in "teacher salaries" and your zip code. This will bring up salary ranges in your area for teacher aides as well as for day care, kindergarten, elementary school, high school, and adult education teachers. It will also give you information about base pay, benefits, bonuses, teachers' unions, and the cost of living in the region in which you wish to work. If you're employed by a nonprofit, www.guidestar.org is a terrific resource for information about salaries at nonprofit organizations. If you work for the government or want to work for the government, every government entity—at the city, state, and federal levels—maintains a Web site with information about job grades and pay scales.

In addition to www.salary.com, hundreds of other sites allow you to select your job category, type in your zip code, and, for free, get a report on the median salary paid to people performing your job in your region. For a fee, you can get information customized to your particular circumstances. The U.S. Bureau of Labor Statistics (www.bls.gov) is another great resource. There are also sites focused on particular professions, such as www.HealthJobsUSA.com and www.physiciansearch .com for health care industry jobs, www.marketingpower.com for jobs in marketing, www.datamasters.com for information systems jobs, and www.TheLadders.com for law jobs. And many many more.

**LEADING WEB-BASED SALARY
INFORMATION RESOURCES**

- www.monster.com
- www.jobstar.org
- www.hotjobs.com
- www.salarysource.com
- www.payscale.com
- www.salarydirectory.com
- www.rileyguide.com
- www.salaryexpert.com
- www.jobweb.com
- www.careerbuilder.com
- www.compare-fun-jobs.com
- www.vault.com
- www.collegegrad.com
- www.acinet.org
- www.careerjournal.com
- www.abbott-langer.com
- www.dol.gov
- www.opm.gov/oca/07tables

Benazir—THE RIGHT JOB AT THE RIGHT SALARY

A reproductive endocrinologist (a specialist in treating infertility), Benazir spent five years after completing her residency doing research at a prominent Massachusetts hospital. When she was thirty-five she decided that she wanted to scale back her research and get a clinical job working with patients. She had great qualifications and knew she could command a hefty salary. She just wasn't sure exactly how much she could get.

Benazir identified the job she wanted, at a small practice that provided individualized care. This practice was advertising for two new doctors to join the staff. With her academic and research credentials, Benazir figured she had a pretty good chance of getting one of those spots. To be safe, she applied to four other practices in the area, even two that had no openings, and to two practices out of state. She researched pay rates in Massachusetts and around the country on Web sites specializing in medical careers (her first search, for "endocrinologist salaries," produced over eighteen thousand hits). Although she didn't want to move out of Boston, she figured that knowing what she could earn elsewhere would be a good negotiating tool. Using all this information, she identified the salary she wanted to earn.

In the end, she received two offers, one from her first-choice clinic and one from another larger practice in the area. Neither offered her as much as she wanted, and the larger clinic actually offered her more than the clinic where she wanted to work. Having done her homework, she felt confident that both offers were too low. She had objective evidence that she was worth more. She presented the information she'd gathered to the senior doctors at the clinic where she wanted to work, mentioned that she'd received a higher offer from the other practice without giving details, and successfully negotiated a salary that was 28 percent higher than she was initially offered.

Kayla—THE RIGHT TITLE

Kayla had worked for ten years as the data manager for a small market-research organization. She was initially hired to manage the technicians in the computer services support group, but the organization grew rapidly and soon Kayla was supervising the maintenance of all of the company's databases, directing the construction and management of new databases, and working with an outside consultant to customize security software to protect the company's proprietary research. She was also supervising the company's IT training programs.

When her boss put her in charge of purchasing new hardware and software for the company, Kayla decided that her job title no longer described what she did. She'd received an ample raise every time she took on a new function, but she was still classified as a data manager.

To identify a more appropriate title for her current role, Kayla launched a theoretical job search. She scanned job listings on several employment Web sites, looked through past issues of influential information technology magazines and journals, and even called a few headhunters. What she found was pretty clear-cut: People with responsibilities similar to hers typically held the title of vice president or chief information officer (or both). Her current title was woefully inappropriate for her level of responsibility and the importance of the job she was doing. She took this research to her boss and within a few weeks he made a company-wide announcement changing her title to vice president of information systems.

LOCATION, LOCATION, LOCATION

Researching the cost of living in different regions should also be an important part of your preparation, because you may need to earn a lot more to maintain your current standard of living if you move to a different city or state. For example, using the salary calculator at www.realtor.com, you'll discover that a homeowner who can live comfortably for $100,000 in Pittsburgh needs to make about $170,000 in Boston to maintain the same standard of living. This information can help you calculate how much you'll need to earn to make it worth your while to move from Pittsburgh to Boston—good preparation for your salary negotiation if a Boston employer offers you a job. You'll also need cost-of-living information if you're negotiating to buy a house in your new location, expanding a business and preparing to hire employees in a new region, or working out a price structure for your products or services when you're entering a market where overhead costs may be higher. Dozens, maybe hundreds, of Web sites post regional cost-of-living comparison data. The University of Michigan Document Center publishes one of the best, www.lib.umich.edu/govdocs/steccpi .html. Another option is simply to search for "regional cost of living index." You should also research tax rates in cities or towns where you contemplate purchasing property or opening a business. The taxes paid by the previous owners of a property may be far lower than those you'll pay if your property is reassessed because you'll pay more for the property than it sold for before. To research municipal tax rates, go to the Web sites of the cities or towns in which you're thinking of buying property or setting up shop.

USE YOUR CONTACTS

Once you've collected enough general information about salaries and qualifications, talk to your colleagues and peers. "Wait!" you say, "this is totally off limits where I work." This may be true. A lot of us know more about our colleagues' sex lives than we do about their salaries, and many organizations know that it works to their advantage to keep employees in the dark about what their peers earn. Some employers even let their workforce know that talking about salaries is a sackable offense. And at companies where that threat is not explicit, the taboo may nevertheless be powerful. Many people are also reluctant to discuss their qualifications—perhaps their résumés have conspicuous holes in them, or they talked their way into positions above their qualifications, or they're simply uncomfortable talking about themselves.

In some situations (where you're not likely to be fired, for one example), the easiest way to deal with the salary taboo can be simply to ignore it. Linda has a friend named Susan who received a job offer at another university. Susan was trying to gather information about what professors at a certain level earn and she took Linda out to lunch to get her advice. She hemmed and hawed and danced around the issue for several minutes until Linda finally realized what she was trying to ask.

"I'm happy to tell you what I earn if that would help you," Linda said. Not everyone is as courageous and comfortable flouting convention as Linda is, however, and not everyone enjoys her level of job security. So if this is a danger zone for you, for whatever reason, there are other ways to get the information you need.

Rather than simply asking people outright what you want to know, try framing your questions like this:

- "What do you think would be an appropriate salary for someone performing my job at my level?"
- "Do you know the approximate salary range for this position [the job you have or the job you want]?"
- "What do you think this job [the job you want] would pay someone who has this amount of experience [your experience]?"
- "What are the qualifications needed to do that job [the job you want]?"
- "How many years of experience are usually required before one is given this degree of responsibility or can expect to earn [X] amount?"
- "What are the necessary steps to get from here [where you are now] to there [where you want to go]?"
- "Are there any hidden requirements—ways you're expected to prove yourself—before you can be considered for this job?"
- "Do you know of anyone who's made the switch from this function [the one you're doing now] to that function [the one you want to do]?"
- "Do you think the company makes an effort to pay people equally who are doing the same job?"
- "If someone were going to ask for [X—whatever you want], when would be the best time?"

- "If I were to go after [X] job [the job you want] what would be the best strategy?"

You could even try:

- "If a man were doing my job [or the job you want to get] what do you think he'd be paid?"

In this way, instead of asking people for personal information about themselves, you're asking them to share their expertise, which most people are happy to do. These contacts can also help you tease out crucial tactical information such as whether your boss never fails to be impressed if someone takes the initiative in a particular way or if there's someone else who has to like you, even though that person isn't your immediate supervisor, for your request to succeed.

You should also draw on the expertise available from your social and professional networks outside of work, and make the most of every networking opportunity you can find. And be sure to talk to men as well as women. Since men typically earn more than women doing the same job and often advance more rapidly into new positions, they may have a more realistic sense of the range of salaries available or the bottom-line requirements for what you want to do.

Rita—USE YOUR NETWORKS

Rita had just graduated from a master's program in electrical engineering. She was offered a job by an enormous software development company, a leader in the field, which employed 55,000 people worldwide—almost half of them at corporate headquarters, where Rita was offered the job. She accepted the offer without negotiating because she'd heard that the company paid well by industry standards and she thought the salary offer was generous. Six months later, she learned that three other people who were hired for the same position at the same time had negotiated their offers and were earning 10 to 15 percent more. She felt angry and confused. How had those other hires known that they could negotiate for more?

Rita had been a starter on the women's track team in college and she joined a running club as soon as she settled in to her new job. She struck up a friendship with a woman who'd worked for Rita's employer before switching to a smaller start-up firm. When Rita told her new friend what had happened, her friend said, "Did you ask around at all before that salary negotiation? Because there are a lot of people in this town who would have been able to help you. It's pretty much common knowledge what they'll pay people entering at your level. They start by lowballing everybody. But if you push back, they'll pay more."

"But I was new to town," Rita protested. "I didn't know anyone here."

"Sure you did," her friend said. "Doesn't your alumni association have a big chapter here? I bet your university's career services department could have put you in touch with half a dozen people who were hired at the same level in the past few years. You also could have looked on the Web. Dozens of sites report daily on every twitch and sneeze over there."

If Rita had taken advantage of the various sources of information available to her, she would have known that the offer was too low. She could have asked for more money, backing up her request by saying, "I know that the salary you're offering falls at the low end of the range for that job and that you pay more to people with my qualifications. I'd love to work here but I need to be paid as much as my peers."

Deena—CHECK WITH PEOPLE WHO KNOW

Deena had worked as a lawyer in Kansas City for five years when her husband's employer transferred him to its Los Angeles office. After passing the California bar, Deena applied to six L.A. law firms doing the type of work she enjoyed. All six asked her to list her salary requirements. Deena thought she'd ask for 12 to 15 percent more than she'd been earning in Kansas City because the cost of living was so much higher in L.A. But she was worried that this was too much. Before responding, she called a man she'd known in law school who'd become a headhunter and worked exclusively with lawyers. When she told him what she was planning to ask for, he burst out laughing.

"Wow, that's much too low," he told her. "And I'd say you were being underpaid in Kansas City. I've been recruiting lawyers for fourteen years and women always underprice themselves. The average man will ask for 20 percent more than a woman with better qualifications." He also warned Deena that asking for a lower salary might make her a less attractive candidate. "They figure if you ask for more you must be worth more—you must be better," he said. Convinced, Deena asked for 33 percent more than she'd been making in Kansas City. She received job offers from three firms, including her first choice. None of them balked at her salary request.

GO STRAIGHT TO THE SOURCE

Don't overlook one potentially fertile source of information—the person who has the authority to give you what you want. In most cases, if you're being underpaid your boss will know this; if you ask for more he or she may readily make the adjustment. Instead of looking at your boss simply as someone with power over your future, try approaching her or him as a partner with a shared interest in seeing that you make the most of your talents.

Georgiana—A LOT TO ACCOMPLISH

Georgiana had a graduate degree in architecture and worked for a large, prominent New York firm. After six years at the job she was promoted but told she needed to produce more original design work in the next two years if she wanted to stay at the firm and become an associate partner. She was carrying a heavy project management load, however, and serving on a task force developing affordable low-income housing at several city sites. She couldn't possibly fulfill all of these commitments and clear her drafting table to do any original design work at the same time. Unsure what to do, she approached her boss, one of the senior partners, and asked for advice. Together, they prioritized, rearranged, and reduced her other responsibilities over the next two years and identified a few small-scale design projects that she could take on. With her boss's ongoing help, she was able to fulfill all her other professional commitments, design two small buildings—one of which was a runner-up for a national design award—and earn the promotion to associate partner when the two years were up.

The best managers know that people do better work when they're making steady progress in their careers and enjoy what they're doing. These managers recognize that it's good for business when everyone is working at the peak of his or her abilities. With this in mind, tell your boss that you'd like to discuss your professional goals and your future at the organization. Ask how your qualifications measure up to those of your peers and what skills you need to acquire in order to move ahead. If you're primarily interested in getting a raise, try asking your boss where you fall in the salary distribution—how your pay compares with that of other people with similar training, experience, and skills in the organization. Not every boss will tell you what you want to know, but you'll be surprised at how much you can learn simply by asking.

7

WHAT DO YOU KNOW
ABOUT THE OTHER SIDE?

IN EVERY NEGOTIATION class she teaches, Linda shows her students a short video made by the Visual Cognition Lab at the University of Illinois. In the video, six people duck in and around each other, tossing basketballs back and forth in a hallway. Three of the people are wearing black T-shirts and the other three are wearing white shirts. Linda instructs her students to count how many times a player in white catches the ball. The video lasts twenty-four seconds and a member of the white team catches the ball fifteen times. In the middle of the video, a man in a particularly silly-looking gorilla suit walks right into the group of ballplayers, turns to the camera, and beats his chest. Then he walks off. A majority of the students who watch the video never notice the gorilla. They're so focused on their own goal—counting the number of times the ball changes hands—that they don't even see the gorilla.

Linda uses this video to illustrate a crucial point about good negotiation practice: Don't focus too intently on your own goals or you may miss something important—something that, in a negotiation, can have a big impact on how things turn out. When you're preparing for a negotiation, and even when you're in the middle of one, it's natural to focus on yourself—what you want and how to get it. But a key to any successful negotiation is knowing how the other side sees the problem. You need to be well informed about how they make decisions and recognize what's most important to them.

Twyla—MISSING THE POINT

Twyla, a screenwriter who wanted to make the leap to directing, was looking for the right project. Tooling around on the Web, she discovered a self-published novel by an obscure Louisiana writer about the experiences of an extended family during Hurricane Katrina. She loved the book and figured that she wouldn't have to pay too much for the rights since the book was practically unknown. Before meeting the author, Twyla sat down with her producing partner and they put together a provisional budget for the film. They decided what she should offer, how much it would be great to pay (their aspiration value), and the most they could afford to pay (their reservation value). Then she flew to New Orleans and made her pitch. Twyla thought her offer was fair, but the author refused to sell. He didn't care about the money. He was much more interested in how Twyla planned to tell his complex story. He wanted to make sure that she was passionate about the material and that her vision for the movie was in sync with his own. Twyla blew the deal because she didn't arrive prepared to discuss her creative ideas. She came across as not having sufficient passion for the content. Because she hadn't paused to consider what might matter most to the other negotiator, she failed to get what she wanted.

Holly—WHAT YOU WANT, WHAT THEY NEED

Holly worked for a large pharmaceutical company. Her job involved identifying, interviewing, and selecting appropriate candidates to participate in clinical research studies. As part of the nonprofessional staff, Holly was required to work from 8:30 to 5:00, which caused problems because a lot of potential research subjects could only come in to be interviewed after regular business hours or on weekends. These scheduling constraints meant that it took Holly a long time to recruit enough suitable subjects for each study. She knew she'd have much better luck if she could switch to a more flexible schedule. Holly felt trapped between the company's regulations and the requirements of the job she was being asked to do. She'd already received one lukewarm performance review and knew she could do a much better job if given the chance.

Holly decided to talk to the head of the research lab about her problem. He told her that the lab was preparing a proposal to submit to the National Institutes of Health. The goal was to get funding for a series of clinical trials aimed at getting their drug approved for public use. It was essential that they have enough data from their preliminary studies to make a strong case that the drug actually worked. Getting the drug on the market would be enormously valuable for the company, and the sooner the better. Holly took this information to the director of human resources. She explained that she could help the researchers get the data they needed sooner if she could adjust her schedule. Presented with this argument, the HR director immediately agreed. The key for Holly was collecting enough information about the needs of the organization to show that her solution would address an important business priority.

BONE UP ON INTERNAL POLITICS

To learn as much as you can about what really matters to the other side, there's nothing like "ground-level intel gathering," or what those of us outside the military call gossip. Is your boss desperate to impress *her* boss? Has the wife of one of your supervisors been offered a job in another state, and are there rumors that he'll follow her? Does one of the senior people in your office detest one of your mentors? What is your boss worried about? Has your group fallen short of its performance targets? Does she think her own job may be at risk? Has technology or the business climate or something else changed recently in ways that make it harder for her to do her own job well?

You already talk to your friends at work about your boss's moods. Dig a little deeper and find out what really makes your boss tick. What are his pet peeves? Are there any projects that she's particularly committed to or sentimental about—that she sees as her "babies"? Does he have favorites on the staff? The answers to these questions extend far beyond the realm of gossip: They can tell you a lot about your boss's goals and interests, about the qualities that he values in employees, and about his priorities. They can help you think about how your interests and his (or hers) are either aligned or conflicted. This type of information often won't be summarized in a financial report but may have a big impact on how you approach your negotiation.

Ericka—KNOWING THE INSIDE SCOOP

Ericka worked as an assistant buyer for a large family-owned retail cooking equipment store. She felt ready to be promoted to senior buyer, but when she approached the store's owner he dismissed her request with a wave of his hand. Everyone in the store agreed that the boss had been irritable lately, though no one knew why. Ericka had the idea to ask the store's shipping manager, Ron. Ron had been at the store for twenty years and played poker with the boss on Friday nights. Ron told her that a national chain, the most recognizable name in the cooking tools business, was about to open a store two blocks away. Her boss was afraid that this powerful chain would destroy his business. He'd decided to try to rebrand the store for the luxury products market, to turn it into the city's premier destination for stylish European kitchen hardware. Knowing this, Ericka put her promotion ambitions on hold and focused on familiarizing herself with the world of super-high-end kitchen faucets, sinks, cabinet knobs, and lighting. Eighteen months later, when the rebranding looked as though it would be a success and Ericka had demonstrated her knowledge of the new product sector, she asked for and got her promotion.

Even in negotiations outside work, you'll do better if you understand what's important to the other side. Linda knows, for example, that her husband will agree to go on any vacation as long as she invites his brothers and his mother to go too (which she's happy to do because she adores his family). Sara knows she can always convince her busy brother to visit if she can scare up Red Sox tickets, because he'll drop almost anything to see the Sox play.

Make Sure You Know How Decisions Are Made

Sometimes the critical piece of information you need involves your organization's policies and precedents. Get clear on who makes the big decisions—about promotions, raises, and bonuses—and find out as much as you can about the criteria they use. Does your organization have a fixed system for filling jobs that open up? Does the company allow people to make lateral moves? Is there only one way to get where you want to go or can you take a more winding road? Also important is *when* decisions are made. You'll have a lot more room to maneuver if you make your pitch at the right time.

One of the best ways to access this type of information is by talking to vendors, distributors, subcontractors, or business partners who've worked with your organization for a long time. They usually have an interesting point of view on how things work (or don't work) and what really drives decision making. Administrative assistants within your organization are another great resource. They often possess nuts-and-bolts information such as how and when certain kinds of decisions get made, who really has the final say about issues you care about, and what kinds of exceptions or special provisions the company has made for valued employees in the past. People who've been with the organization for a long time can provide insight into how the organization's history may be influencing current strategy or the balance of power, and they often understand the impact of quirky institutional rules or unspoken policies. In addition to learning more about what you need to know, collecting information in this way enables you to cement existing personal ties and build new alliances that may serve you well later on. And don't forget about asking your boss directly for information. He or she may tell you more than you think.

WHO HAS THE INFORMATION YOU NEED?

Certain kinds of revealing and useful information won't be written down anywhere. To find out what other people know, you need to talk to the right people. One of the first steps in laying the groundwork for your negotiation will be figuring out who those people are.

- Who are the "power brokers" in your organization, the ones who really make things happen?
- Who has access to information about how well your organization is doing financially?
- Which assistants to powerful people know the most about how the organization works?
- Which of your coworkers has been with the organization the longest?
- Which subcontractors or suppliers have worked with the organization for several years?
- Who always seems to be up on the recent gossip?
- Who socializes with the boss?
- Whom does your boss go to for advice?
- Which group of people routinely goes out together after work?
- Who plays tennis or golf, or goes fishing or boating together outside work?
- Whose kids go to the same school(s) as the boss's kids?

Maggie—WHAT'S THE SYSTEM FOR AWARDING BONUSES?

Maggie, a pharmaceutical rep, traveled around a wide territory in the Pacific Northwest, visiting doctors' offices, clinics, and medical schools to inform health professionals about the benefits of her company's drugs. She was paid a salary plus commissions based on the volume of sales she generated. She also received a yearly bonus. When she started at the company, she received fairly small bonuses because she was just learning the job and her sales figures were relatively low. But she rapidly became one of the most productive reps in the western United States. Her commissions increased accordingly but her bonus only inched up a little every year. Compared to the value she knew she was bringing to the company, her bonuses began to look really small— "totally not keeping pace with my contribution," she said.

Thinking about it, Maggie realized that she didn't know how bonuses were determined and who made those decisions. The umbrella organization that owned her company was a huge multinational corporation. Was there a formula in place to assure that everyone was treated fairly? That seemed unlikely. Did different divisions or regions follow different standards? Was it all arbitrary? To find out, she took one of the older reps to lunch and asked if he could explain how things were done. He told her that bonuses were decided by regional management committees. Every year, the corporation allotted money for bonuses to each region based on the year's profits. The management committees for each region split up the pot based on the requests made by supervisors on behalf of their employees.

He also told Maggie that a lot of reps met with their supervisors every year to ask for the bonuses they wanted. "But talk to your boss by October 15 or it'll be too late for this year," he said. "They lock those numbers down before Thanksgiving." With a little more legwork, Maggie confirmed that she was getting far smaller bonuses than other reps at her level. Since she hadn't asked for bigger bonuses, her supervisor apparently concluded that she was perfectly happy getting less. But that was about to change. Maggie made an appointment to meet with her supervisor on September 30 and asked for a 50 percent increase over her bonus of the previous year. Her supervisor agreed, "without even blinking an eye," she said. "He just nodded and wrote down my figure. I got the feeling he was thinking, 'She finally figured it out.' I should have asked for more a long time ago."

Lois—TIMING CAN BE CRITICAL

One of the important things Maggie learned from the senior rep was when to make her bonus request. To time your request strategically, you need to know when the important decisions are made: when budgets are set, promotions considered, raises distributed, and bonuses calculated. Timing can be a critical factor in determining whether your negotiation succeeds or fails.

Lois worked as a paralegal in the law office of a city government in the Southwest. The city was growing rapidly and the cost of living was rising too, making it harder and harder for Lois to pay her bills. After she'd been at the job for three and a half years, she decided she needed more than the small percentage increase the city handed out to all employees every July. She put together a memo citing figures she'd obtained from the Paralegal Association of America, the Association of Government Employees, and the city's own manual detailing hiring standards and practices. She described the projects she'd worked on and her contributions, and made a strong case that she should be reclassified at a higher pay grade.

Although Lois felt confident that she deserved to be reclassified, she still felt uncomfortable asking for more money and delayed going to her boss. When she finally worked up her nerve and gave him her memo, he called her into his office. "You make a good case," he said. "But it's too late for this year. Let's talk about it again next spring." Even though the next fiscal year wouldn't start until July 1, he explained, department directors had to submit their budgets by May 15.

Lois had asked for her raise during the first week of June, too late for her boss to put through any changes. "Give this memo to me again next March," her boss said. "I'll see what I can do then."

Unfortunately, when March rolled around, Lois's boss had left and she was forced to make her pitch all over again to a new boss who didn't know her work. He decided to get better acquainted with all his employees before making any changes, and Lois struggled through yet another year with barely enough money to get by.

What could she have done differently? After her conversation with the new boss in which he turned down her request, Lois described her predicament to the department director's secretary, who'd held the job for twenty years. "I wish I'd known what you were thinking two years ago," the woman said. "I could have told you to get your salary request in before May 15. That's the way the city's been doing it for as long as I've been here."

QUESTIONS TO ASK ABOUT HOW
DECISIONS ARE MADE

- What are your organization's hiring policies? Are all jobs posted on a department Web site or advertised in an industry publication? Must a job be posted for a certain amount of time before it can be filled? Are jobs sometimes filled without a formal search? Is the system much more informal?

- When are decisions about raises made in your organization? When is the best time to provide input to the decision maker? What about bonuses, pension benefits, stock options, vacation days—what's the process for handing out those and any other parts of the compensation package?

- Who decides how work is allocated? Does the same person assign projects, set schedules, and determine responsibilities or are these functions split up? If these functions are not performed by the same person, what is the chain of command among the people involved? Who is the most senior person with the most power?

- How does your organization collect information regarding performance? Are all employees evaluated according to a well-understood and standardized system? Which data are used? Who collects the data and when? How heavily do personal (possibly subjective) evaluations influence the process?

- Are promotions made according to a strict schedule or are they made on an ad hoc basis? Who participates in the decision-making process and how much does each person's opinion or recommendation count?

- Who makes decisions about eligibility for special benefits such as extra training, tuition reimbursement, or flextime arrangements? Are there written rules about how these benefits are distributed or are decisions made on a case-by-case basis?

- What are the rules about early retirement—when it can be taken, who can take it, and the benefits provided? Are these rules strictly enforced and universally applied or are exceptions made?

DOES YOUR COMPANY OFFER HIDDEN PERKS AND BENEFITS?

Companies vary widely in the types of special arrangements and discretionary benefits they offer to individual employees. Likewise, one organization may distribute perks freely (Sara started out her career working at a fashion magazine, where makeup and accessory giveaways were a regular occurrence) while another may offer none or dole them out only on rare occasions. To find out about both benefits and perks, you certainly want to talk to the people in your HR department. But don't stop there. Often the benefits that people receive in practice are more generous than those officially on the books.

Margot, a female executive at a large car-rental company, told us that she'd worked for her employer for over twenty years, the last eight as a director and vice president, without knowing that she could receive a reimbursement of $1,500 a year for her health club membership dues. And she only learned this in a casual conversation with a colleague, not from a personnel manual!

Jesse, an in-house lawyer for a huge Rocky Mountain medical center, was told by the HR office when she got pregnant that the company would only allow her a stingy three weeks of paid leave after her baby was born (she thought this was particularly shocking for a medical facility). She'd have to use a combination of short-term disability, sick leave, vacation, personal days, and unpaid family leave if she wanted to stay away from her job any longer. To see if she could do better, she began combing through a confusing thicket of federal statutes and state codes. Bogged down, Jesse attended a women's networking luncheon organized by the hospital and brought up the issue with a few of the women at her table. They told her that the company would give her as much as twelve weeks of paid leave but that her senior manager needed to submit a special request for her. Going straight to HR didn't work.

Eliza—FIND OUT WHAT'S AVAILABLE

Eliza, an interior designer at a large firm in Atlanta, was engaged to be married. Her fiancé, Greg, was a captain in the army reserves, and shortly after they became engaged he'd been sent to Afghanistan. He was about to return after eleven months away and the two of them planned to get married quickly. Neither had a lot of money and they didn't care about having a big wedding, but Eliza wanted to take Greg on a wonderful honeymoon so that he could begin to recover and re-group. Eliza knew that her firm owned a condo in Miami because it had a lot of Florida clients, and she asked her supervisor, who was one of the partners, if there was a "company rate" for renting it.

"For your honeymoon?" her supervisor said. "What about Paris?" It turned out that the company also owned an apartment in Paris for designers to use on buying trips for European antiques. "Now that the trend is toward less formal interiors, it doesn't get used much," her supervisor told her. "And there's no charge for staff." The company's travel office found Eliza a good deal on round-trip airfare from Atlanta to Paris and, kind of stunned by how glamorous it all was, Eliza and Greg went to Paris for their honeymoon.

How Well Is Your Organization Doing?

Now that you've learned a lot more about the person you'll be negoti-ating with and about your company's policies and perks, it's time to think about the broader context. For negotiations at work, this means finding out about the financial health of your organization. Is your business or your department or your division growing, just keeping pace with the competition, or falling behind? Learn what you can about your organization's financial stability and long-term goals, and the current state of your profession. Doing this kind of research is par-ticularly important for women because many of us, when we want a raise, worry that our employers can't afford to pay more. The economy is in flux, global competition threatens various sectors of American in-dustry, and both outsourcing and downsizing have become common-place. In this climate, we worry that if we ask for more money we'll be canned because money is tight. Or we don't want to put pressure on our supervisors when we know they have a lot on their plates. These are legitimate worries, but don't let them determine how you behave until you learn more.

Publicly Traded Companies

How can you find out how well your company is really doing? If you work for a publicly owned company, you can learn most of what you want to know about your company's finances online at the Securities and Exchange Commission's Web site, http://www.sec.gov/index.htm. There you'll find annual and quarterly financial reports as well as information about your company's cash flow, investments, benefits programs, taxes paid and owed, and product lines (and much more if you're interested). You'll also find information about issues of concern in your market sector and learn whether your company is planning any acquisitions, mergers, or restructuring. If you work for a large organization, you should look at the financial health of both the organization as a whole and of your specific division, department, or plant.

Initially, the volume of information on this site can seem daunting, but the SEC offers an online tutorial called "How Do I Use EDGAR" (EDGAR stands for Electronic Data Gathering, Analysis, and Retrieval). The site also provides descriptions of different forms as well as tips about how to search most effectively for the information you need.

If you still can't understand crucial parts of the SEC's reports (and this is not uncommon), dozens of online sites explain how to read quarterly and annual reports, proxy statements, and other types of business documents. The Web sites of major business magazines and independent research organizations also provide links to the best sites for different kinds of business information. Without much searching, you should be able to find a recent summary of your company's financial status, assessments from stock analysts of your CEO's performance, commentary about the company's problems, management initiatives, likely next moves, and a lot more. The amount of information available, and the level of detail, may shock you. You can sometimes even learn what your boss is being paid—kind of a fun tidbit when you're heading into a discussion of your future. Decisions that you thought were hush-hush or potentially damaging information about company problems may be clearly reported on the Web, and in many cases analyzed by independent researchers.

You should also start reading what industry analysts are saying about your company's stock. This will give you insight into what professional business research organizations think about how your company is being managed and about its short- and long-term financial prospects. Many books and Web sites can help you understand how the stock market works if you're not sure or need a brushup. You might even consider taking a course at a local community college or adult education center. This can be an excellent long-term investment if you want to understand more about the financial health of your organization.

Betsy—A STEP AHEAD OF LOSING HER JOB

Betsy worked for a huge food company with supermarkets in ten states. The company also owned a large wholesale food distribution service with its own trucking division to deliver food to the company's stores as well as to hundreds of other groceries. Betsy worked as a dispatcher in the trucking division. Business in her region was growing, she was working longer hours than ever before, and she felt ready for a raise and a promotion. But her company had been in the news lately, with allegations of shoddy accounting at corporate headquarters, and she decided to do a little homework before approaching her boss.

She discovered that the company's stock prices, which had been soaring, had dropped 15 percent since the accounting irregularities had come to light. The company was still making plenty of money, and posting higher earnings each quarter than it had for the same quarter the year before, but to her surprise the trucking division was losing money. Several prominent analysts in the food service industry thought it was inefficient for a food service company to be in the trucking business too and recommended that the company outsource the distribution function to a subcontractor. Betsy realized that she might be on the verge of losing her job.

Looking through the job openings in the company's other divisions, she realized that many of her skills would be useful in inventory management and control. She applied for and got an inventory management position, and six months after she made the switch her company sold the trucking division and contracted with the buyer to provide all of its trucking services. Most of the drivers and mechanics were rehired by the new trucking service, but all of the dispatchers lost their jobs. Betsy felt lucky that she'd had the foresight to bone up on the company's plans and problems, and she never lost a day of work or any of the benefits she'd accrued.

Privately Owned Companies

If you work for a privately owned company, it will be a little more difficult, though not impossible, to get an accurate picture of your employer's financial situation. Regional business journals and the business pages of local newspapers typically do a good job of tracking the ups and downs of important businesses in the community. The Web can also help you here. One site alone, www.hoovers.com, collects information about 12 million companies worldwide and provides in-depth analysis of about 40,000 of the world's top businesses, including many privately held companies. Some public libraries, most universities, and many businesses subscribe to this Web site. If you can't find free access, you should be able to download a detailed report about your organization for a small fee.

For smaller companies, gathering information through public sources may not be possible, although the local business press may tell you some of what you need to know. For the rest, your internal contacts may be the best source for help in understanding the big-picture issues. Try to find people who can tell you what your organization's power players are worried about. Has unusually high turnover damaged productivity? Are there new initiatives coming down the pike that could change the structure of the organization or the types of skills that are rewarded? Is a powerful competitor planning to expand?

Liz—KEEP YOUR EAR TO THE GROUND

Liz was one of three senior managers in the compensation and benefits department of a privately owned biotechnology company. After five years as an assistant, Liz felt ready to do more, but her boss didn't show any signs of leaving. Liz figured that this meant she would have to change jobs. Knowing that expertise in compensation and benefits is a very portable skill, she went to several job Web sites, including one directly targeting the biotech industry, to see what was available in her region. She also began reading the local business press to find out as much as she could about the financial health of businesses in her area because she wanted to work at a thriving company where she could earn what she felt she was worth. Six weeks after she started exploring new job possibilities, she noticed an item in the local business weekly about her current employer. According to this article, the company was negotiating with a world-renowned scientist to join the company and planning to hire a dozen researchers to work in his lab.

Liz was friendly with an executive assistant to one of the partners at her firm and asked her what she knew about the story. It turned out that the company had already signed a contract with the scientist and was currently looking for a building in which to house his lab. "A building?" Liz asked. "For a dozen researchers?"

"Oh, no," said the executive assistant. "It's going to be much larger than that—probably a hundred scientists or more when they're staffed up."

Liz went straight to her current boss and said she wanted to apply for the job of director of personnel at the new site. Much as she liked what she was doing, she said, it was time for her to move forward in her career. But she loved the company and didn't want to leave. Putting her in charge of hiring at the new site would be a perfect solution, she argued. The company could dedicate an experienced employee to the tricky process of assembling a large research team in a very short time. She could ascend to the next level professionally.

Good results all around. After considering a few other options, including trying to manage the lab's personnel requirements from the main location, Liz's boss gave her the job.

Nonprofits

If you work for a nonprofit, you can obtain copies of your organization's recent tax filings at www.guidestar.org, the National Database of Nonprofit Organizations. You must register but many of the services are free. This site offers information about revenues (and revenue sources), expenses, the salaries of the five highest-paid employees, and reports of newsworthy events such as fund-raising successes and awards won. Many nonprofit organizations also post their annual reports on their own Web sites. In addition to financial information, these reports typically include information about the organization's future direction and financial objectives, giving you insight into where your organization is headed and what your bosses see as key challenges.

Government Organizations

The Web is also a great resource for government workers. If you're a city employee, your city's Web page (most are www.ci.cityname. statename.us—for example, Long Beach, California's, page is at www.ci.long-beach.ca.us) will contain information about budgets, expenses, the salaries of employees (by grade and by level within each grade), challenges facing the city, and any problems that may force the city to shift resources from one area to another. State Web sites (e.g., www.wyoming.gov) post information about state-level budgets and expenses, new programs started in response to recent legislation, and salaries (broken out by department and by function within each department). If you work for the federal government, go to your department's Web site, locate the budget, and study financial details such as expenses, salaries, future initiatives, planned changes in direction or focus, et cetera.

Janet—WHAT CAN THEY REALLY AFFORD?

Janet worked for the federal government as a data analyst. She was one of the most senior people in her division, and the salary range for her grade level was high ($63,000 to $89,000). Janet's salary, $77,500, fell squarely in the middle of the range. In the past year, she'd begun managing a group of junior analysts working on a new data set. With her new responsibilities, Janet thought she should be earning more, and a little research convinced her that she qualified for a $6,000 to $8,000 increase. She'd never really thought about her boss's budgetary concerns, but since her group was working in a new area she decided to look into the federal allocation for her division. To her surprise she discovered that the division's budget had been increased by 11 percent for the upcoming fiscal year. Armed with this information and with her research into the market value of her skills, she approached her boss with great confidence, and won herself a $6,750 raise.

SOURCES OF INFORMATION ABOUT
YOUR ORGANIZATION

- http://www.sec.gov for information about publicly owned companies
- www.hoovers.com for information about privately owned companies
- www.guidestar.org, a national database of nonprofit organizations
- www.ci.cityname.statename.us for information about government jobs in many cities
- www.statename.gov (for example, www.ny.gov) for information about jobs with your state government
- www.department.gov (for example, www.commerce.gov) for information about jobs with the federal government

To prepare thoroughly for any negotiation, Linda tells her students, they need to see themselves as data detectives. What information can they dig up that they assumed was classified? Which major players (or anonymous sources) can they convince to confide in them? How many treasure-trove sites for information can they bookmark in their Web browsers? How creative can they get in tracking down the answers they need? Like detectives, she tells them, they need to accumulate clues, assemble the puzzle, and then interpret what they see. What are the stakes and what are the odds? How confidently can they predict what will happen next? How do their own plans fit into the larger picture? The trick is to collect the right information, she explains, analyze what they discover, and tease out the implications.

Sometimes what you find may not be such good news, of course (think of Betsy, the supermarket truck dispatcher). Your company may be in trouble or planning to outsource your function or on the verge of implementing stringent cost-cutting measures. But whatever you learn will help you adjust your plan accordingly. In most cases, you'll probably find a lot to encourage you too. Think how much more confident you'll feel asking for a raise if you know that your company has just rebounded from a slump? Or asking for a promotion if you learn that your boss is expanding your division? Or asking to switch to a more flexible schedule if you find out that one of the senior vice presidents who has kids works the same schedule? The bottom line when it comes to negotiation is that ignorance is never bliss. The more you know, the better you'll do.

8

Boost Your Bargaining Power

There's been a lot of talk about women and power in the past few decades—how women can exercise their power without producing negative reactions, feel comfortable reaching for more power, and reap the benefits of their growing financial clout. A lot of us assume, however, that when it comes to negotiating we have no real power over the outcome—that the person who has something we want, the person with something to give, holds all the cards. The best we can do, we figure, is ask for what we want and hope for the best. But that's rarely the case. You probably have far more power to sway the course of most negotiations than you realize. This is because, in every negotiation, there are at least two sides and each side has something the other side needs.

Recognize What You Bring to the Table

Linda frequently has the following conversation with a graduating student who's just been offered a job.

"I'm afraid to negotiate my offer," the student says. "It's a big, successful corporation. Why do they need to negotiate with me?"

"Did they interview a lot of candidates for the position?" Linda asks.

"Oh, yeah," says the student. "The original pool of candidates was huge. The interview process was grueling."

"And they selected you out of lots of candidates, right?"

"Yes, but—"

"So they think you're the best of the bunch. Doesn't that give you some leverage? Why do you think they chose you?"

With some careful probing, Linda can usually identify the student's special attributes—a rare skill, uncommon experience, strong commitment to the company's goals, or any number of other factors—that made her or him the most attractive candidate for the job. In this way, she's helped hundreds of her students discover the sources of their bargaining power and accurately measure the value they bring to the organization that wants to hire them.

If you're applying for a new job, think about what you can do that your potential employer needs: why you're well qualified for the job you want. Don't just consider your degrees and test scores and the relative prestige of the college you attended or the previous places you've worked, although all those are important. Will the job require public speaking and is that one of your strengths? Will you be managing a complex operation and are you especially organized and efficient? Have you done a lot of volunteer work in which you've been able to focus the energies of different stakeholders to get things done? Have you participated in your local government and understand the protocols and political rivalries that influence decision making on public projects? Are you a "connector"—do you know how to build fruitful alliances? Do you have children and does the job require an understanding of issues important to families? What are your hobbies and do they enhance your understanding of your organization's business challenges? Are you athletic and applying for a job in a sports-related industry? Or musical and looking for work in the music industry? Or a beach lover and interested in a career in tourism? Does your potential employer have several overseas offices and do you speak French (or German or Chinese) fluently? Have you traveled widely? Are you willing to move around? Is the company short of women in professional positions and eager to change this? Do they need more women in marketing or sales (or both) because their target market has shifted to include a lot of women?

If you're not looking for a new job but want a change in your current situation, do you know more about how your department functions than anyone else, including your boss? Would losing you inflict a major hit on the company's ability to serve customers efficiently and quickly? Do you possess important "knowledge capital" (which the company will lose if it lets you go)? Perhaps you're the only one who has kept abreast of changing government requirements for your industry or who knows how to fix a technical "work-around" that leaves a manufacturing process or database vulnerable to failure if it breaks. Maybe you're one of the few people left over from a previous regime and carrier of the organization's "institutional memory"—you remember what's been done and tried and the steps that led to certain decisions. Does this enable you to prevent periodic attempts to reinvent the wheel? Are you the person an important client prefers to work with or the only one in your group with the social skills to smooth over conflicts and keep everyone happy and working at their peak?

If you own your business and you're negotiating a new partnership, think about the special qualities you bring—your leadership skills and vision for the company's future, your contacts in the regional business community, your special relationship with suppliers, your popularity with the local press, your community service record, anything that can be construed as a business asset and a bargaining chip.

While some people overrate their abilities, women often make the opposite mistake; they're too self-effacing. To avoid this trap, look for ways to objectively evaluate your skills. Solicit the help of people who know you (either inside your organization or out) to identify your particular strengths. Remember to factor in any unusual aspects of your situation that might not immediately be recognized as bargaining points but could make a difference. The source of your bargaining power may not be something you can list on your résumé or quantify in concrete terms. Sometimes your power to negotiate comes from value you bring that's hard to measure but very real all the same.

Lydia—CALM AT THE CENTER OF THE STORM

Lydia worked in the secretarial pool of a high-pressure personal injury law firm in Detroit. Certain lawyers at the firm regularly blew up and shouted at the administrative staff and as a result a lot of secretaries only lasted a few months. Those who stayed often refused to work with the notoriously difficult lawyers. But Lydia remained calm whenever a lawyer lost his cool and the office manager relied on her to work with the worst of them.

When Lydia had been at the firm for twelve years, her eighty-year-old mother fell and fractured her hip. Since Lydia was an only child and her father was dead, she had to pack up and sell her mother's house and move her into a nursing home. This was a big job. Her mother lived three hours away, the house needed a lot of repairs, and her mother was too frail to do much. Lydia took her full three weeks of vacation time to get started and then tried to do the rest on weekends. After five draining months of driving back and forth every weekend, she decided to quit her job. She'd get her mother settled and then look for a new position.

When she informed the office manager that she was leaving, he actually stumbled out of his chair, she says. "But you can't leave!" he said. "What do you need? What can we do to help?" He immediately offered to give her two months of paid leave and a third if she needed it. If Lydia had realized how valuable she was to her employer she could have negotiated for the leave she needed much sooner. She could have saved herself five months of stress and exhaustion. Instead, she drove herself to the breaking point.

Natalya—A TOWN INSTITUTION

For thirty years, Natalya taught dance to small children in a prosperous midwestern suburb, renting studio space in a small building on Main Street. When the owner sold the building and gave Natalya thirty days to vacate, she thought her career was over. There was no way she could afford to rent new space in the town at going rates. The town's arts center contained a studio but the center was used exclusively by nonprofit arts organizations.

Sadly, Natalya sent a notice to the parents of her current students saying that she would have to stop giving classes at the end of the month. Her announcement sent shock waves through the family-centered community. Several parents called her immediately. In talking to one of them, she mentioned the studio at the arts center. "I'm on the board of the arts center," the mother said. "Let me look into this." Ten days later the mother called to tell Natalya that she could use the studio every afternoon between 1:30 and 5:00. She would be charged a nominal fee and allowed to use the theater in the building to present her students' recitals, pending schedule conflicts. She started teaching at the arts center the day after she moved out of her old space, with no interruption to the children's schedules.

Helen—LOCATION, LOCATION, LOCATION

Helen worked at a large New England dairy farm as an assistant manager of the dairy's busy ice cream stand. When the dairy opened another stand fifteen miles from the main location, she applied for the job of manager at the new location. The other applicants had more management experience but Helen had several advantages over all of them—she lived half a mile from the new location, she was single, and she could work nights. She pointed this out to the farm manager, who needed round-the-clock oversight at the new stand, and he gave her the job.

Unlike Lydia and Natalya, Helen recognized that she brought something special to the table, factors that didn't appear on her résumé but made her particularly well suited to negotiate for, and get, what she wanted, in her case a job for which consistency in staffing was key.

They Need You as Much as You Need Them

Many of the most profitable businesses today, in the United States and around the world, regard their workforce as one of their most valuable assets. The CEO of the SAS Institute (a large software firm), Jim Goodnight, has been widely quoted as saying, "Ninety-five percent of my assets drive out the front gate every evening. It's my job to bring them back." Goodnight regards "bringing them back" as critical because replacing good workers is incredibly costly.

HOW MUCH DO BUSINESSES SPEND REPLACING WORKERS WHO QUIT?

The U.S. Bureau of Labor Statistics reports that 23.1 percent of the 134 million nonfarm workers in the United States voluntarily quit each year. The Hay Group estimates that a quit costs a company between 50 percent and 150 percent of a worker's annual salary. The U.S. Bureau of Labor Statistics reports that in 2006, median annual earnings were approximately $35,000. Using the more conservative 50 percent cost figure, this means that attrition costs American companies at least $541 billion a year.

Jim Goodnight's commitment to keeping his workers happy reduced annual turnover at SAS to just 3 percent, saving his company between $60 and $80 million a year. Most software firms, in contrast, let 20 percent of their workers leave every year—workers who take their training, knowledge, and skills elsewhere, and cost their employers millions to replace. If your employer would have a hard time replacing you if you quit, or if replacing you would be expensive, that gives you negotiating power, power that comes not just from the value you bring to the table but from the cost to the other side of losing you or what you're offering.

The following table, based on a Hay Group report, illustrates the massive impact attrition rates can have on a company's bottom line.

ANNUAL ATTRITION COSTS FOR A MIDSIZE COMPANY	
Number of employees	5,000
Average salary	$35,000
Total revenues	$500,000,000
Profit margin	10%
Attrition rate among clerical workers	14%
Attrition rate among professional workers	12.5%
Annual cost of attrition	$20,000,000
Cost of attrition is 4 percent of revenues and 40 percent of profits	

The costs of attrition are not the only issue, however. For managers to excel, they need to do more than just run their own groups and see that they function well. They also need to have a long-term vision for their organization's future. This requires more than simply retaining employees and reducing attrition costs. And it requires more than simply hiring good people. They also need to cultivate the talents and make the most of the skills and experience of the people they hire. For this reason, one of the basic mandates of good management is knowing what your employees want—what they want now, what they want to do in the future, and how they foresee getting from here to there.

Recognizing that your boss has a strong stake in keeping you happy and promoting your professional development also gives you bargaining power.

Mindy—IF JOB PRESSURES MAKE YOU WANT TO QUIT, YOUR BOSS NEEDS TO KNOW

Mindy worked for a woman named Claire who'd started a private housecleaning business. After Claire's father was diagnosed with Alzheimer's disease, caring for him began to eat up a lot of Claire's time, forcing Mindy to take over most of Claire's duties. Since she was putting in fifteen to twenty extra hours a week and shouldering so much more responsibility, Mindy thought she deserved a raise. But Claire never acknowledged the extra work Mindy was doing. "She basically dumped her business on me and I was carrying it for her, and she barely noticed," Mindy said. She liked Claire and sympathized with her tough personal situation but she felt caught between two unsatisfactory solutions: either accept her situation or leave.

In truth, Mindy had a third option, which was to tell Claire that she wanted more money because she was doing more work. Claire needed Mindy to be working at full capacity; she surely didn't want her best employee to feel disgruntled and unfairly treated. This gave Mindy a lot of bargaining power. Instead of using it she waited until the pressures on Claire eased up a bit and then quit, an unsatisfactory solution all around. "Claire was really surprised and upset when I said I was leaving," Mindy said. "But I was just too burned out to continue at that point."

WOMEN—IN HIGH DEMAND

In American business today, women have become a highly prized resource. With the pool of talented men entering the labor market shrinking—potentially threatening the ability of many organizations to thrive and grow—the high rates of attrition among female managers have become a pressing concern. Business leaders have begun to realize that they need to make special efforts to retain female employees, many of whom leave organizations before reaching the upper ranks. Very often women leave not because they're stepping out of the workforce to raise their families but because they find their organizational culture inhospitable to women or see few opportunities to rise into the ranks of upper management. In the article "Winning the Talent War for Women," Douglas M. McCracken, writing about Deloitte Consulting's attrition problems in the early 1990s, articulated the problem this way: "In professional services firms . . . the 'product' is talent, billed to the client by the hour; and so much of our firm's product was leaving at an alarming rate." The decline in male college enrollments has also raised a red flag. Women currently represent 57 percent of entering college freshmen (and men only 43 percent). In "Off-Ramps and On-Ramps: Keeping Talented Women on the Road to Success," Sylvia Ann Hewlett and Carolyn Buck Luce report that, "Given current demographic and labor market trends, it's imperative that employers learn to reverse this brain drain. Indeed, companies that can develop policies and practices to tap into the female talent pool over the long haul will enjoy a substantial competitive advantage." Felice N. Schwartz, author of "Women as a Business Imperative," explains that "there simply are not enough capable men available today to fill all of the managerial jobs. . . . The nation's labor pool isn't growing fast enough to keep up with management demand." To ensure that they have high-quality managers at every level, businesses need to cultivate the talents of the women they hire.

In making this point to his senior management team, J. Michael Cook, the CEO of Deloitte Consulting who created the firm's famous Women's Initiative, wrote:

> Half of our hires are now women, and almost all of them have left before becoming partner candidates. We know that in order to get

enough partners to grow the business, we're going to have to go deeper and deeper into the pool of new hires. Are you willing to have more and more of your partners taken from lower and lower in the talent pool? *And* let the high-performing women go elsewhere in the marketplace?

The business world has also discovered that helping women fulfill their professional goals and rise into senior positions is good for business. Studies have shown that women's leadership style, often called "transformational leadership," frequently differs from men's in ways that inspire commitment, increase creative thinking, improve morale, and solicit more input—providing management with more information on which to base critical decisions. Other research suggests that achieving greater gender diversity in the upper echelons of an organization may increase productivity and profitability. As a further incentive, retaining female employees and helping them rise into high positions in an organization enhances an organization's public image. As Schwartz writes in "Women as a Business Imperative":

Today companies compete through their values as well as their products. Customers want to know what a company stands for. When a company can demonstrate that it has moved aggressively in the way it recruits, trains, promotes, rewards, and values women... it will speak directly to the millions of men and women who care deeply about this issue.

Schwartz concludes, "A company's reputation for good human values is as valuable an asset as capital equipment."

Charlotte—HER VALUE NOT REFLECTED BY HER
LEVEL OF RESPONSIBILITY

Charlotte was an executive, the only female executive in senior management, at a computer software company. She was well liked, respected by colleagues and clients, and savvy about the ins and outs of
the business. Everyone in the firm came to her for advice. When her
firm bought another, smaller software company, the CEO consulted
her daily during the rocky process of merging the two firms. After ten
years at the firm, though, she realized that she had a lot of influence
but very little real authority. "Everyone leaned heavily on me," she
said, "but I never got the title and salary that would have reflected
that." Angry and ready to quit, she hired a personal career coach to
help her figure out what to do next. "I'd put in a lot of time at the firm
and if I wasn't going to get to the next level there, I wanted to find another place where I could."

Instead of pointing her in a new direction, the career coach advised
her to use the power of her position—as the most senior woman in the
company, a central figure in the organization who was trusted by both
senior and junior staff—to see if she could get what she wanted.
Without much optimism that it would work, she agreed to give it a
try. "Since I'd already made up my mind to leave I figured I had nothing to lose," she says. She approached the CEO, enumerated her contributions to the work of the firm, and asked to be promoted to vice
president. "I didn't say, 'And by the way you'll be losing your only senior woman,' but he got the point." Taken aback, he thought about it
for a day and called her into his office. "I can't imagine how I'd replace
you," he said. "Not to mention how I'd explain losing you to the
board." He hadn't been thinking about her career goals, he said, and
he wanted to do everything he could to make her happy. Within
weeks, he made her the company's first female vice president and put
her in charge of a new customer services group that would work with

all the product development divisions to build up their customer base. "It was a lot more than I ever hoped for," she said.

The Power of a Good Alternative

We introduced the idea of a BATNA—the best alternative to a negotiated agreement—in Chapter 5. A strong BATNA can be a great source of bargaining power because a strong BATNA gives you a lot of freedom. You don't have to agree to anything that's worse than your alternative. This forces the other negotiator to offer you something great in order to convince you to accept. The opposite is also true: If the other negotiator has a *bad* BATNA, this increases your bargaining strength. In Charlotte's case, both conditions applied. She had a strong BATNA (she was ready to leave) and her boss had a weak one (losing her would be a major blow). Although Charlotte was more than qualified, even if your credentials or experience are less than outstanding, if the other side is in a bind and has no other good choices, that strengthens your position.

Immediately after graduating from college, Sara briefly held a temp job as one of two administrative assistants to the producer of an old soap opera, *The Edge of Night*. She and the other assistant spent their days answering the producer's phone, photocopying scripts, and reading the voluminous fan mail sent in by viewers, some of which was very weird and entertaining. Sara wasn't interested in a permanent job in television, but the other assistant, who wanted to work in TV production, was desperate to "get up to the fourth floor," where the show was filmed. At the beginning of a week of intensive shooting, one of the show's temperamental male stars blew up at a PA (production assistant), insulting her intelligence, her competence, and her looks. The PA quit. Sara's friend, the other administrative assistant, asked the producer if she could have the job. Although she had no experience or formal training, she knew that the producer was in a bind and had no time to look for a replacement outside the current employee pool. Sara's friend got the job.

Debbie—PERFECTLY HAPPY WHERE SHE WAS

Debbie was the managing partner in the Chicago office of a consulting firm with offices all over the world. She loved her job and she loved Chicago, where she'd grown up. One day she received a call from a senior vice president in the United Kingdom who wanted her to apply for a job in the London office. Although the job sounded attractive, Debbie didn't think it could possibly beat her current situation. The vice president was persistent, though, and eventually she agreed to apply. After many rounds of interviews and trips back and forth across the Atlantic, she was offered the position. She was torn. The London job paid more than she currently made and she thought she'd enjoy spending a few years in Britain. But London was a long way from her family and friends.

If she was going to make the move, Debbie decided, the company would have to make it worth her while. She asked for a lot more money and a company apartment because it was expensive to live in London, a car and driver because she didn't know the city well, a generous travel fund, and more vacation time so that she could return often to the United States. Because she would be perfectly happy staying where she was and she understood the power of her strong BATNA, she got everything she wanted.

SOURCES OF BARGAINING POWER

- Education
- Previous employment experiences
- Special skills or training
- Depth of knowledge or expertise
- Unique talents
- Demonstrated performance excellence
- Reputation in your field
- Social or interpersonal skills
- Leadership or team-building abilities
- Client connections
- Internal alliances (if you're already employed)
- Powerful outside contacts (both professional and social)
- Support of a powerful mentor
- Knowledge of the organization's culture, processes, history
- Good alternatives (a strong BATNA)
- Limited choices (weak BATNA) on the other side of the table

MAKING A BAD BATNA BETTER

What if you have a bad BATNA—your fallback position is objectively inferior to your goal? This, of course, happens often. We ask for more because we want something better than we already have. If you're negotiating for a promotion and your BATNA if you don't get it will be the status quo—staying in your current position—you're not on a particularly strong footing. If you're unemployed and applying for jobs, your BATNA is pretty weak. In both cases, you may be able to improve your BATNA by getting another job offer, whether from a different organization or from another department or division within the same organization. If your boss or potential employer doesn't want to lose you, he or she may be more motivated to reach a satisfactory agreement knowing that you have another job to go to. (When Linda's students go out on the job market she tells them to get more than one offer or their BATNA may be moving back in with their parents.)

Ashanti—IN HIGH DEMAND

Ashanti worked for a large bank as the general manager of a busy branch office. She liked her job and knew she was good at it but she felt underpaid. "My job is ten times more stressful and demanding than any other job at the branch but I wasn't earning much more than some of my employees," she said. She pointed this out to her supervisor at the corporate office several times, even providing documentation of all she'd achieved at the branch, but her supervisor was never persuaded. She wondered if perhaps she was mistaken. She didn't know for a fact whether she was fairly paid or not.

To find out, Ashanti took what felt like a bold step. She applied for jobs at three other large banks in the area. She received offers from all three, each paying about 25 percent more than she was earning. When she told her supervisor about the offers, he immediately said he would match them. Taking a deep breath, she said, "Can you beat them, though? I'd like to stay here but these other banks really want me." After some discussion, he agreed to raise her salary by 30 percent instead of the 25 offered by the other banks, and she agreed to stay, which is what she'd wanted all along.

Having these other offers really boosted Ashanti's bargaining power with her current boss. They gave her leverage so that he would take her attempts to negotiate her salary seriously. But is getting another offer always a good idea? Is it dishonest to apply for a job, go through the interview process, and persuade another organization to make you an offer you're not planning to take? Not at all. Most organizations want to know who's out there—who's good, who's restless and ready for the next step, and who may not be getting the recognition he or she deserves. They're also grateful for the chance to woo away good people if they can. And you may surprise yourself and de cide to take the new job after all. But remember, don't accept a new job without giving your current boss the opportunity to counteroffer. And use your willingness to stay where you are to negotiate the terms of the new position.

What about antagonizing your present boss by using another offer as a bargaining chip? This is a valid concern. If the offer is credible (it's a good offer and you'll take it if your boss won't negotiate to keep you), then there's really no risk. Your new offer is better than your BATNA (your current job). If your boss does decide to keep you, so much the better. Of course, it's never a good idea to burn bridges, so always make your proposal in a good-natured way. Making ultimatums usu- ally backfires.

You're on less secure footing if the new offer doesn't match your current position—if you don't really want it and you're only using it as leverage. This doesn't mean you shouldn't get the other offer or stay silent about it if you do. But you need to be mindful of how you pre- sent the other offer to your boss—not as a threat or a club to get him to do what you want but as one factor in a decision-making process about your future (see Chapter 14, "The Likability Factor," for a broader discussion of this). Here are some ways to approach the dis- cussion:

- "I don't want you to hear through the grapevine that I've received a job offer from another company. I haven't decided what I'm go- ing to do and I'd like to ask your advice. Are you open to dis- cussing my salary?"

- "I've received another offer and I'm really torn. I'd rather stay here but I'm not sure how I fit into the company's future plans. I'd like to talk about that with you."

- "I've received another offer but I do love working here. How much flexibility do I have? Can we look at making a few changes?"

- "I'm mixed about accepting this other offer I've received. Can you give me any advice about what I need to do to move ahead here?"

- "This other job has a number of attractive features. Can we make some of those things happen for me in this job?"

In some situations, unfortunately, none of these tactics may work. Although in certain fields collecting outside offers as a negotiating tactic is time-honored, respected, and no big deal, in others it's a dicier proposition. Some supervisors, told by an employee that she's received another offer, will point to the door without hesitating, and say, "Congratulations. We wish you well" (and don't let the door hit you on your way out, et cetera). Experienced managers also tend to have good radar—they can tell when another offer is just a ploy and an employee is angling for leverage, not seriously considering the other job. In these situations, if you really don't want to leave, using another offer can be a risky tactic. If you've been recruited by another firm and you're genuinely torn, however, sharing this with your boss may prompt him or her to try to keep you. You'll need to read your circumstances carefully and proceed accordingly.

BUILDING MUSCLE

Sometimes you simply don't have enough bargaining power to get what you want right now. You don't have all the qualifications you need or something in your circumstances has prevented you from showing what you can do, making you appear less capable than you really are. Maybe you're not missing a particular skill or qualification, you just haven't achieved the performance levels necessary to move up. Or maybe you haven't reached higher performance targets because of constraints inherent to your organization.

To improve your credentials, start by working backward from

where you want to be to where you are now. Do you need more years of experience, a different kind of experience, or some type of additional training? Check out local community colleges, university extension schools, and executive education programs to see if they offer courses that will help round out your résumé. Are you part of a team with low-functioning members, and is your work evaluated solely on the basis of the team's performance? Talk to your supervisor about establishing evaluation criteria that rate the contributions of individual team members. Or get the whole team together and brainstorm ways to improve your overall productivity. If you don't think this will work, ask to be switched to another team, one in which you'll have more opportunities to show what you can do. If you need to demonstrate your leadership ability, offer to take on an unpopular project, agree to coordinate a special event, or volunteer to work with a difficult client whose business is important to your employer. In addition to giving you a chance to show your stuff, you'll win points for extra commitment. Be imaginative, think long-term as well as about the immediate future, and remember that any way in which you can increase your value to your employer also increases your power to negotiate for what you want, whatever that is.

Sandy—THE ENTREPRENEURIAL EMPLOYEE

Sandy, the development director for a nonprofit in a small southern state, faced this dilemma. Her job was to write grants and solicit gifts to the agency from individual donors and corporations. She'd been fairly successful but she'd never landed any really large grants. She felt as though her career was stagnating.

Sandy asked a few of her friends who worked in development to help her figure out what to do. They concluded that a major factor holding her back was her limited contacts outside the region. Establishing personal relationships with granting officers could mean the difference between success and failure, but so many of the largest granting organizations were far away. To solicit those large donations successfully, Sandy needed to visit potential donors and discuss her organization's needs face-to-face. Spurred by this advice, Sandy asked the director of her agency if the organization could invest a small amount of money in a travel budget, arguing that the return from winning larger grants and donations would far outweigh the costs of sending her on a few trips. The director agreed, but he couldn't manage it—the organization just didn't have the funds.

After mulling it over, Sandy decided to invest some of her own money, and time, in travel. She'd been planning a long weekend in New York to visit her sister. She took a full week of vacation instead, spent four days in New York visiting foundations and then took the train to Washington to meet with granting officers at several government agencies. A few months later she visited her best friend from grade school, who'd moved to Seattle, and met with a couple of corporate donors while she was there. She made a third trip, again paying her own way, to Los Angeles for a beach vacation interspersed with a few visits to funding sources. After each meeting, she followed up with phone calls, e-mails, and press clippings about her organization's contributions to the community. Within fourteen months of her first trip to New York she'd brought in four grants that together doubled her organization's budget. She approached the director of the agency again and persuaded him to include funds for travel in the next year's budget. She also negotiated for a promotion and a raise. In less than three years, Sandy increased her own salary by 27 percent and began receiving job offers from other nonprofits.

Ileana—MAKING HERSELF A KEY PLAYER

Ileana worked as a junior designer at a small graphic design firm. The firm's two founding partners handled all the important design work themselves, leaving the grunt work to Ileana—mocking-up proposals and laying out corporate brochures and annual reports. She considered getting another job but hesitated, not sure what she wanted. One day, paging through client portfolios in search of lost contact information, something caught her attention. Several customers had recently requested Web site design services. Since the firm didn't have a technical person on staff to produce the Web sites, the partners farmed out all this work to a consultant.

Ileana fancied herself something of a closet computer geek. She subscribed to several computer magazines, was an early adopter of new technology, and loved getting into the guts of a software program and playing around with what her computer could do. She also liked to shop and browse for information on the Web and had strong opinions about what made a Web site effective and user-friendly. She thought she'd have no trouble learning to translate a design concept into a functioning site.

Getting on the Web, Ileana discovered that business budgets for Web site design and support were growing faster than budgets for every other category of design work, and that more and more graphic design firms were entering the lucrative Web-design business. Scanning the course offerings at a local technical college, she found what looked like an excellent two-semester course in Web site programming. Ileana asked the partners if they would pay her tuition to take the programming course. Training her in this area would make the firm more of a full-service shop, she argued, and would cost far less than outsourcing this function every time a client asked for a Web site design. The partners agreed. Ileana rapidly became so proficient that they made her director of Web design programming within a year and began actively marketing Web site design as one of the firm's specialties. (She didn't tell us how much, but they also gave her a *big* raise.)

POWER SURGE

A fundamental part of laying the groundwork for a negotiation involves assessing the various ways in which you bring value to an employer, partner, or client. Eugene Carr, the founder and president of PatronTechnologies, an e-mail marketing service for arts organizations, says that, compared to his male employees, far more of the women he's met in his career prize "job satisfaction, personal growth, office camaraderie, respecting their boss, and belief in a larger goal" as desirable parts of their work experience. Women's commitment to those intangibles makes them great employees, he says—easier to work with, more likely to enjoy what they're doing, with a better attitude toward teamwork. Not enough women recognize the value of these traits, he says, and therefore underestimate their own value as employees. When assessing your own bargaining power, it's crucial to remember that value comes from a combination of quantifiable factors—the "hard stuff" on your résumé—and intangibles such as those described by Gene Carr. And don't forget that power is not static. You can and should actively work to boost yours where you can.

PHASE THREE

Get Ready

9

AIM HIGH

Gwen worked for six years as the business manager of a winery in northern New York State. During those six years, wine sales more than tripled, the permanent staff grew from eleven people to twenty-six, and the winery won two prizes at international winemaking competitions. Given how well the company was doing and how much her responsibilities had grown, Gwen thought that maybe she could ask for a 10 percent increase rather than the standard 3 percent she got every year. But she liked the job and didn't want to spoil things by making a ridiculous salary request. Unsure what to do, she did a little poking around on the Web and called a few contacts she'd made at winemaking competitions. She learned that business managers at comparable small California wineries typically earned more than twice what she was making.

Because New York State wines are not California wines she thought that asking to double her salary would be way too much. After a week of anxious nights, she decided to request a 25 percent raise. The owner didn't even hesitate. "You're absolutely right. You're doing a lot more than we hired you to do," he said. "You practically run this place." (We've heard so many stories from women whose

145

bosses said the same thing—you practically run the place.) Although pleased by the compliment and by the raise, Gwen wondered afterward if she'd actually set her sights too low. Since the owner had agreed so readily to a 25 percent increase, would he have given her more if she'd asked?

SHOOT FOR MORE AND YOU'LL GET MORE

For many women, the fear of overestimating what they're worth, poisoning a good relationship, or being ridiculous drastically limits how much they try for when they negotiate. Research has consistently shown that there's a direct correlation between your target—what you aim for in a negotiation—and what you get. Women typically aim too low. This phenomenon cuts across all professions and all levels of seniority. Even extraordinarily successful women often underestimate the value of their skills and expertise.

This is a simple but critical point: One of the most important determinants of your success in a negotiation occurs before you open your mouth—before you even walk into the room. So if the voice in your head says that what you want is "too much," make sure that it's not actually far below what's realistic and appropriate. By the time you start the conversation, you've already lost half the battle if you haven't set a high enough target for yourself. If you walk in aiming to get less, you're guaranteed to walk out with less.

Negotiators who set higher targets get better results, first, because they make higher initial requests than people who set lower targets, which prevents them from prematurely cutting off the upper end of what's possible. If Gwen had asked for the 10 percent increase she'd originally planned to request, it's doubtful that the owner of the winery would have insisted on giving her 25 percent instead. If you ask for less, it's the rare employer who will voluntarily give you more.

Making higher initial requests also defines the parameters for the rest of the negotiation. If you're negotiating over the price of a new car and you start by offering the salesperson $500 below the sticker price, that sends a message that you're willing to pay close to the sticker price. If you instead offer $3,000 less than the sticker price, you signal that you want a better deal. A salesperson might make only a minimal concession to a buyer who offers $500 less than the sticker price, dropping the price perhaps $100 or $150, or he might hold firm, saying that he can't go any lower. To a buyer who makes a more aggressive first offer, a salesperson knows he has to make a better counteroffer or risk watching the customer walk away to another dealership. Of course, offering $10,000 for a $30,000 car isn't an effective strategy. Your target should be ambitious but not impossible. An unrealistic target won't get you very far.

AIMING HIGH OVER A LIFETIME

Two colleagues differ in their approach to negotiating: One consistently sets high targets for her annual salary increases and the other aims lower. The one who always aims high averages 4.3 percent raises every year. The one who sets lower targets averages 2.7 percent annual raises. If both start out earning $35,000 when they're twenty-two, by the time they reach sixty-five, the person who aimed higher will be earning $213,941. The person who consistently aimed lower will be earning only $110,052—$103,889 less. The person who aimed higher will also have earned $1,485,603 more between the ages of twenty-two and sixty-five than the person who aimed lower. If she invested this difference in an account with a 3 percent interest rate, she'd have an extra $2,120,730 saved.

Jan—NO IDEA HOW MUCH SHE WAS WORTH

Jan was the housekeeping manager at a large luxury hotel in Bermuda. Housekeeping is a critical function in the luxury hotel business, involving hundreds of low-skilled workers, long days, tight schedules, massive inventories (linens, soaps, shampoo, hand lotion, cleaning products, uniforms), and—in the best hotels—no margin for error. The luxury hotel world in Bermuda is a small one, and when someone is good, everyone knows it. And Jan was very, very good. As a result, rival hotels constantly tried to recruit her. Since she was happy where she was (she had a very strong BATNA), she would only want to switch jobs for a big jump in salary. So every time this happened, Jan decided to ask for an outrageous amount of money. Before each interview, Jan's husband, a hotel general manager, asked her how much she thought was outrageous—how much she planned to ask for. If she said $5,000 more than her current salary, he'd say "Ask for $10,000 more." If she said $6,000 more than she was making, he'd say, "Ask for $12,000." Every time Jan followed her husband's advice, and every time she got what she asked for. And whenever she told her current employer that she was leaving for another job, he would match the offer and convince her to stay. In six years, she increased her salary by $36,000. (One general manager told her that she was making more than he made.) Truly a star, at the top of her profession, Jan still drastically underestimated what she was worth, and therefore what she should aim for. Even when she met Sara and told her this story, she still couldn't quite believe that she was paid so well.

YOU'RE GOOD, YOU'RE READY, YOU DESERVE IT

You might wonder why we're dedicating a whole chapter to the importance of setting a high target. It seems like a pretty straightforward idea: higher target, better outcome. Unfortunately, for many women, it's not so simple. We're smart, we're hardworking, and we know we're doing good work, but we still find all sorts of reasons for questioning whether we deserve more than we already have.

That annoying voice says: "If you really deserved more, someone would have given it to you by now."

It says: "Okay, you work hard, but lots of people work hard."

It says: "What makes you think you should have so much more than other people?"

Of course, hardly anyone, male or female, is immune to self-doubt. At some point, we all question whether we deserve what we want. But women tend to ask this question much more frequently than men do. In study after study, researchers have found that women have a low sense of what psychologists call personal entitlement.

One study asked undergraduate business students applying for similar jobs to predict two things: what they'd be offered as a starting salary and how much they were likely to earn at their career peak, the year they earned the most. Although the women in the group were just as qualified as the men, they expected to earn starting salaries that were 11.5 percent lower than those the men expected to get. Their guesses about their career-peak pay were 24 percent lower than those of the men. The women didn't think they were less talented or had less potential. They simply underestimated what their abilities were worth and how much prospective employers would be prepared to pay them.

In another study, researchers compared women's and men's estimates of what would be fair pay for a variety of jobs. They found that women's estimates of fair pay for first jobs were 4 percent lower than men's; women's estimates of career-peak pay were 23 percent lower than those of men.

A 2007 study published by CNN/*Money* asked thousands of MBA students about their expected future earnings. Female MBA students' estimates of what they would be earning one year after graduation averaged $89,599 while male MBAs thought they'd be earning $97,519 on average, almost 9 percent more. Five years after graduation, women expected to be earning $164,046 while men expected to be earning $204,372, almost 25 percent more.

In Chapter 6 we described a study in which researchers asked college students to review the admissions folders of a number of (fictional) college applicants and then pay themselves for the work they'd done (the men paid themselves 63 percent more on average than the women). Similar studies have been conducted with schoolchildren. Researchers asked the children to perform a small task and then pay themselves what they thought they deserved (the six-year-olds paid themselves with Hershey's Kisses). The results dramatically demonstrated that women's depressed sense of personal entitlement starts young. In first, fourth, seventh, and tenth grades, girls consistently paid themselves less than boys—between 30 and 78 percent less.

Petra—NOT SURE HER BOSS WOULD THINK SHE WAS READY

Petra worked for her friend Naomi, who had a wedding and events planning business in the northern suburbs of Washington, D.C. Naomi's business was extremely successful and Petra knew that she was an asset—she was meticulous, organized, and had great social skills. Clients loved her and so did the point people at the various venues (hotels, banquet halls, historic buildings) where she and Naomi staged their events.

After working for Naomi for five years, Petra married and moved south of D.C. to a town in Virginia. Petra now had an hour-long commute to work and frequently found herself stuck and fuming in Beltway traffic. She wondered whether Naomi would be receptive to expanding her business into Virginia by opening a second office that Petra would run. She did a little asking around and convinced herself that there would be enough business to justify the second location, but she didn't know how Naomi would respond to the idea. Although she'd staged over a hundred events and taken charge of the office when Naomi went on vacation, she still worried that Naomi might think she didn't have enough experience to run a satellite office by herself.

"I was afraid to ask her," Petra said. "There were all sorts of reasons that she might have said no—it wasn't the right time, or she didn't have enough capital, or whatever. But all I could think about was that she was going to say she didn't trust me to do the job myself. Then of course I'd be humiliated and have to quit and it would ruin our friendship and my career would be in the toilet, and so on. And the thing is, Naomi isn't even like that. She doesn't humiliate people. But I was still afraid to ask her."

Petra had been living in Virginia for fourteen months when she met someone at a party who asked her to organize a huge event in Richmond, an hour south of D.C. When Petra told Naomi about the job, she hesitantly added, "You know, I've been thinking we should open a Virginia office. Maybe I could run it."

Naomi pounced on the idea at once. "Grow the business!" she said. "That's my next step. Absolutely, set it up." Petra had been so worried that Naomi would think she wasn't qualified that she never considered the possibility that her idea might help Naomi fulfill some of her own goals, that Naomi might welcome the suggestion rather than bat it down.

Tamlyn—DOING MORE? GET PAID MORE

Tamlyn worked in the administrative offices of a large health care services corporation. When her boss, Marie, left for an extended maternity leave, the office supervisor asked Tamlyn to take over Marie's job while continuing to do her own. To keep up, Tamlyn was forced to work late most nights and come in over the weekend too. Since she was putting in so much time and carrying such a heavy load of responsibility, she thought about asking for a bonus, a larger contribution to her 401(k) plan, or perhaps an extra week or two of vacation when her boss returned. She'd heard stories about the organization rewarding high-performing employees in all three of these ways at different times. The office supervisor never offered her any additional compensation, however, and Tamlyn suspected that this was because her performance wasn't good enough. She knew she wasn't doing Marie's job as well as

Marie did it, or as well as she could do it herself if the demands of her own job didn't siphon off so much of her time. And she wasn't doing her own job as well as usual for the same reason. She decided to forget it. Marie would be back in a few months anyway.

Like Tamlyn, many women hold themselves to unrealistically high standards of performance. And of course doing good work is admirable, important, and an overarching goal. But sometimes we're asked to do something else: We're asked to do *more* rather than *better*. This was true in Tamlyn's case, and she deserved to be rewarded for taking on extra responsibilities and working so many additional hours. Since this was not a permanent situation, she might not have been able to negotiate a permanent salary increase, but asking for some sort of bonus as a reward for the six months in which she carried dual responsibilities would have been perfectly appropriate.

RELY ON THE FACTS

In many cases, women don't ask for as much as they can get because they lack knowledge about the marketplace—they don't know what other people are getting. This problem is particularly acute in industries without fixed and well-known pay standards. One of Linda's studies discovered that the gap between men's and women's average salaries in industries without standardized pay structures is more than three times as large as the gap in industries in which pay scales are well publicized and widely understood. Women are also at greater risk of undervaluing themselves when they work in unique situations in which comparisons can be hard to make.

The remedy in every case is to track down as much information as you can. If you do work in an industry without standardized pay structures or easily available data, figure out whom you can trust, take a few people to lunch, and be imaginative in pinning down what you need to know. (Refer back to Chapters 6 and 7 for guidance.) Make sure you're comparing yourself to the right people, though. Don't tumble into the trap of comparing yourself solely to other women (who still make only three-quarters of what men earn) or to women who are your social peers but not necessarily at the same level professionally. Finding out what comparable people get—people performing similar work with similar experience to yours—can help you fight the inclination to undersell yourself. There's nothing like solid evidence to help you set the right target and send you into your negotiation feeling confident that you deserve what you want.

YOU NEED MORE INFORMATION

Researchers asked participants to negotiate in pairs over the price of a single item, with one member of the pair acting as the buyer and the other as the seller. Among buyers who had no information about the typical price for the item, women paid 27 percent more on average than men in the study paid. But when buyers were given information about the approximate value of the item, the gap closed substantially (though not completely), with women paying only 8 percent more on average than the men.

Nina—BETTER CREDENTIALS BUT ASKING FOR THE SAME RATE

After graduating from college with a double degree in child psychology and education, Nina passed the tests needed to get her teaching license. While looking for a full-time position, she took a temporary job at an elementary school, filling in for a kindergarten teacher who had to have back surgery. The town only had half-day morning kindergarten at the time, and the regular teacher had prepared a curriculum guide for the three months when she'd be away. This left Nina free every afternoon, and since the substitute job didn't pay very well she replied to an ad on

Craigslist for a part-time nanny. The woman who had posted the ad (a friend of Sara's) needed someone to pick up her two children after school, play with them, help with their homework, and give them dinner before she and her husband arrived home at seven. Nina took her college transcript to the interview as well as recommendations from her professors and from other families for whom she'd worked. The kids liked her immediately and Sara's friend offered Nina the job on the spot. She asked Nina what she wanted to be paid. Nina had not checked out what nannies typically earn. She'd been getting $10 an hour for babysitting so she asked for $10 an hour. Sara's friend laughed, and said, "Let's try that again. Nannies around here usually get $15 an hour and most of them don't have any training at all. You have a degree in child psychology, you're a certified teacher, and you're going to drive an hour each way to get here. You're going to be doing homework with my kids, not just changing diapers. I don't typically insist on paying people more than they ask for but I don't want to take advantage of you."

Taken aback, Nina hesitantly asked for $20 an hour.

"Much better," said the mom. "How about $17?"

NEGOTIATE AS HARD FOR YOURSELF AS YOU WOULD FOR SOMEONE ELSE

When *Women Don't Ask* first came out, our publisher sent the two of us on a book tour to promote it. During one five-week period, we visited eight cities. We spoke to women's professional associations, gave readings at bookstores, and talked about the book on television and on the radio. By the time we hit Los Angeles, Linda was exhausted, she'd lost her voice, and she was running a fever. Fortunately, Linda grew up in Pasadena, not far from L.A., and she stayed with her mother during that leg of the trip. The morning after we arrived, Linda's mother called her own doctor to get Linda an appointment. The receptionist who answered said that the office was swamped and there was no way she could squeeze Linda in. Rather than accepting this refusal, Linda's mother asked to speak to the nurse. The nurse said that one of the doctors in the practice was out that day and it was impossible to find time for Linda. Again, instead of accepting this answer, Linda's mother asked to speak to the doctor. The nurse reluctantly paged the doctor to pick up the phone. Because Linda's mother had been a patient for many years, the doctor agreed to see Linda right away. Through every stage of the process, Linda's mother remained pleasant and polite. But she didn't give up.

If Linda's mother had been sick herself, Linda feels sure that the negotiation would have stopped when the receptionist said there were no openings. Linda's mother would have waited a day or two to see the doctor no matter how sick she felt. But because it was her daughter who was sick, Linda's mother persevered until she persuaded someone to do what she wanted.

One additional point about this story is important. Linda's mom didn't worry that Linda wasn't entitled to special treatment. But she surely would have questioned that if the appointment had been for herself.

WOMEN KNOW WHAT OTHERS ARE WORTH

In one research study, students were asked to write a series of opinions about campus-related issues. Half the students were then asked to indicate how much they thought they should be paid for the work; the other half were asked how much they thought someone else should be paid for doing the same work. Women paid themselves much less than men—19 percent less. But they paid other people more—about as much as the men paid themselves. This tells us that women can often accurately assess the value of a task as long as it's being performed by someone else. It's when they're trying to calculate the value of their own work that self-doubt swoops in.

We told the following story in *Women Don't Ask* but we want to repeat it here because it's so revealing. Gabriela, fifty, was the general manager of a leading symphony orchestra. On behalf of the orchestra she routinely negotiated with musicians' unions, charitable foundations, record companies, and concert halls. She was known and respected as a tough and skillful bargainer. She knew that she was good at her job and a huge asset to the organization. Nonetheless, she could never bring herself to ask the symphony's board of directors for what she thought would be a fair raise. Every year she presented the board with a list of salaries earned by the general managers of other orchestras, and every year she accepted what they offered her. "I think they'd respect me more if I said something back," she told Linda. "They're probably wondering, how good can she be at negotiating for the orchestra if she can't even negotiate for herself?" Even though the benefits of asking are obvious to Gabriela (not just more money but greater respect from her board), she can't bring herself to do it.

This story may seem hard to believe, but Gabriela is not alone in her discomfort around negotiating for herself. Most women negotiate far more effectively on behalf of others—setting higher targets, arguing the merits of their case, and resisting concessions—than they negotiate for themselves. This is true both of younger, less experienced women and of older, highly successful women working at the peaks of their professions. One of Linda's studies looked specifically at senior executives from private industry and government agencies (company presidents, directors, chairwomen, chief executive officers, chief operating officers, chief financial officers, agency heads). When they were negotiating for someone else, these ambitious, experienced, and successful women reached agreements that were 18 percent better on average than the agreements they accepted when they were negotiating for themselves. Men, in contrast, negotiated equally good agreements for themselves as they did for others.

Once you recognize your ability to set more appropriate targets for others, it becomes easier to do the same for yourself. Ask yourself, if you were negotiating for your sister or your best friend, what goals would you set? How much would you think she deserved? If you were negotiating for your daughter, a colleague you respect, or a woman you're mentoring, would the situation look different? How much more would you think was fair? The chances are you'd aim much higher. Step away and look at your own situation objectively. If this is hard, ask a friend or colleague who admires your work to weigh in. Doing so should give you a more accurate perception of what a person with your skills, years of experience, and qualifications deserves. It should make you feel entitled to more of what you want, convince you to set higher targets, and help you hang in there and hold out for what you deserve.

Eleanor—OKAY FOR MY HUSBAND BUT NOT FOR ME

Eleanor was married with two kids. Both she and her husband worked full-time, she as a pediatrician and he as a management consultant. She had a busy practice, worked late two nights a week, and was on call one weekend a month. Her husband also worked hard, putting in sixty to seventy hours a week and traveling constantly. Every August, to recharge his batteries, he took a three-week fishing trip to Canada with his brothers. Although this made August a tough month for her, Eleanor could see that the trip was good for her husband. He always came back in a great mood, far more relaxed than when he'd left, with more energy for the kids and for her.

When a group of her medical school friends invited her to join them for a five-day "girls' getaway" at a spa in Arizona, however, the situation didn't seem as clear-cut. Eleanor wanted to go and knew she could use the break. But it would be hard for her husband to handle the kids by himself while she was away, and the spa was expensive. How could she justify being so extravagant? Most of all, Eleanor didn't think she deserved to take so much time away from her children when the kids were always hungry for more time with her as it was. She decided not to go.

Eleanor could see clearly that her husband worked hard and deserved to take his annual fishing trips, and she could see that taking those trips was not just good for him but good for the family. But like Tamlyn she expected an awful lot of herself. She couldn't see that she too deserved and needed a break, and that the whole family would benefit if she paid attention to her own emotional and physical health once in a while.

IT'S NOT ABOUT HOW MUCH YOU NEED; IT'S ABOUT HOW MUCH YOU'RE WORTH

What if your needs are modest, though, or you're getting by fine on what you're already making? Do you *have* to set a high target? Is it really necessary to get as much as you can? In most cases, the answer is still yes. You should aim high in your salary negotiations anyway because, as the saying goes, money is never just money. More than just a way to pay your bills, your salary functions as a gauge of your professional progress and an important source of information about your abilities. Employers use applicants' compensation records as one measure of their talent and potential. If two applicants with similar qualifications apply for a job, a prospective employer may conclude that the person who has consistently been paid more must be the better candidate. Like most of us, employers often assume that the more "expensive" choice is superior to the "cheaper" alternative. (A high school math tutor told us that the number of her clients doubled when she raised her fee from $40 to $80 an hour. Because she was more expensive, the parents in the area assumed she was better.) By not earning as much as you're worth, you risk communicating something inaccurate about your abilities. If you allow yourself to be chronically underpaid, you may inadvertently disqualify yourself from opportunities that come your way down the line.

Frances—I HAVE PLENTY

Shortly after completing a master's degree in urban planning, Frances was offered a job at a nonprofit organization dedicated to developing and managing low-income housing. When the executive director of the organization proposed a starting salary of $48,000, Frances accepted without negotiating.

Soon after Frances started the job, the executive director's secretary knocked on her office door.

"Can we talk for a minute?" the secretary asked.

When Frances nodded, the secretary came in and closed the door.

"I probably shouldn't be doing this," she said, "but you know Evan and José?" Evan and José and Frances had all been hired at the same time. "They're both making a lot more than you are. A lot more."

The secretary told Frances that the two men had negotiated for higher salaries before accepting their jobs, and she encouraged Frances to talk to the executive director about adjusting her salary to match theirs. Frances wasn't sure, though. She thought $48,000 was a good salary to be earning right out of school. She could live comfortably on that salary. It seemed somehow greedy to ask for more money when the whole agency was about helping poor people. Maybe Evan and José had better qualifications. Maybe there were good reasons why they deserved more than she did.

The secretary insisted that this was not the case. If anything, she said, Frances was the most qualified of the three. She was certainly the one the executive director had been most excited about hiring. "I really think it's just that the men asked for more and you didn't," she said.

Frances turned this information over in her head for several weeks, confused about what to do. In the end, she decided not to ask for the salary adjustment. She was okay with what she was earning, she didn't need more. It didn't occur to her that when she applied for her next job, the salary she'd accepted at this one would be among the data considered by her future employer.

NEVER MIND WHAT YOU CAN LIVE WITH— WHAT WOULD YOU LOVE TO GET?

One of the lovely consequences of writing our last book is that we get lots of fan mail from women who want to share their tales of negotiation success. These remarkable stories have revealed the breadth of issues that women have felt inspired to try to change, and provided glimpses into the ways in which our readers have truly remade their lives by shaking their heads free of old constraints and hesitations. Every aspect of your life has the potential to be transformed by negotiation. So rather than worrying about asking for too much, start thinking about what you really want. Reflect on what would delight you, not what you're willing to settle for, what would make you feel terrific, not what you know is an easy bet. Revisit the hopes and goals you identified in Chapter 2. Consider whether some of those goals might be revised upward, whether wishes that seemed extravagant at the beginning of this process may actually represent less than you can get. The key here is to think big and commit yourself to achieving your goal.

DON'T THINK	THINK
"I can manage with an extra $25 a week."	"I'm going to ask for twice that much because that's how much I'm worth."
"They probably won't balk at 5 percent more."	"I'm going to shoot for 10 percent more because that would make me feel fairly recognized for my hard work and dedication."
"I know I can get this promotion without ruffling any feathers."	"I want a position that allows me to show how much more I can do."

DON'T THINK	THINK
"I'll apply for that job, everyone knows I can handle it."	"I'm ready to stretch myself—what would I like to try?"
"My contractor will probably agree to do the job for 5 percent less than his bid."	"Let's see if he'll shave 15 percent off the price."
"I'm sure my partner will do the grocery shopping occasionally if I ask."	"I'm going to work out a truly fair division of responsibilities at home."
"I'm pretty good at this job."	"Where can I add the most value? That's what I want to do."
"I'm well paid. My title doesn't really matter."	"What title would describe my real responsibilities and convey the authority I need to do my job?"
"I can't expect to enjoy work too much. That's why they call it work."	"What would be really fun?"

COMMIT TO YOUR GOAL

To commit to a goal, you have to believe in it. It might feel out of the question to ask for a 25 percent increase (like Gwen at the winery) when most people only get 3 or 4 percent a year. But don't make your decisions about what you deserve based on what most people get. Start from the premise that you're not most people. You're you, your situation is unique, and you should be paid what *you're* worth. And that's probably more than you're getting now. Review the sources of your bargaining power and remind yourself of all the reasons why you deserve what you want. Those reasons could include:

- "I've been here for five years. I've more than paid my dues."
- "The standard pay for someone with my experience is 10 percent more than I'm making now."

- "I'm the only one in the office with my particular set of skills. No one else can do what I do."
- "It would take them months to train someone else to do my job."
- "My clients love me. I always figure out a way to get them what they need."
- "Two people were doing this job before they hired me."
- "Everyone turns to me for advice because *I know more than everyone else.*"
- "I have two advanced degrees, contacts throughout my field, and a great reputation."
- "I'm the only person on the team who can see the big picture as well as all the little ones."
- "Feeling guilty isn't good for my kids or me."

Focus on the positives—all your qualifications and experience—and resist the temptation to doubt yourself. Ask for promotions when you deserve them, ask for more money when you're being asked to take on more responsibility, and last but not least, remember that perfection can't be the goal. You're doing your best, and that's probably a lot better than you think.

10

THE POWER OF
COOPERATIVE BARGAINING

ASKING QUESTIONS, listening closely, thinking creatively, and working together to solve problems—these are skills many women possess. They're also skills that make for great negotiators. When people work together to achieve a mutually satisfactory solution, they're more likely to feel committed to the terms of that agreement. When negotiators forgo competing for dominance and instead work together to solve problems, rather than straining their relationship they more often improve it. No one feels bullied or mistreated, and no one leaves the negotiation angry. Both, or all, parties learn more about each other, show that they're willing to be flexible, and build trust.

When we imagine negotiating, however, many of us picture the sort of interaction we described in Chapter 5. To do well, we think we need to stake out an extreme position, conceal information from the other side, and bluff. We have to be able to endure bullying, stonewalling, and the anger of the other negotiator without faltering. We should be prepared to propose ultimatums and hold firm even when we see that our stance is making the other negotiator frustrated or unhappy. Rather than use these hardball strategies and risk ruining our relationship with the person on the other side of the table, many of us decide not to ask at all.

The good news is that this is a false choice—we don't have to choose between what we want and the relationships we want to protect. We don't have to embrace the "I win/you lose" style of negotiating in order to succeed. The hardball style is far from the only way, or even the best way, to get what you want. The past thirty years of negotiation scholarship have shown that taking a collaborative, problem-solving approach to negotiations produces better agreements than approaching them as wars to be won. You may have heard this referred to as a search for "win/win" solutions or as "cooperative bargaining." Although this is not a new idea, it is a powerful and important one, and particularly useful for women.

WIN/WIN

Why is cooperative bargaining superior to competitive bargaining? Perhaps most persuasively because cooperative bargaining tends to produce better outcomes, not just for you, but for both sides. Two people who take a cooperative, problem-solving approach to a negotiation will each "get more" than either will get if they stake out an aggressive position and try to "win" the negotiation. How can that be?

Imagine that a young married couple, Sophia and James, who live in Los Angeles, sit down together to plan their one week of summer vacation. Sophia wants to rent a house on the beach near San Diego but James wants to take a camping trip in the Sierra Nevada Mountains. They approach this difference as a win/lose dispute: Either Sophia will "win" and they'll go to the beach or James will "win" and they'll go camping. They eventually decide to compromise—after three days at the beach they'll pack their bags and go camping. Although this might be good for their marriage, it won't be as relaxing as staying in the same place all week. And neither will get what she or he wants, which is a full week in a place with all the desirable features of their dream vacation. Suppose, instead, that Sophia tells James that she wants to go to the beach because she loves swimming and sailing and nothing's more relaxing for her than lying on the sand reading a novel. James tells Sophia that he prefers the mountains because they're less crowded and he likes to go hiking. Together, they go to their computer, do a little research, and find a resort in Costa Rica where they can both get what they want—a beach (but not a crowded one), swimming, sailing, *and* hiking. With this solution, both Sophia and James can have the vacation they want—both sides can "win." They reach a decision that's better for both of them than splitting their vacation week between two locations.

Once they resolve to work together to find a mutually satisfactory solution, negotiators can often find imaginative ways to address everyone's interests. They may also identify additional resources, opportunities, and concessions that they can use to reach an agreement that suits them both. Negotiation experts call this "enlarging the pie."

Here's an example of how it can work. Imagine that Lilly, a veterinarian, owns and operates a small veterinary hospital. A national chain of veterinary hospitals approaches her about selling. Lilly loves being a vet, she feels loyal to her customers and their pets, and she doesn't want to stop working. But if she gets the right price, she could *afford* to stop working. And her kids are teenagers now. She'd like to take them to Europe for a month; she'd like to take them to China. But she can only ever find another vet to cover for her for a week at a time. She's also sick of spending her nights and weekends doing paperwork—that was never why she wanted to become a vet.

Assuming that this is a one-issue negotiation in which the only issue is the sale price for her practice, Lilly could go back and forth with the representatives of the national chain. If they offer her enough money, she could sell. If she sells for a price that's her bare minimum (her reservation value), the chain would "win"—they could get her practice for a good price. If she persuades them to spend more, Lilly would "win."

What if they approach the negotiation differently, however? Could Lilly and the chain both "win"? Could they reach an agreement that both sides would prefer? What if, in exchange for selling the practice for a good price, Lilly asked to be rehired as the principal vet? This would allow her to take longer vacations because the chain could bring in vets from other sites to cover for her when she goes away. She could still do the work she loves, continue to earn a good salary, and be relieved of running the business. On the other side of the ledger, without any disruption because of the sale, the chain's management could get an experienced vet to run the practice, a vet who knows the clientele and has a loyal following. This solution could represent a pure "win," with both sides getting everything they want. Instead of negotiating over one thing (price) they could put all these other things on the table as well—Lilly's experience and reputation, the value of stability and continuity for the practice, as well as more vacation time, freedom from paperwork, and a good salary for Lilly. By enlarging the pie, they could negotiate an agreement that's better for everyone.

Unfortunately, many people don't understand the benefits of this type of negotiating—they don't realize that enlarging the pie is possible. They assume that every negotiation involves splitting a finite set of resources between the negotiators. This assumption is so common that experts have named it the fixed-pie bias. To people suffering from the fixed-pie bias, the techniques we describe in this chapter may seem too "soft." They think taking a cooperative approach to negotiating conveys weakness or gives away too much information. But they're wrong. Decades of research have conclusively shown that a cooperative approach produces better outcomes than a combative one. First and foremost, it increases the likelihood that you'll get what you want and reduces the risk that your negotiation will end in an impasse, with neither side happy. A cooperative bargaining approach also elicits greater buy-in and follow-through all around. In addition, taking this approach can help safeguard and even improve your relationship with the other negotiator. Last but not least, cooperative bargaining makes the whole process of negotiating more enjoyable by reducing conflict and promoting collegial problem solving.

INTERESTS, NOT POSITIONS

In their groundbreaking 1981 best-seller *Getting to Yes,* Roger Fisher and William Ury described how interest-based, rather than position-based, bargaining could be used to reach successful agreements. In position-based bargaining, negotiators announce what they want or what they're determined to see happen and spend the rest of the nego-tiation defending that position. In interest-based bargaining, negotia-tors try to understand the interests—the needs, goals, constraints, and pressures—behind each position and then look for a variety of ways to satisfy those interests. Since compatible interests often lie beneath op-posing positions, negotiators who try to understand each other's inter-ests can often find several solutions that satisfy both sides.

As an example, Linda's boss (the dean of the Heinz School) wanted her to chair a strategic planning committee to consider the future of the school. Linda wanted to say no because she needed to finish this book. When Linda and the dean talked about their underlying inter-ests, Linda explained that she needed to finish the book but her heavy teaching load already limited the amount of time she had to work on it. The dean said that he didn't want to prevent Linda from finishing the book on time but he also really wanted her to chair the committee. He was less concerned about how many courses she was teaching. He offered to reduce her teaching load until the work of the committee was finished. Would that give her enough time to finish the book? Linda said that it would, and agreed to chair the committee.

Sheila—WHAT THEY WANTED, WHAT SHE WANTED

Here's another example. Sheila, a journalist, spent four years as the editor of an alternative weekly aimed at college students and young professionals and then two years as a reporter for a Web site devoted to uncovering corruption in the state government. When she was hired by a big-city daily newspaper, she was elated; she'd finally broken through to big-time investigative journalism. Sheila arrived for her first day of work with several ideas for stories already churning around in her head. To her dismay, the executive editor told her she'd be working in the Style section for now. Formerly the province of cooking tips and fashion news, Style sections have long been considered a "female ghetto" in the newspaper business, and no place for serious reporters. Sheila fumed all morning, tempted to march into the executive editor's office to complain. But she wasn't prepared to walk out if he refused to switch her to the news desk, and she knew that bawling out her boss on her first day was not a good idea. She called Sara, whom she'd met when they both worked for the *Boston Phoenix* years ago. Sara suggested that she ask her boss about his underlying interests instead: why he'd assigned her to Style.

Sheila's boss explained that the editorial board wanted to "juice up" the Style section with the hope of attracting younger readers, many of whom rarely read a daily paper. Rather than posting Easter brunch recipes, the editors wanted Sheila to target younger readers and make the section edgier and more timely. The former Style editor was retiring and the editorial board wanted a real reporter to take over the section, someone who would research and track down emerging trends as they were happening. Sheila's background made her the perfect combination of a good reporter and someone in touch with youth culture.

"I can see why you chose me for this," Sheila said, "but I thought you hired me to cover hard news. That's what I really want to do."

"Okay," said her editor, "good to know. How about a compromise?" He offered to make Sheila editor of the Style section—quite a coup for a new hire—in return for an eighteen-month commitment to the section. Work with the paper's art director to redesign the section, he said, partner with some of the other cultural reporters on the staff, and recruit a stable of good freelance writers whom the paper can rely on to propose significant style-related features. Get the section noticed. In the meantime, he promised to hire a deputy Style editor to help her out. When the section is well established, he said, you can turn it over to the deputy editor and move to the news staff.

Sheila was happy to learn that the editorial board actually wanted someone with her skills and recognized what she brought to the paper. She was glad the executive editor knew what her goals were too. She agreed to his compromise with only two amendments. She asked him to meet with her every six months to assess where the section was going so she could adjust course if needed. She didn't want to reach the end of her eighteen-month trial period and find out that she hadn't done what he wanted. Also, she said, "I'd like to have a record of this conversation, in case you leave. Can we put it in writing?" Her editor told her to send him an e-mail summarizing what they'd discussed and he'd put it in her personnel file.

Position-based bargaining can lock negotiators into a tug of war in which neither side will relinquish its stated goal, ending in an impasse. If Sheila had insisted that she would only write news stories and her editor had said sorry, he needed her elsewhere, the odds are that one or both of them—Sheila almost certainly—would have been unhappy with the result. Interest-based bargaining allows negotiators to look for creative solutions. To do this, you need to volunteer information and ask a lot of questions, focus on the interests and goals you have in common, trade things you care about less for things that matter to you more, and think of yourself and the other negotiator as partners in problem solving.

NEGOTIATE OUTSIDE THE BOX

In the third week of every negotiation class she teaches, Linda has her students conduct a two-party negotiation in which one student is selling something and the other student is trying to buy it. She gives each student detailed instructions about his or her reservation value, target value, BATNA, and underlying interests in the negotiation. What she doesn't tell the students is that she's constructed the case so that there is no contract zone—the most the buyer is willing to pay is less than the minimum the seller will accept. The only way for the students to reach an agreement is by talking about each side's underlying interests, which Linda has laid out in detail in the case material, and expanding the set of issues on the table. However, 95 percent of her students walk away with no deal because they go into the negotiation assuming that it's a straightforward negotiation about price. They never stop to reconsider their initial assumption or to use their case materials to broaden the scope of the negotiation.

COMMON GOALS

In a conversation with the editor of our first book, Sara remarked that an editor's goal when buying a book is always to pay as little as possible. Our editor corrected her, saying, "My goal is to pay enough to make it possible for the author to write the book." Although editors do want to keep their costs down and writers always need more money, editors and writers have a shared interest as well—making a project happen. Similarly, in almost all negotiations, the parties have common goals as well as conflicting ones. Conflicting goals often stand out: You want a higher salary and your employer wants to keep costs down; you want your brother to do more to take care of your aging parents and he wants to do less; you want your teenage kids to come home early and they want to stay out late. But all of these situations contain shared interests as well. You and your employer both want you to feel appreciated and to be as productive as you can. You and your brother both care about the health of your parents. You and your kids are both concerned about their safety.

A few years ago, Linda led a negotiation workshop for the executive directors of large arts organizations with unionized employees. She assigned half the directors to play themselves and the other half to play union negotiators trying to resolve eight issues. She gave each side private information about their priorities over the issues, what mattered most to them, and what they cared about less. She had written the case so that for two of the issues both sides actually wanted the same thing. (These are called compatible issues.) But the directors assumed that the union negotiators wanted the opposite of whatever they wanted, and vice versa. Both sides assumed they had no shared interests. As a result, most of the negotiating pairs actually reached bad deals—they missed agreeing to things that they both actually wanted. When you focus too intently on how goals conflict, you may miss where they intersect.

Marissa—FIXING HER OWN PROBLEM AND EVERYONE ELSE'S

Marissa was one of five salesclerks who worked in a small boutique that sold handmade jewelry. The store's owner, Eliza, scheduled two clerks for every shift, and posted the schedules a week before the first of each month. No two months were alike and no two weeks within a month were alike, making it difficult for the clerks to arrange their personal schedules to fit around their hours at the store. As a result, the clerks traded shifts all the time, and occasionally there was a mix-up and only one clerk showed up for a shift. Eliza hit the roof when this happened, but she blamed the clerks themselves rather than her scheduling system.

Eventually Marissa decided she had to find a way to talk to Eliza about the problem. She wanted to say, "Your scheduling system causes problems for everybody and you should let me do it because I can do it better." But she knew that was the wrong approach. Instead she said to Eliza, "We all want the store to run smoothly. You don't want only one clerk here, and we don't want to miss our shifts. No one wants to be stuck all alone in the store on a busy day."

To meet their shared goal of ensuring that the store was fully staffed for every shift, Marissa offered to take over the scheduling function herself. She proposed constructing a standard weekly schedule that would accommodate each clerk's regular personal commitments. The clerks would only be allowed to trade shifts if both people contacted Marissa at least twenty-four hours in advance, and every clerk would be "on call" one day a week when she wasn't working in case someone got sick or had a personal emergency.

Rather than feeling attacked for her scheduling ineptitude, Eliza was thrilled to hand off the scheduling responsibility to Marissa. The store ran more smoothly, Eliza had fewer reasons to get irritable, and Marissa and the other clerks got what they wanted.

As this story demonstrates, your own wishes and the interests of your employer may be closely aligned, or even one and the same. Sometimes getting what you need requires little more than pointing out an oversight, identifying a problem, or sharing a crucial piece of information with your employer.

Suparna—EVERYONE WANTS THE SAME THING

Suparna was an administrator at an international relief agency that coordinated food delivery to starving populations in Africa. The agency's distribution system was inefficient, though, and a lot of the food shipped to Third World countries never reached the people it was intended to help. Suparna respected the agency's distribution manager, but he was "massively overworked," she said. She had a lot of ideas about how to improve the system but no time and no authority to implement them. "People were dying and we had food that could help them!" she told us. "It was really getting me down. I thought I'd find another place where I would feel as though I was making more of a difference." In a last-ditch effort to change the situation before looking for another job, Suparna wrote up her ideas and proposed that her boss create a new position for her, a position dedicated to removing some of the kinks in the distribution system. She fully expected her boss to say he didn't have the funds, but things turned out far better than she hoped. The agency had just received a large private donation, and the director decided to use a portion of that money to create a new half-time position. Suparna would still have to spend half her day doing administrative work, but after that she was free to apprentice herself to the distribution manager and try out some of her ideas. She didn't get everything she wanted—she'd hoped for a full-time position—but she got enough to make her feel as though the work she was doing made a difference, and she decided to stay.

The key for Suparna was that she and her boss shared two important goals: They both wanted to see the food distribution program run as efficiently as possible and neither of them wanted her to quit.

INFORMATION SHARING

What if you don't know what the other side wants? What if you can't even guess at the interests motivating the positions they stake out? Your best move then is to ask. Ask what they really want, why they want it, why they think what they want is fair, and why they think their solution is superior to any alternative. Many people believe that sharing information in a negotiation will leave them open to exploitation by the other side and they communicate as little as possible about their underlying motives. This is a mistake. Asking questions is one of the key techniques in cooperative bargaining—asking questions, and listening carefully to the answers. You'll get the most benefit from asking questions if you ask them in an open-ended way. Rather than asking if your negotiation partner likes your proposal, for example, ask about his or her reactions to what you've said. This will elicit more information—and much more useful information. If you're confronted with a tight-lipped negotiator, one effective tactic can be to reveal information about yourself first without asking for information in return. The norm of reciprocity in this situation can be quite strong, and your frankness may spark the other side to share important information too.

In a lab study, participants were paired up to attempt a multi-issue negotiation. In some pairs, the researchers instructed one negotiator to ask questions and try to learn about the other side's preferences. In other pairs, they instructed one negotiator to *volunteer* information about his or her preferences. In a third group of pairs, the researchers gave no instructions to either negotiator. Those pairs in which one of the negotiators either asked for or volunteered information judged the preferences of the other side far more accurately and reached better agreements than the pairs in which neither negotiator shared or sought more information. The impulse to share information, whether it took the form of asking questions or offering explanations, prompted opposing negotiators to reciprocate.

Not only does this demonstrate that exchanging information about preferences and priorities produces better outcomes (for both sides), it also shows that both sides don't need to know this. One side walking into a negotiation determined to take a cooperative approach is enough. In other words, approaching your negotiations prepared to bargain cooperatively increases the likelihood that you'll make a better agreement whether or not the other negotiator understands the benefits of this approach.

If volunteering information about your side of the equation doesn't prompt many revelations in return, try asking a few unthreatening questions to get the other side to open up. Here are some ideas:

- "I want to be sure I have a clear picture of the pressures you face. Can we talk about that?"

- "Among the issues we're discussing today, price is most important to me. Is that true for you or is another issue more important?"

- "I know you're balancing a lot of competing interests here. Can you describe them to me so I have a better idea of what they are?"

- "I can tell that giving me what I want would present some challenges for you but I'm not sure I totally comprehend the nature of those challenges. Can you sketch them out for me?"

Getting the process moving in a cooperative direction usually creates some momentum. Once the other side sees that you truly care about their point of view, they'll often loosen up and share more information. And once you know more about each other's needs and interests, the better the odds are that you'll find areas of overlap. Discovering that you have more in common than you thought will also promote the feeling that you're allies in the process rather than adversaries.

Masha—WHY DID HE SAY NO?

Masha had been offered a job as the vice president of a firm that imported Italian shoes for the American market. She and the firm's president had agreed on her title, her salary, her responsibilities, and her starting date, but he was resisting her request to remodel the office she would occupy, which was shabby and dark. Although the rest of the firm's offices had been updated quite recently, Masha's position was important, and she would be meeting with distributors and advertising sales representatives in the office, she still couldn't get the firm's president to yield. Masha was perplexed and angry. She certainly wasn't going to take the job if he didn't think her position was important enough to merit a decent-looking office. But when she pressed him he responded gruffly and dismissively. She was considering walking away from the job when it occurred to her to ask the president why he kept refusing—was it a budget thing, or was there another reason? Sheepishly, he explained that his sister, who was an interior designer, had remodeled all the other executive offices at the firm, but she'd just had a baby and wouldn't be returning to work for six months. He didn't want to hurt his sister's feelings by using another designer.

Masha had an easy answer. As long as her boss made a commitment to remodel her office within a year, she would start on the day they'd agreed to and use the unrenovated space. Masha would have preferred to move into a beautiful new office, but she could survive and function for a limited time in an office that fell short of her ideal. Both sides felt happy with the agreement, which set a good tone for their future interactions.

LET'S MAKE A DEAL

Of course, sometimes what you want actually conflicts with what the other side needs and it's not possible to present your request as a mutually beneficial change. When this happens, you can try another cooperative tactic—offer to make a trade. You can give up something that's not especially important to you, but matters a lot to the other side, in exchange for something you want more. Early American settlers helped their neighbors clear land by rolling off and burning felled timber and then their neighbors would do the same for them. Today, the term *logrolling* is used to describe any type of bargaining in which both parties trade things they care about less in exchange for things they want more.

If you're negotiating a job offer and you want a signing bonus so you can buy a new car (and you know the company doesn't typically give signing bonuses), you could ask if there's any way you can make it worthwhile for the company to give you the bonus. Maybe it would help if you started earlier than you'd planned. Or maybe they need someone to work an overnight shift for three months. Or maybe they just need an extra pair of hands to help get a crucial project out the door, and then you can start the job they're hiring you to do. You could also take another approach. Rather than asking if there's something your prospective employer needs, you can see if there's something you could *give up* that would make it possible for the company to give you that bonus. If you're relocating, you might offer to rent a truck and move yourself if your new employer will give you some or all of the money budgeted for your moving expenses. If you're being hired by a small business and you can get health insurance under your husband's plan, you could offer to waive health insurance coverage if the company will give you a portion of the savings as a signing bonus.

If you're negotiating the salary for a new job and the company can't give you as much money as you want, you might ask for a better title in exchange for accepting the lower salary. In many cases, giving you the better title won't cost the company anything and it could be valuable for you down the line. If you want to be promoted early, you could offer to spend six months straightening out a poorly functioning department in exchange for the promotion. Or you could offer to cover a vacant position, essentially doing two jobs, in exchange for being promoted to the position you want as soon as the vacant job is filled. If your employer really needs someone to fill a position in Florida and you don't mind relocating, you could offer to move to Florida in exchange for an early promotion.

Never forget, however, that when you're logrolling you need to negotiate multiple issues at once. If you negotiate each issue separately, you'll find yourself in a series of competitive win/lose entanglements. Discussing several issues at once and linking them together makes the process more reciprocal. Always emphasize that you're willing to make a concession on one issue *in exchange* for something else you want. Don't yield on one issue and then expect a good-faith concession on something else later. You need to negotiate these simultaneously. Be explicit that your offer to give something to the other side is conditional on getting something back that you want.

In some cases, however, you may not know enough to propose attractive trade-offs. If that's the case—once again—ask questions. If you want to ask your boss for a raise but know his budget is tight, here are some questions to try:

- "Is there any way that I could help save the organization money and make it possible for me to get this raise?"
- "Do you feel as though we could control costs better in one area?"
- "Would it help if I worked a few extra hours a week?"
- "Do you need someone to train new recruits?"
- "If you could devote more resources to reducing costs, what would be your first step?"

Open-ended questions like this will give you raw material to work with. If you can figure out ways to reduce costs, you may achieve even more than you hoped. While helping him solve his problems, you may also enhance his impression of your abilities and set the stage for future negotiations that yield big dividends. Keep in mind, however, that it can be difficult to move some people from "negotiation" to "problem-solving" mode. Don't give up immediately, and always frame your questions in terms of a quest to "figure this out together." The conversation should never sound like an interrogation. A positive cooperative attitude breeds cooperation, while a negative attitude usually encourages defensiveness.

LOGROLLING

- List the issues to be negotiated.
- Determine your priorities over the issues. What's most important to you? What do you care about less?

- Think about the other side's priorities. How do they differ from yours? Can you easily identify anything that's very important to the other side but not as important to you, and vice versa? Remember that having different priorities is a *good* thing; it gives you more areas to negotiate.
- Think about what you'd be willing to trade to get what you want. What can you do or what can you give up that might be of value to the other side?
- Can you add anything to the negotiation that would make it easier to logroll, possibilities that aren't on the table but might be attractive to the other side?
- Sketch out several different ways to fit together your differing priorities, making sure to negotiate over multiple issues simultaneously, offering concessions on certain issues in return for receiving concessions on others.

You can also logroll away from the office. When you're negotiating with a contractor to do work on your house, your first priority will be to agree on a fair and reasonable price for the job. But you may also care about other things, such as when the job gets done. Perhaps you'd like the job completed while you and your family are on vacation. You may be willing to pay more if the contractor will commit to doing the job according to your schedule. You can trade something valuable to the contractor (more money) for something valuable to you and your family (timing). Or perhaps the opposite is true—the contractor you like can't start the job for six months. You could offer to postpone the project if the contractor charges you less for the work, offering to give up something less valuable to you (getting the project done sooner) in exchange for something you want more (saving money).

Or suppose that you and a housemate are deciding how to allocate household chores. The ideal would be to do this so that each side doesn't get stuck doing something he or she absolutely hates, and no one feels exploited or overtaxed.

You: "Let's think about the chores we have to do. Tell me what you hate doing and name some things you don't mind as much."

Housemate: "That's easy. I hate cleaning toilets and I always forget to take out the garbage and it piles up. I don't mind vacuuming, though, and I like to keep the kitchen clean."

You: "Okay, I don't like cleaning toilets either but I really hate cleaning out the fridge. How about if I clean the bathrooms and take out the garbage, and you keep the kitchen and fridge clean and vacuum? Vacuuming takes a little longer than taking out the garbage, but cleaning the bathroom is more disgusting than cleaning the kitchen. Does that seem fair?"

Continue to ask questions until you've gotten all the information you need and you're convinced that your housemate likes the plan. Of course, this will be easier if you have a good relationship with your housemate. In other situations, especially when you're negotiating with someone you don't know, it can be more difficult. But the benefits are great, so keep working at it until you discover enough information to help you reach a good agreement.

A quick note about gamesmanship. When logrolling, you might be tempted to overstate how much it will cost for you to make a certain concession. By suggesting that you're conceding a lot you may hope that you'll win a bigger concession in return. Although this can be effective in situations in which you have no ongoing relationship with the other side, this tactic has a number of drawbacks and may backfire. First, the other person may know that what you're offering doesn't represent much of a sacrifice, and so your exaggeration will suggest that you're not bargaining in good faith. Second, if you exaggerate too much, the other side might decide that what they're asking is too much for you to give, change tacks, and ask for something different, something that's actually more costly for you. Furthermore, down the road, if the other negotiator discovers that you exaggerated, this could damage your relationship. If he or she talks about your deception, it could damage your reputation.

CREATIVE PROBLEM SOLVING

Taking a cooperative approach offers another important benefit. When people aren't worried about angry eruptions or afraid of conflict, when they feel a strong incentive to work something out together, and when they've identified multiple possible trade-offs, they tend to think more creatively. A negotiation that otherwise might have ended in an impasse sometimes produces an unexpected and imaginative solution that works for everyone.

If you find yourself in a situation in which no obvious solution presents itself, try organizing a brainstorming session.

- Get the parties together in a room with a chalkboard, whiteboard, or flipchart.
- Volunteer to be the "scribe."
- Define the problem to be solved.
- Encourage people to come up with ideas, even radical ones, to solve the problem.
- Write down every idea.
- Don't allow people to evaluate, comment on, or criticize the ideas yet. The objective is to encourage creative problem solving and free people from worrying about details, constraints, or, for now, questions of fairness.
- Assure participants that no idea is too silly or off base to share. You want to separate the process of thinking about solutions from the process of deciding among them.
- Ask everyone to imagine solutions that they may have overlooked. Have you been framing the negotiation in only one way

and might there be other ways to fit together the pieces of the puzzle?

- Once you've recorded all of the group's ideas, go through them one at a time. Is this one at all workable? Does that sound great but impossible to implement? Winnow down the list to four or five possibilities. Then break down the constituent parts of each proposal. Who likes this idea? What are its pros and cons? Who has a huge problem with it? What would balance it well? If one side yielded on a particular issue, what would be a good trade-off for doing so? Does this trade-off suggest others? Keep talking until you've cobbled together two or three solid alternatives for solving the problem. Once you've established some workable proposals, see if a consensus emerges around one particular solution. If not, is there one clearly inferior solution? If no one can agree about which solution is best, can you find a way to modify one of the solutions so that it meets all sides' basic interests?

Joyce—NOT PERFECT BUT PRETTY GOOD

Joyce worked as an executive assistant to one of the vice presidents of a large financial services firm based in New York City. She'd worked at the firm for eight years when her husband was asked to relocate to China for a year. Joyce knew that this move would be great for her husband's career, and the whole family (she had twin eleven-year-old boys) thought it would be an exciting adventure. But Joyce loved her job and didn't want to lose it.

Joyce asked her boss if she could take an unpaid leave for a year and return to her job when she got back, but her boss turned her down. Unfortunately, he couldn't leave the position vacant for a year, her boss said, and it was impractical to hire a temporary worker for the job. He liked Joyce and valued her work, however, and he thought it would be a loss to the company if she were forced to quit. "Let's think about this for a few days and see if we can come up with a solution," he said to Joyce.

The two of them sat down the following week to brainstorm about options. Joyce couldn't do the job remotely using e-mail, phone calls, and overnight mail because her boss needed his assistant to be close by. Could she come back once a quarter? No, that wouldn't work. Could she work on a project for her boss that didn't require her presence in the office every day? No, he didn't have any work like that to give her. After much back-and-forth, her boss exclaimed, "I've got it! This company has over thirty vice presidents and dozens of other high-level corporate officers. Someone's going to need a new assistant by the time you get back. What if I get Human Resources to keep you on the books? That way you won't have to start all over at the bottom of the benefits ladder. I'll make sure they commit to paying you the same salary when you return and consider you for the first executive assistant's job that opens up."

This solution didn't give either Joyce or her boss everything they wanted. He didn't want to lose Joyce, and Joyce wanted to work with him when she got back. But both of them came away with a lot. Her boss held on to a valuable employee with a lot of experience and knowledge about the company. Joyce left for China confident that she'd have a job when she got back, and a job at a company she knew and loved.

The two of them were able to negotiate this solution because they refused to give up when it looked as though their interests were totally incompatible. They worked together to find a way for each of them to get some of what they wanted. This type of flexible, open-minded, think-outside-the-box approach can be a powerful tool for resolving impasses and reaching agreements that satisfy both sides.

COOPERATIVE BARGAINING: A CASE STUDY

Four years ago, Laura founded a small New York–based dance company. A Chicago theater invited her to bring part of the company's repertory to Chicago for a short summer run, which would be great exposure for the company and a chance to develop a good relationship with this particular theater in Chicago.

The theater offered Laura the following contract:

- A three-day run that would include five performances, one Thursday night, two on Friday, and two on Saturday (matinee and evening performances)
- Payment of $7,000 per show
- Reimbursement of travel receipts within sixty days (for a tour bus and the cast and crew's food and hotel expenses), with a cap of $8,000 in costs
- Start date on the second Thursday in July

Laura offered this counterproposal:

- A five-day run with only one performance a day, Wednesday, Thursday, Friday, and Saturday nights, Sunday matinee
- $11,500 per show
- Travel paid upfront by the theater
- Run to start the third Wednesday in July (six days later than the theater proposed)

By phone and e-mail, Laura and the theater's general manager went back and forth, restating their initial proposals, not getting anywhere. They needed another approach.

Laura couldn't do two performances in a single day because some of her star dancers had language in their contracts saying that they wouldn't be required to perform more than once a day. She could do the earlier start date but she'd rather not: She wanted to give her dancers a short break before the Chicago run. Her company also had a perpetual cash-flow problem, typical of small arts organizations, and she couldn't afford to pay upfront for transportation. And Laura was convinced that the higher price-per-performance figure was totally justified because all her New York shows had sold out and she was sure the Chicago theater would sell out too.

Looking for a solution, Laura flew to Chicago and sat down with the general manager. She started by asking why the theater preferred to book them for the earlier week. She received a straightforward answer: They already had another show booked for the later date. Since the start date was so important to the theater, Laura asked if they would be willing to give the dance company travel money upfront in exchange for Laura yielding on the earlier start date. They agreed.

The next issue to tackle was the number of performances. Laura proposed a compromise—she would agree to starting Thursday (what the theater wanted) instead of Wednesday (what she wanted) in exchange for having only one performance a day but adding the Sunday matinee. This would mean four performances instead of five, which would make the trip to Chicago less profitable overall, but she couldn't get around that provision in her stars' contracts. The theater manager refused to budge. Laura asked why they couldn't eliminate the Friday and Saturday matinees, especially if they added the Sunday afternoon show. The theater manager explained that one of their biggest donors was a local foundation dedicated to introducing kids to the arts. This foundation insisted that they have at least one weekday matinee performance that they could invite local youth groups to attend for free. Well, then, if the matinee performances would be for school kids, Laura asked, how would the theater feel if Laura scheduled understudies to perform for those shows? This would allow her to sidestep the contract provisions of her star dancers. The theater manager had no problem whatsoever with this.

The only remaining sticking point was the price per performance. Laura needed a minimum of $8,500 per show, for a total of $42,500 for the five performances. This was her reservation value—it wouldn't be worth making the trip for less. She still wanted to get closer to $10,000, her target value.

The theater manager increased his offer from $7,000 to $8,000 for each of the five performances. She gave the theater manager a packet of rave reviews of the company's New York performances, assuring him that the Chicago run would sell out too, but he was unconvinced. "I just can't take that big a chance on a dance company that's never been to Chicago before," he said.

What could be done? "Let's try to be creative around this issue of the ticket sales," Laura said. "Anything less than $8,500 per performance and I'll be operating at a loss. But I'm willing to take a little risk because I'm so confident that we'll surprise you. How about this?" She asked the general manager to agree to $8,500 with these conditions: If the theater sold fewer than 75 percent of the seats for any given performance, Laura would accept $1,000 less for that performance. In exchange, the theater would agree to pay a $2,000 bonus for any performance that was more than 95 percent sold out. This was easy for the theater manager to accept because the arrangement limited the theater's risk, and he didn't think the performances would sell out. It was valuable for Laura because she was so confident about ticket sales. The beauty of the arrangement was that even if the theater manager was wrong and the house did sell out, the extra ticket sales would make it easy for him to pay the $2,000 bonus. They had an agreement.

By asking questions, logrolling, and thinking creatively, Laura was able to reach an agreement that was good for both sides. But could she have done any better? Both Laura and the theater's management cared about selling a lot of tickets. What could they have added to the contract to further this shared interest? Perhaps a special VIP party with the dancers after the Friday night show to attract patrons and spread positive word-of-mouth? Or Laura could offer to invite talented high school dancers for a Saturday morning master class if the theater would arrange for press coverage. Now that their interests were so closely aligned, could they find other ways to enhance the deal and add value for both sides?

When people work well together, they communicate more about what they need and what they expect. They appreciate the risks and uncertainties driving each other's reluctance to sign off on certain provisions, and they understand the different barometers of success they each bring to their joint enterprise. This knowledge enables them to take imaginative but well-founded chances together, and to support and participate in each other's achievements. The process helps form strong personal and professional alliances that will enrich their later encounters and provide unexpected benefits long into the future.

II

Refine Your Strategy

You've done your background research and established an ambitious target. You understand the benefits of cooperative bargaining and you're ready to go. What's your next move? How do you initiate the negotiation? Should you use e-mail, write a formal letter, leave a phone message, or broach the subject in person? What do you say? Should you make the first offer and wait to hear how the other side responds? If you do make the first offer, *what* should you offer? And when should you do it? Are there right and wrong times to negotiate? Right and wrong places?

In Person? On the Phone? E-Mail?

Your first strategic choice should be about how to communicate. Whenever possible, a face-to-face interaction is the best choice. Face-to-face communication makes it easier to use the cooperative bargaining tactics we described in the previous chapter and guarantees you immediate feedback (though not necessarily your final answer), saving you uncomfortable hours or days waiting for an e-mail message or phone call. You also get *more* feedback—the information conveyed by the other negotiator's tone of voice, facial expressions, and body language. If the other negotiator says, "I'll consider your request," while facing you, making eye contact, and smiling, you'll know that your chances of getting what you want are probably better than if she swings her chair away and squints at her computer. If the other negotiator nods and appears interested in what you're saying, you can feel reasonably confident that he understands you. If the other negotiator looks distracted instead or keeps checking her watch, she's probably not paying close attention. At the same time, you can use nonverbal techniques of your own—warm eye contact, a relaxed posture, a smile—to present your request in a positive, let's-work-this-out-together way.

Making your request in person also allows the conversation to flow back and forth between the two (or three or four) of you. Observing the other person's nonverbal cues, you can adjust your presentation accordingly. If a quick frown tells you that the other negotiator doesn't fully understand what you're saying or may be confused, you can offer more information or rephrase. If a shake of the head suggests that the other negotiator doesn't agree with a point you've made, you can pause and ask why not. If the other negotiator gestures impatiently, you'll know to pick up the pace or reschedule for a better time. You can also stop to ask a question if you're not sure *you* understand.

Of course, people can and do misunderstand each other even when they're negotiating face-to-face. Linda requires her students to write up the agreements they reach during in-class negotiations—a useful exercise, since they so frequently describe the terms of their agreement quite differently, even though they reached those agreements only moments before. Linda's point is to emphasize the need to check in regularly with the other side, summarize what you've agreed to, and sketch out what you plan to do next.

If a face-to-face discussion is out of the question, your next-best choice is to pick up the phone. You can still have a back-and-forth conversation over the phone although you miss out on the extra information provided by nonverbal cues. Phone conversations can also be misleading because people's phone manners differ. Some personalities come through loud and clear over the phone while other people speak with relatively little affect, their tone flat and hard to read. Sara's father-in-law (he died in 2004 at ninety-two) was like this: Although he was charming, warm, and even courtly in person, over the phone he sounded distant, distracted, and in a hurry to get off. Sara's husband made a point of discussing anything important with him in person.

Submitting your request in writing, either on paper or by e-mail, presents the greatest challenge to a successful negotiation. Although this route may appeal to you because it allows you to present your proposal in its entirety, detailing your argument in an organized and precise way, that also represents its greatest weakness. Not only do you risk overwhelming the other negotiator with too much information all at once, but in a written request you essentially state your position and wait for a response, leaving little space for the give-and-take so central to good cooperative bargaining. A staged approach during a face-to-face conversation makes it possible for you to adapt your argument in response to input from the other side as you go along. Staking out your position and waiting for an answer discourages the collaborative problem solving necessary to reach good agreements. Making your proposal in person allows you to change areas of emphasis, bring out a particularly salient point, or delay presenting certain aspects of your proposal until the optimal time. In writing, the subtleties of language (and humor) are often lost, making misunderstandings common.

Of course, even when face-to-face communication is possible, it may not be the best choice for you. A friend of Linda's was preparing for a negotiation and wanted to submit a written request. Linda described the advantages of a face-to-face approach but her friend was unconvinced. She worried that she wouldn't be able to make her case as persuasively in person and nothing Linda said could quell her anxiety. Linda realized that her friend's nervousness was too big a barrier and might undercut the benefits of a face-to-face encounter. (Her friend submitted her proposal in writing.) In Chapters 12 and 13, we provide tools to help you control or mitigate your nervousness about face-to-face encounters, but if you still feel that this is not the right choice for you, and you're not comfortable using the phone, sending an e-mail or written memo may be preferable.

You also need to take into account what you know about the preferences of the person or people from whom you'll be making your request. Some bosses want a written proposal or preview of a negotiation before they meet with you. Others can't slow down to read dozens of e-mails filled with employee requests. Some managers set aside a particular time each week when their door is always open. Others want their employees to make appointments to see them. During the research phase of preparing for your negotiation, try to find out what the people on the other side prefer.

SHOULD YOU MAKE THE FIRST OFFER?

When you're offered a job, a prospective employer typically makes the first offer—"We'd like to hire you, and this is what the job pays." (Putting the ball in your court to make a counteroffer.) It's not uncommon, however, for organizations to ask prospective hires upfront about their salary requirements. What do you do then? If you're unsure what they're willing to pay and don't want to ask for too little (or way too much), you can try to "punt"—to hold off answering and hope the other side will make the first move. Here are a few graceful ways to avoid committing yourself too soon:

- "I'd like to learn more about the position and the responsibilities before I give you a firm answer about salary."
- "I'm not comfortable talking about salary at this early stage. Can we postpone this part of the conversation?"

- "It's a bit too early in the process for me to estimate that."
- "I'm not quite ready to talk about money. Can we discuss the position a little more first?"
- "Can you tell me more about the job before we talk salary?"
- "What is the salary range for the position?" (Put it back in their court.)

If they press you to give them a number, forcing you to make the first offer, say something very flexible, such as:

- "I'm considering job opportunities in the range of $[X] to $[Y]."
- "I know that the market for people with my skill set is between $[X] and $[Y]."
- "I'm looking at jobs that pay between $[X] and $[Y]—aiming for the high end of the range, of course (laugh)."

The range you describe should be broad, with $X low enough not to eliminate you from consideration and $Y high enough to signal that you know your value and you're not a pushover.

But what if the situation is ambiguous and it's not clear who should make the first offer? If you're talking to a vendor who sells a product you need, you could ask the vendor to name her price or you could name a figure. The same is true if you have your own business or consultancy and you're going after a job: You could ask what the job pays or you could propose a fee. Then what are the pros and cons of going first? If both sides recognize that a negotiation will ensue but it's not clear who will make the first offer, going first can sometimes work to your advantage. The benefits of going first derive from what is called anchoring—influencing the other side's perceptions about what you want and what you'll accept (your reservation value).

When Sara moved four years ago, she and her husband liked a property in Lincoln, Massachusetts, but they thought it was way overpriced. Sara checked the appraised value of several other houses on the market in Lincoln and noticed that the owners had listed those properties for about $50,000 more than their appraised value. The owner of the house Sara and her husband liked had listed the property for $350,000 more than the appraised value. Sara couldn't possibly afford the house at that price but she understood what the owner was trying to do. By listing her house for so much more, she was telling prospective buyers that the house belonged in the same high-priced category as a lot of other houses in Lincoln, where real estate is extremely expensive. The owner was trying to anchor perceptions about the house's value by starting the bidding so high, forcing anyone who wanted the house to counteroffer against her inflated price. She was also sending a message that she was not prepared to accept a price more in line with the house's appraised value.

In the same way, by taking the lead and making the first offer in an ambiguous situation, you can create a focal point for the ensuing negotiation, starting the bidding where you want it to start and influencing the other side's perception of your reservation value. If your reservation value for a consulting job is $60,000 but you go first and ask for $70,000, you could anchor your client's perceptions of what you will accept at a higher point. Concluding that your reservation value is higher than it really is, he might offer you $65,000 even though he'd originally planned to offer you $60,000.

Regarding the house in Lincoln, Sara tried to reanchor the negotiation by making a counteroffer that was $50,000 more than the house's appraised value and $300,000 less than the asking price, which she thought was fair and appropriate for the size, condition, and location of the house. The owner, offended, refused to counteroffer, and Sara and her husband bought another house in a nearby town, where they're very happy. After waiting eighteen months, the owner of the Lincoln house found a buyer willing to pay her price and sold. Her anchoring strategy had paid off.

Whether or not you should go first and try to anchor the negotiation in an ambiguous situation depends on how much information you have. If you know the other side's reservation value and they don't know yours, you should definitely take the lead because you know exactly what to ask for: a number higher than their reservation value that leaves you enough room to back down to the top amount you know they'll pay. If, on the other hand, you have no idea what they'll pay, making the first offer can be tricky. If you're sure they'll pay at least $50,000 but think they might go as high as $80,000 to get you (basically you have no idea), you could take the safe approach and make a low offer, such as $55,000, but then you'd rule out the possibility of getting more. Or you could take a daring approach and ask for $75,000, but if their real reservation value is closer to $50,000, you'll lose credibility if you have to backpedal from $75,000 to $55,000.

For this reason, when you don't have much information about the other side's intentions or resources, it's usually a good idea to let them start the negotiation if you can. Their first offer will give you a rough idea of their reservation value and help you calibrate your counteroffer. If they have no idea what you're going to want, however, they may press you to go first in the hope that you'll lowball yourself. In that case, follow the advice above and name a broad range, with the bottom end not too low and the high end not wildly out of the question.

Of course, in certain situations you'll need to go first because you're the one who has decided to initiate a negotiation. You want a change and the other side is happy with the status quo, which means it's up to you to propose something different. You need to go first.

WHEN'S THE BEST TIME TO ASK?

Does it matter when you ask? Can you increase your chances of success by timing your negotiation strategically? Absolutely, although there are no simple rules to help you choose the best time. Is Monday morning better than Friday afternoon? After lunch better than the end of the day? Will you do better after the Christmas party or after the

first of the year? In September when everyone's back from their summer vacation or in May when things start to slow down? Any of those
times might be good choices depending on your circumstances. The
key is to ask when your bargaining power is high and when the other
negotiators will be most receptive to your proposal. But don't delay
unnecessarily. The sooner you ask, the better you'll do, and the easier
it will be.

Ask When Your Bargaining Power Is High

You were just named your company's top regional salesperson, or your
most recent project was a huge success, or you've received a prestigious
award for your work, or an article you published in a leading industry
journal is getting a lot of attention. Asking for what you want on the
heels of events like these can be especially fruitful because your talents are particularly visible. Other good times might be when there's
been a lot of attrition in your division, or when your department is
growing rapidly, or when a new boss has come onboard who needs you
to teach her or him the ropes—times when losing you would be especially costly. You don't want to crow over your accomplishments or
hold your employer over a barrel when things are tough, but if you can
make a persuasive case for what you want at moments like these, your
chances of success increase.

Grace—THE PERFECT MOMENT

Grace, a sales representative for a large computer software company,
knew she was underpaid. Although she earned a commission on every
sale and her annual compensation was ample, her base salary had increased very little since she'd started the job. Six weeks before two of
her largest client contracts were scheduled to come up for renewal,
Grace approached her boss about her salary. She'd determined that a
15 percent increase would bring her base salary in line with that of her
peers, other reps who racked up similar sales figures every year. But in

addition to the 15 percent, she wanted something more. She wanted a onetime bonus of $30,000 as acknowledgment of her value to the company and compensation for the years when her base salary should have been higher. Although this seemed like a lot to ask, she knew that her boss couldn't afford to lose her right before those two large contracts were renewed. She considered getting another job offer to further bolster her position but decided this was unnecessary. Her position was strong enough. "I told him that this was what the market was telling me I was worth," she said, "and that I needed the bonus to feel like I was a valued member of the team." Her boss gave her both the raise and the bonus.

Read the Smoke Signals

A second factor to consider is whether the timing is good for the other side. You don't want to pipe up with your request right when your boss is besieged with demands or under too much pressure to focus on your situation. You don't want to ask for something relatively small in the middle of a big emergency. Find a time when you know the other negotiators won't be impatient to move on to another topic, when they're likely to be in a good mood, and not hungry, overtired, cranky, or disappointed about something totally unrelated to you.

Leticia—WHEN YOU REALIZE IT'S THE WRONG TIME

Leticia was the head of the costume department at a major regional opera company. Talking to her counterparts at other companies convinced her that she was underpaid, and after she completed the bulk of her work for the new fall season she decided to ask the general manager for a 15 percent raise. She thought she had a good chance of getting 10 percent but she was really hoping to get 12.

When Leticia arrived for her appointment, her boss was meeting with the head of the musicians' union, which was threatening to strike just before the season opened. Half an hour later, the union head

stormed out and Leticia's boss called her into his office. As soon as she
started to speak, he exploded. "You're asking for more money too?" he
shouted. "Does anybody have a clue where all this money's going to
come from?!"

Leticia realized that she'd picked the worst possible day to ask for a
raise. "He was incredibly professional and I'd never seen him lose his
cool like that," she said. Rather than apologize and back down, as she
was tempted to do, Leticia said, "Why don't we talk about this another
time? There's no rush." Her mild response calmed down her boss and
he apologized for losing his temper. A month later, when the orchestra's contract had been signed and it was clear that the new season was
going to be a smashing success, Leticia went back to her boss. He said
he didn't have enough money to hike her salary by 15 percent, but he
gave her 10 percent, which, under the circumstances, she regarded as a
massive success. Her quick thinking had rescued what could have been
a disastrously mistimed negotiation.

Sooner Is Better Than Later

Once you've prepared for your negotiation, can it hurt to wait a little
while, get up your nerve, and look for that elusive perfect moment?
Yes, for a number of reasons. First of all, perfect moments are hard to
spot in advance and often pass before we realize they're over. Second,
and more important, waiting too long can interfere with your ability
to ask well. If you keep putting off a negotiation, perhaps hoping that
the powers-that-be will give it to you on their own, by the time you finally do ask you may be too soured on your organization to ever be
happy there again. Frustration and pent-up feelings do not make a
good recipe for success.

Sara—UNAPPRECIATED AND TIRED OF WAITING

Less than two years after she graduated from college with a degree in
English literature, Sara was offered a job as the acquisitions editor of a

small literary book club. The club involved working with the best literary and intellectual books being published by the most prestigious
publishers, and she felt lucky to get such a great job when she was so
young. On her first day, however, she discovered a lot of problems.
Her desk was piled high with overdue contracts to be signed, books
that should have been delivered to the club's warehouse hadn't arrived,
and the club's monthly brochure was six or seven weeks behind schedule. Sara quickly brought the situation under control. She sorted
through and finalized all the contracts and tracked down the missing
books. She set up a regular schedule for meeting with the club's publisher and senior editors to choose books, and she speeded up production of the monthly brochure and got it back on schedule. At the same
time, in response to an attractive new promotion, membership began
to rise and orders were up. For the first time in a long time, the club
was making money and running smoothly.

Sara's bosses were clearly pleased by this turnaround, and she expected a nice raise in recognition of the job she'd done. The club didn't
operate according to strict schedules or regular review periods, however, so a year passed with no raise, and then another six months, and
three more months yet, and she was beginning to feel impatient. The
salary she'd been offered when she started was meager, but she'd accepted it because she was young and inexperienced and it was such a
great job. But after twenty-one months, the strain of living on so little
money—in Manhattan—began to take its toll. She wanted a raise, she
needed a raise, and she knew she deserved a raise.

Just a month short of Sara's second anniversary at the job, the owners of the book club handed out 3 percent cost of living increases to
everyone on the staff, including Sara. She received the same percentage
as the women who processed customers' orders and the men who
packed books in the warehouse. She was particularly incensed because
this 3 percent increase raised her salary to $19,800 (she really was
badly paid) and she thought it was a slap in the face that her bosses

hadn't even rounded up her salary to $20,000. Without stopping to think, she strode into the publisher's office. "At least you could have rounded the figure up to $20,000!" she said. Embarrassed by her outburst, she fled back to her office. The next day, the publisher sent Sara a note saying that her new salary would be $20,000, not $19,800. The publisher clearly hadn't understood. The point Sara had wanted to make was that they hadn't thought for a moment about what a difference her work had made to the success of the club. They'd treated her just like everyone else. They hadn't noticed or acknowledged her contribution.

Sara's mistake was one that many women make. She waited and waited for her salary to be increased and the longer she waited the more frustrated she became. By the time she finally got a raise, she was too worked up about the situation to explain what she wanted in a clear or rational way. A better approach would have been to assemble documentation, long before she became so angry, showing how she'd improved the club's internal workings and transformed it into an efficiently run, professional operation. She could have identified the best time to approach the publisher and made her case in a calm and persuasive way. Waiting until you're fed up and angry tends to make you ask badly when you finally make your move.

Jane—TOO ANGRY, TOO LATE

Sometimes, the consequences for letting things go too long can be even graver. Jane was a senior manager in the customer service department of a cellular phone service provider. After Jane had been at the job for over eighteen years, the company launched a wildly successful national advertising program that began attracting thousands of new customers every day. Human resources had to scramble to hire new representatives to handle the huge volume of calls but they couldn't keep up, or find enough senior managers to train and supervise them.

Jane began working double shifts, training new managers, training new reps, and often answering customer calls herself. Night after night, she arrived home exhausted and crawled into bed.

Jane's children were grown and her husband had recently retired. He'd been hoping to spend more time with his wife but instead he never saw her anymore, causing real strains in their marriage. Jane's health was also suffering from the lack of sleep, the fighting with her husband, and the stress. Senior management didn't seem to appreciate the pressure the new ad campaign was putting on customer service, and she saw no signs that they were taking the necessary steps to fix a system on the verge of breaking down. They hadn't acknowledged the enormous sacrifices made by people like Jane, with bonuses, raises, or even some simple gesture of thanks, like a gift certificate to a local day spa or flowers delivered to her office. They just kept piling on the work and taking it for granted that their capable employees would shoulder the heavier load.

Jane finally reached her breaking point. One of her husband's nieces was getting married in Florida and he'd been pressing her to take a week off and spend some time relaxing in the sun after the wedding. They'd bought their tickets, but she'd delayed asking for the time off because she couldn't see how the office could get by without her for a whole week. Finally, on the Thursday before the wedding weekend, she couldn't delay any longer. "I need next week off," she told her boss. "My niece is getting married and you have to find someone to cover for me."

Her boss, struggling with her own problems, felt threatened and undermined. "There's no way I can find someone by tomorrow and you know it," she said. "We're in crisis management mode here. You come in next week or don't come back at all."

Unable to face another day on the job, and unwilling to go home and tell her husband she had to back out on the vacation, Jane walked out the door and didn't go back. She left a job where she had almost two decades of seniority at a time when many similar companies were outsourcing her function to lower-paid employees overseas. She left a job she'd hoped to stay in until she retired. Her mistake was in waiting for her supervisors to change what had become a bad situation instead of speaking up sooner and trying to push for the needed changes herself. Even if she'd just asked for the week off sooner, she might have been able to work out a better solution. Surely her manager would have preferred to keep Jane from quitting.

Both of these women delayed taking action and suffered because of it. Sara didn't get the raise she deserved and behaved in what felt like an unprofessional and embarrassing way. Jane lost her job. Even if you want to give your organization a chance to make things right, by the time you've "had it" you may be too angry to ask for what you want in a calm and persuasive way.

Procrastinating Makes It Worse

In new research on how people experience dread, scientists found that postponing something unpleasant can actually make the thing they dread feel worse when it finally happens. Apparently our brain imposes costs when we worry about something, and the longer we worry, the higher the cost. Although it may seem counterintuitive, the sooner you ask for what you want the better the negotiation itself will feel. If you're worried about the negotiation and keep postponing it, your anxiety will make the process harder. Pulling off a Band-Aid slowly hurts more than ripping it off fast. "Getting it over with" actually makes the experience itself easier.

Millie—DO IT NOW

Millie, the founder of a nonprofit agency serving deaf and hard-of-hearing adults, needed the agency's Web site revamped. Her cousin had offered to do it pro bono but was taking forever. Millie found a design firm willing to do the work for a reduced fee, but before she hired them she knew she had to call her cousin. On a Friday afternoon, after procrastinating all week, she decided to make the call first thing Monday morning. Then, impulsively, she picked up the phone and made the call. Her cousin was actually relieved to be off the project— she was overcommitted, which is why it was taking her so long. The conversation went well, there were no hard feelings, and Millie had a much better weekend than she would have had if she'd delayed.

DOES LOCATION MATTER?

In the film classic *It's a Wonderful Life,* the sinister banker Mr. Potter invites George Bailey into his office to offer him a deal: He'll pay George $20,000 a year (a fortune in 1946 when the film was made) to come work for him. Sitting behind a large desk, Potter gestures for George to take a chair so close to the floor that the younger man's chin barely grazes the desk. This arrangement conveys a lot about Potter's attitude toward the negotiation—he thinks he's smarter and tougher and more important than impractical George Bailey and he's confident that George won't be able to resist his offer. George looks around the room and quickly realizes that he wants no part of this skewed business relationship, a relationship that bears no resemblance to the more collaborative practices he favors in his family business, the Bailey Building and Loan.

Although Potter probably wouldn't have persuaded George to accept his deal in any case (George knows Potter too well to trust him), the physical layout and the atmosphere of the place you choose for your negotiation can help set the tone and signal how you want the negotiation to go. If you feel at a disadvantage in your boss's office because of the arrangement of the furniture, ask to meet in a small conference room or in the cafeteria, if you can. If you want a collaborative discussion with a colleague, sitting at opposite ends of a long table is not the right strategy. You would do better in a more informal setting—a lounge at work, over a drink, or side by side looking at supporting documents on a desk or table. For negotiations that include more than two parties, consider a round table or a conference room in which the layout doesn't imply a subtle (or not so subtle) hierarchy. Try not to position yourself at the front of a room, which can convey the impression that you're telling everyone else what to do. Avoid spaces that are too large for the gathering. People tend to feel more connected to each other when they're in closer physical proximity (though not *too* close). Inviting someone to lunch or a ballgame or a charity event can set a collegial tone conducive to building alliances and sharing information.

For negotiations that take place at home, remove as many distractions as possible. Turn off the TV, make sure the kids are otherwise engaged, and don't try to do the laundry at the same time. We know, we know—if your home life is anything like ours, that's a tall order. But do the best you can to minimize disruptions that will cause you to lose focus.

WHAT SHOULD YOU ASK FOR?

You've picked the right time and identified a good location. Now it's time for the actual negotiation. How should you start? Should you cut to the chase and name your figure? Should you just say what you really want? Unfortunately, that's almost always a mistake. Negotiation by definition involves a series of offers and counteroffers in which both sides make concessions. For this reason, experienced negotiators never start a negotiation by making their best offer (although they may try to convince you that they have). They don't expect you to ask for the minimum you'll accept either. They assume you'll ask for more than you want, they'll counteroffer for less, you'll come down a bit, and you'll meet in the middle.

If you hire people yourself, you'll recognize the pattern. You don't offer a candidate your reservation value—the absolute most you're willing to pay. You'd like to pay less if you can, and—expecting a negotiation—you want to leave yourself some room to move. If you're a small-business owner making a major purchase for your business (or renting office space or contracting for services), you don't begin by offering the full amount you've budgeted. You start lower, hoping to save money and leaving yourself room to negotiate.

Of course, the negotiation you're planning may not be with an experienced negotiator, or it may be very informal, or you may know for certain that there won't be too much back-and-forth. But even in less formal negotiations, unless you ask for far too little, your first proposal frequently won't be accepted. Unless you leave enough wiggle room between what you ask for and what you really want, you risk being forced back down below your real goal.

But you've already told me to set such a high goal, you may be thinking. *I can't possibly ask for more than that!* But if you've set the right goal (done your research, talked to colleagues and friends), that's exactly what you should do.

Here's an example of how asking for more than you want can make a big difference:

ASK FOR MORE THAN YOU WANT

- Abby is offered a salary of $48,000 from an employer, which is close to the bottom of the range for that job in her region.

- Based upon her research, her expenses, and other offers, she decides that she would have to get at least $50,000 to accept the job. This is her reservation value.

- Abby really wants $54,000, however, and her research tells her she's worth it and that her employer can afford it. $54,000 is her target value, her goal for the negotiation.

Employer Offer	Reservation Value	Target Value
----| ----------	--------------------	---
48,000	50,000	54,000

Scenario 1: Abby asks for what she wants

· Abby asks for $54,000, her target. The employer counteroffers with $51,000 (splitting the difference between $48,000 and $54,000).

Employer Offer	Reservation Value		Target Value
----	----------	----■ --------------	---
48,000	50,000	51,000	54,000

· Abby concedes $2,000 and asks for $52,000. The employer offers to split the difference and they agree to $51,500.

Employer Offer	Reservation Value		Target Value
----	----------	------■ ------------	---
48,000	50,000	51,500	54,000

Scenario 2: Abby asks for more than she wants

· Abby asks for $57,000, which is $3,000 more than her target of $54,000. The employer counteroffers with $52,500 (splitting the difference between $48,000 and $57,000).

Employer Offer	Reservation Value		Target Value	
----	----------	-------- ■ ----	--------	
48,000	50,000	52,500	54,000	57,000

> • Abby concedes $2,000 and asks for $55,000. The employer offers to split the difference and they agree to $53,750.
>
> | Employer Offer | Reservation Value | | Target Value |
> |---|---|---|---|
> | ----\|---------\|-----------------■-\|--- | | | |
> | 48,000 | 50,000 | | 53,750 54,000 |

In Scenario 1, in which Abby asked for exactly what she wanted, she successfully raised the employer's offer by $3,500, which was $1,500 more than her reservation value, but $2,500 less than her target of $54,000. In Scenario 2, in which she asked for more than she wanted, Abby raised the employer's offer by $5,750, which was $3,750 more than her reservation value, and only $250 less than her target. It was also $2,250 more than she got in Scenario 1, when she asked for what she wanted instead of asking for more.

Beginning a negotiation by asking for so much may seem scary or outrageous or just plain nutty, but trust us, it's not. It's actually common practice, and in certain situations, it's the law.

WHEN NOT NEGOTIATING IS ILLEGAL

The idea that negotiation involves give and take on both sides is so pervasive that in some contexts, such as union negotiations, it's actually *illegal* to put an offer on the table that you're not prepared to negotiate. This is called Boulwarism after Lemuel Boulware, a former vice president of General Electric, who told the International Union of Electrical Workers (IUE) at the beginning of negotiations to prevent a strike that the company was making its "first, last and best offer." Boulware used these tactics during labor disputes throughout the 1950s and 1960s and eventually abandoned it after a 122-day strike in 1969. The National Labor Relations Board ruled these tactics to be in violation of federal labor laws and the federal courts upheld the decision in 1969 and 1970.

There's not only a direct correlation between the target you take into a negotiation and how much you're able to get, there's a direct correlation between how much you ask for and how much you get. If you start out asking for what you want, you'll get less than you want. So whether the negotiation is about your salary or something else, if you've identified a high but reasonable target, resolve to ask for more than that.

Marnie—NAMED HER FIGURE TOO EARLY

For years, Marnie, a friend of Linda's, looked for a Victorian dining room table that would fit in her high-ceilinged, oblong dining room. When she finally found one that she loved, the table was priced high at $5,000, which was $1,000 more than she'd budgeted and more than she thought the table was worth.

Without thinking it through, Marnie told the dealer that she didn't want to pay more than $4,000 for the table. The dealer counteroffered with $4,600, and Marnie immediately realized her mistake. "He was expecting to negotiate with me," she told Linda. "Of course he wasn't just going to give me my price." Marnie felt obliged to increase her offer to $4,200. The dealer countered with $4,300, and at that point they were so close Marnie decided to agree. Paying $300 extra for something you love might not seem like an enormous mistake but think of it this way: $4,300 is 7.5 percent higher than $4,000. If you pay 7.5 percent more for every major purchase you make during your lifetime, that can add up to a lot of money you could have saved or spent elsewhere.

WHAT IF IT'S MORE COMPLICATED?

In a negotiation over a single issue (such as the price of Marnie's table), your major strategic decisions will involve whether or not to make the first offer and how high (or low) that offer should be. A multi-issue negotiation requires a completely different approach. Before you can focus on offers, you need to identify the issues to be discussed. And instead of laying out your position from the get-go, you'll do better to start with a general discussion of both sides' underlying interests. In broaching the subject of a promotion, for example, rather than asking outright for the title, responsibilities, salary increase, start date, and anything else you want, you could say, "I think I have more to contribute and I'm ready to take on some new challenges. Can we discuss what's next for me?" This introduces what you want more broadly and sets the stage for a more wide-ranging discussion of your career plans and the company's future. Instead of jumping right into a traditional back-and-forth negotiation in which offers are exchanged or refused, you begin with your goals (I'm ready to move to the next level) and postpone nailing down ways to advance them. This kind of introductory conversation also allows you to scope out the situation and identify the issues of greatest concern to the other side. By initiating the negotiation without making a traditional offer or proposal, you leave room for an open-ended discussion of interests and alternatives.

Irma—A LOT TO SORT OUT

Irma's parents owned a beach house on a lovely island off the coast of Georgia. During the four decades in which they'd owned it, the island had become one of the more desirable beach communities in the area and the value of the cottage had multiplied many times. After Irma's father died, she and her husband, Roy, took on more and more of the cottage's upkeep. They lived relatively close by in Savannah and spent most of each summer at the cottage with their two kids. Irma's only sibling, her unmarried brother Andrew, lived further away in Atlanta and didn't come as often. Three or four times every summer, usually with a girlfriend in tow, he'd arrive unannounced. He'd relax, enjoy himself, and contribute nothing to the cottage's care and expenses.

Irma knew that her mother's will left the cottage to Irma and her brother equally. She and Roy had replaced every appliance and fixture in the house over the years, repaired the roof and the porch and the stairs, refinished the floors, and fixed up the kitchen. She was happy to do this for her mother, but if her brother was part owner her feelings would change. She knew Andrew thought she overdid it on the cottage, fixing things that didn't absolutely need fixing and replacing things that didn't need replacing. Ramshackle suited him fine, he said. It was a summer cottage. Irma also worried that Andrew might want to sell the cottage because it was now so valuable.

She considered asking her mother to put a provision in her will that prohibited them from selling the cottage, or better yet, to change the will and leave the cottage to Irma's two kids. She thought about telling Andrew that he had to sign a contract promising not to sell the cottage so it would pass to her kids eventually. She wondered if she could persuade her mother to sell the cottage to her for a favorable price—it was only fair, after all the work they'd put into it—and leave the money from the sale to Andrew. None of these were ideal solutions, she knew, and all would breed ill will with Andrew.

Instead of attacking the problem head-on, she drove down to Atlanta and took her brother to lunch. "We need to start thinking about the future of the cottage," she said. "My kids adore it and they would be heartbroken if we sold it, but I can imagine that you might want or need the money. Roy and I would like some recognition for all the work we've done, whatever we decide. Mostly I just want to hear what you've been thinking about it and what would be the ideal solution for you."

Andrew admitted that he'd been thinking about the possibility of selling the cottage, but he loved his niece and nephew and had such happy childhood memories himself of summers on the island. If we sold the cottage, he asked, what kind of price do you think we could get for it? Irma wasn't sure, so they agreed to have the cottage appraised. The price shocked them both. There was no way Irma and Roy could afford to buy out Andrew's half at full price. After more discussion, they hired an independent appraiser to assess the value of Irma and Roy's improvements. With this information in hand, they worked out an agreement that allowed Irma and Roy to buy Andrew's equity in the house from their mother's estate for less than the market rate in recognition of the value of their work. They also agreed to give Andrew full access to the cottage for three weeks of his choice every summer (he had to give them a little advance notice, though). Since Irma had initiated the discussion in a spirit of sibling cooperation instead of making threats or demands, she and her brother were able to find a solution that didn't damage their relationship, and may have even strengthened it.

WHAT'S THE RULE FOR COUNTEROFFERS?

One of Linda's students mentioned a job offer she'd just received and said she was going to ask the recruiter if the salary was negotiable. "What?!" said Linda. If you want to negotiate your offer, she explained, asking *if* the salary is negotiable is an extremely weak opening. It suggests that you're okay with the offer even if it's *not* negotiable. So the first rule of counteroffers is, never ask if something is negotiable. Always proceed under the assumption that it is.

This is especially true when the other side goes first and puts a package—a detailed proposal on a series of issues—on the table. Don't assume that it's all or nothing, and don't feel as though you need to respond immediately with a counteroffer. Try to get more information. Here are some ideas for how to do this:

- "That's a lot to digest. Before I respond, can we talk about your overarching goals for this process?"

- "We have a lot of interests in common and I want to make sure we're on the same page about what those are."
- "Can you give me some background on how you put this offer together?"
- "Would you explain your reasons for breaking down the issues in this way?"
- "There's a lot here. Can you talk about the thinking behind some of the details?"
- "I want to make sure I understand your priorities before I start talking about mine. What matters most to you?"
- "I don't want to miss anything. Can we review the fine print?"
- "Are there any other issues we should discuss before we go further? Have we left anything out?"

The answers to these questions will help you assemble a good counteroffer, make strategic trades, and address the other negotiator's core interests. Make sure your counteroffer leaves you a fair amount of wiggle room, and leaves the *most* wiggle room around the issues that you care about the most. If you make a large concession on one issue while holding firm on another, this will imply something about your priorities over the issues and how much you're willing to move on each. For example, suppose you're negotiating to rent office space and the building owner wants $3,000 a month and a three-year lease. If your target is to pay $2,850 a month and you don't want to commit yourself for more than two years (with the duration of the lease more important to you than the price), a good counteroffer would be $2,750 with a one-year lease. This positions your target value squarely between the two offers. If the owner counters at $2,900 for a three-year commitment, you'll still have enough room to make some concessions and achieve your target. You could offer to meet his price, for instance, *if* he'll agree to a two-year contract.

How many "rounds" of negotiation should you expect? It depends a lot on the context. Complicated negotiations involving the merging of two companies, international arms agreements, and protracted labor negotiations can involve dozens and dozens of rounds, with proposals going back and forth for years. Job negotiations typically involve two or three rounds; so do negotiations over the price of a car or a house. (An acquaintance of Linda's just spent several months and took a dozen rounds to buy a house, but her situation was unusual.) If you aren't sure about what to expect for a particular negotiation, talk to people who've conducted similar negotiations to get a rough idea.

With this information in mind, begin assembling your concession plan. Start by analyzing what your concessions will signal to the other side. If you post your five-year-old car on Craigslist for $14,500, for example, and a buyer offers you $12,000, you might counteroffer by dropping your price to $14,300. This would signal that you're already close to your reservation value and probably won't drop the price much further. If, instead, you drop your price by $1,500, to $13,000, the potential buyer will probably conclude that you overpriced the car initially, you really want to sell it, and you'll lower the price even further. Conceding too much early on can make the other side intransigent because they expect you to make the bulk of the concessions.

As you get to the second or third round of a negotiation, it's typical for the size of the concessions to decrease. Factor this in when you draft your concession plan so that your concessions get smaller and smaller as you near your target. Suppose you see a painting in a small gallery while you're on vacation. The price in the exhibit guide is $1,000. You decide you won't pay more than $900 but you'd like to pay $825 (that's your target). You offer $700 and the artist counteroffers with $900. This is a good sign—he's already dropped the price to your reservation value. A good next offer for you would be $750, which is still lower than your target value. The artist probably wouldn't accept, since his second concession is likely to be smaller than the first. But that's okay because your target is still positioned in the middle of the offers on the table. The artist makes a third offer of $850. You can ask then if he'll split the difference. If he agrees, you'll get the painting for $800—less than your target. Offering to split the difference is a tactic that often works extremely well because it appeals to the other side's sense of fairness. What could be more fair than meeting in the middle? The key to using this tactic is making sure that the middle is where you want it to be.

MAKE A DATE

Once you've decided what to ask for and plotted your concession plan, write down your plan on a note card to take with you into the negotiation. Assemble any other notes, supporting documentation, or projections you'd like to take with you. If you need time to do more background research, set up a schedule for completing your preparation. Track how you're progressing and don't delay without good reason. If you're forced to slow down, don't give up. Pick up where you left off and persist until you complete your advance work.

Once you're ready and you've identified the best time to ask, set a timetable for the negotiation (if it's going to be a multistage negotiation, set a timetable for the interim steps as well as the final deadline). Schedule the meeting with the other negotiator(s) and if necessary reserve a conference room or other space. Decide if it would be useful to have a whiteboard or flipchart in the room so that both sides can write down ideas to be discussed. If it feels appropriate to the setting and context of the negotiation, plan to take notes during the process too. This can help you track the course of the discussion and capture the gist of what was discussed. In most cases, bringing a laptop with you is a bad idea. It can create an artificial barrier between you and the other side and you may spend more time looking at a computer screen than at the other person. If your negotiation will involve complicated financial calculations in which a spreadsheet would be necessary, ask someone to go with you who can run the numbers while you focus on your interaction with the other negotiators.

SHOULD YOU BLUFF?

Once you've embarked on your negotiation, is it okay to lie? To drop hints that encourage the other side to draw the wrong conclusions? If they think you're prepared to walk away long before you really would, they might concede more and give you a better deal than you would get otherwise. Bluffing can be a useful tool for influencing the other side's perception of your reservation value, something that you don't want to reveal in a negotiation. But bluffing carries a lot of risks.

In classroom exercises, some of Linda's students will lie outright to reach a good deal, some students tell the truth unequivocally, and some fall between these two extremes. You need to decide for yourself what works for you, and it's best to do this beforehand because in the heat of a negotiation you might make a decision you'll regret. Remember that the person you're negotiating with may have very different ideas about what's acceptable, so the more you know about her or him the better equipped you'll be to judge how far to go. Context matters too. In a game of poker, for example, bluffing is not only acceptable, it's expected. The same is true when you're buying a used car. But when you're negotiating with your partner, best friend, or spouse? Probably not a good idea.

When you're trying to decide whether to bluff in a particular negotiation, keep in mind that your reputation may be on the line. In Linda's classes, students who bluff aggressively develop very bad reputations. After every practice negotiation, Linda and her students discuss the exercise. Linda distributes the confidential information used by each side to all the students, immediately revealing who told the truth, who out and out lied, and who bluffed. A student who told a whopper of a lie typically has a hard time in class for the rest of the term. Other students avoid negotiating with the extreme bluffers and when they have no choice they distrust everything, take an extremely aggressive stance toward the negotiation, and often end up in an impasse. Their distrust impedes their ability to communicate openly and both sides end up with bad deals or no deal at all.

The class structure ensures that lies and bluffs are quickly detected, which won't always happen. If, however, there's a risk that your bluff will come out, proceed with care. If you tell a client that you can't possibly do a job for under a certain amount and the client later discovers you charged someone else much less, the ill will this engenders may lose you the first client. If you tell a new employee who's pressing for a flexible schedule that everyone works the same hours, the relationship will start on a sour note if she finds out that many people work different schedules. If your company merges with another organization and you tell your new manager that no one else at your level possesses your skills because you're angling for a particular project assignment, this can have negative consequences down the line if it's not true.

If you know for sure that the other side will never discover that you bluffed, you may want to take this chance. But you should never "kiss and tell"—boast to the other side about how clever you were, or even let slip that they could have done better. And remember to calculate the impact, and potential damage, bluffing will have on your relationship before you take that step.

ONE SIZE DOES NOT FIT ALL

Remember that you'll conduct thousands of negotiations during your lifetime (we hope!) and no two of them will be identical (unless you count that regular back-and-forth with your kids about when they can have soda). While we've given you some guidelines to follow, you'll need to customize your strategy to fit the specific situation. How to open the discussion, what to ask for, the order in which you propose different parts of a multi-issue negotiation, when and where to ask, what types of information you want to reveal...it's a lot. But you're ready. It's time to practice.

12

NEGOTIATION GYM:
WORK UP A SWEAT

WHAT IF YOU REALIZE that you've missed more than a few opportunities to negotiate and you're resolved to change that, but you haven't negotiated a lot in your life? Should you start by asking your boss for a raise and a promotion tomorrow? Probably not. You wouldn't start an exercise program by signing up for a marathon, so give yourself a chance to get in shape first.

To help you build your negotiation muscles, we've developed a six-week series of exercises. Consider working through all of them in a systematic way (although you don't necessarily need to do them in consecutive weeks). Linda assigns these exercises to students in her graduate negotiation classes and the students are always surprised by how much they get out of the process, although initially they're often a bit tentative. They wonder if all this practice is really necessary and worry that they'll feel silly asking for things they know they won't get. But this quickly changes. Everyone starts taking bigger chances, setting higher goals, and challenging each other to be more imaginative about what to ask for. They root for each other and begin to have fun, and they return to class each week eager to describe their failures as well as their successes.

If you can, recruit a workout buddy to go through the program with you. The two of you can compare notes, debrief each other, and laugh about the oddball responses you get. In addition to helping you appreciate the gamesmanship aspects of negotiating, going through the workout with a friend will make the process more enjoyable and help you follow through to the big finish in week 6.

WEEK 1:
EASY WARM-UPS

Begin developing your skills by negotiating for several small things. Something "small" means the stakes are low—you won't be devastated if you don't get it. Ask if you can leave an hour early one day to attend a lecture or an art opening or a going-away party for a colleague. Ask if it would be possible for your firm to install a high-speed printer on your floor so that you don't have to waste five minutes running downstairs every time you need to print a long document. If you're self-employed, ask the manager at the office supply store you use if you can get a best-customer or frequent-flyer discount. Or begin outside work. Ask your partner, roommate, or spouse to take a day off from work (instead of doing it yourself) to wait for the cable installer or the refrigerator repairman or the person coming to clean your gutters. Call your credit card company and ask if they can give you a better interest rate since you have a great credit rating and always pay on time. Ask your brother to bring the drinks and dessert to a family party for which you and your sister are doing all the cooking. Ask your next-door neighbor if you can prune a tree of his that's growing onto your property. Ask for at least one thing every day of the week.

- Ask for something that you're pretty sure you can get.
- Ask for something you'd like to get but won't care much if you don't.

- Ask for something from a complete stranger, someone who doesn't know you and whom you'll probably never see again.
- Ask for something that you feel comfortable asking for, where doing so doesn't make you anxious.
- Ask for something that you know will be easy for the other side to give you.

In each case, state your request simply and then wait for the answer. Try to conceal that you're nervous (if you are). Say what you want and let the other person make the next move.

If you practice asking for small things, and do it a lot, you'll discover that people frequently don't respond in the negative ways you expect. It will broaden your sense of what in life is negotiable, because you'll be surprised by how many of these small requests are successful. Many things that you always assumed couldn't be changed—retail prices, schedules set by others, even unspoken agreements about household duties—you'll now see as opportunities for negotiation. You'll get a lot of what you ask for and develop the confidence to tackle the larger, more important negotiations down the road.

Sara—A BUSY WEEK

In one summer week in 2006, to test our week 1 program, Sara attempted several small negotiations to see how well she did. She'd just had her bathroom painted and one of her favorite stores was having a summer white sale, selling all its bath linens at a 20 percent discount. On Sunday, the first day of her trial week, she bought two hand towels in different colors to see which one worked best. When she went back to the store the following Saturday she discovered that the sale had just ended. Although she wanted six full sets of towels, with the sale over she could only afford to buy four. She decided to try bargaining with a saleswoman. "If you'll sell me six sets for the sale price, I'll buy six sets," she said. "If you can't give me the sale price, I can only buy four."

The saleswoman paused for a moment. "I think that would be okay," she said. "I'll give you the sale price."

That same week, Sara was invited to an outdoor picnic. She stopped into a local organic farm that sold heirloom tomatoes—a half peck of mixed tomatoes, customer's choice, in small baskets with plastic bags inside. As Sara waited in line to pay for her tomatoes, she noticed that the cashier was taking the plastic bags out of the baskets, weighing the tomatoes, and keeping the baskets. "That's too bad," she thought. When she reached the checkout counter, she asked the cashier if she could buy the basket too. "I'm taking them to a picnic," Sara explained, "and they look so pretty in the basket."

The cashier leaned forward and lowered her voice. "Just take it. Don't tell anybody. Have a nice picnic."

Sara is also an active user of her local public library, which has an online system that allows her to request a book from her home computer. A librarian e-mails her when the book becomes available and Sara has a week to pick it up. She'd been waiting for almost two months to read a popular book when the notice arrived. She was about to leave on vacation and there was no way she could get to the library before she left. But if she didn't pick up the book on time, she'd drop down to the bottom of the list again. She e-mailed the library and described her dilemma. "Is there any way you could hold the book for two extra days until I get back?" she asked. Half an hour later, a librarian e-mailed to say yes.

Sara also asked for some things she didn't get. She bought a dozen perennials at a local nursery and asked if they'd give her a bulk purchase discount but they turned her down. She and her mother attended a bead show (Sara's mother loves jewelry) and her mother purchased three strands of labradorite, a semiprecious stone, from the same vendor; Sara asked the vendor to give them a discount since they were buying three strands but the vendor refused. Near the end of the day, however, she convinced another vendor to drop his price for an expensive strand of prehnite by more than half (she still couldn't afford it, but it was a very good price).

WEEK 2:
STRETCH OUT

The focus this week is on setting a high target. Again, pick several small things that you want but don't have much riding on. For each one, identify the most you think you can get, and *ask for twice as much*. If you've been planning to offer 10 percent less for an antique lamp you like, ask if you can get it for 20 percent less. If you want to take off the last week in August but you'd also like a few days off at Christmas, ask for both the week in August and the whole week between Christmas and New Year's. If you want a new office chair, ask for the chair and new blinds on your windows.

THE GIGGLE TEST

As a rule of thumb, Linda tells her students to use what she calls the giggle test—to ask for as much as they can without giggling. If you're not a giggler, ask for as much as you can without blushing, or without stammering, or without your voice quavering. Identify your own behavioral cues—how you may unwittingly signal that you don't believe in what you're saying—and consciously avoid behaving in any of those ways when you're asking for something that seems like a lot.

Astrid—ONE MORE NIGHT OR TWO?

Once a year, Astrid and her colleagues attended a large trade show on the West Coast. The show lasted for four days. Astrid and the other members of the sales staff arrived Saturday to set up and then put in fourteen-hour days on the convention hall floor from Sunday through Wednesday. On Thursday they packed up and took the red-eye back to the East Coast so they could be at their desks on Friday morning. The red-eye took a real toll on Astrid, especially after five exhausting days in a row, and it always took her a good week to recover from the trip. She decided to ask if she could stay over on the West Coast for one extra night and fly back on Friday. It meant the firm would have to pay for an extra night in a hotel and she'd miss work that Friday. But if she was going to miss work Friday, she thought, why not stay an extra day, relax a little after the grueling week, pop in on her nephew at UCLA, and fly back Saturday? She doubted her boss would agree but she figured she'd ask. "I could fly back Thursday night and stare at my desk all day Friday," she told her boss. "Or I could fly back Saturday and come in Monday morning fresh and ready to go." To Astrid's surprise, her boss said okay.

Jiao—CONTROL THE SPREAD OF GERMS

Jiao was in her second year as a junior attorney at a large law firm. The firm was preparing for the trial of a corporate client charged with accounting fraud and insider trading. A dozen lawyers and twice as many paralegals were working on the case, and at any given time there were at least ten people reviewing documents and sorting papers in one of the firm's large conference rooms. In January, as flu season set in, Jiao became acutely aware of all the sniffling and nose wiping as people passed documents back and forth around the table. She dreaded getting sick, and she also knew that the firm was barely on schedule. If too many lawyers came down with the flu, they might not be ready when the trial date arrived. Jiao decided to ask the partner in charge of the case if it would be possible to put bottles of hand sanitizer by every seat at the conference table. She also suggested that they ask a local clinic to send someone over to give flu shots to anyone who wanted one. The partner's response was immediate: "Let's do it!" he said. "Everyone at my wife's office is already sick. I'll tell my assistant to order the stuff immediately and send out a memo. And I'll get Human Resources to set up the flu shots."

WEEK 3:
PLAY OUT OF BOUNDS

Now it's time to actively court rejection, to get used to hearing no and not taking it personally or feeling as though you've failed. Linda once tried to negotiate the price of gas. The station attendant—no surprise—turned her down, but seemed amused. Did his amusement hurt her? What if he'd acted disgusted? Or signaled that he thought she was a ridiculous woman who didn't know her way around cars (which happens not to be true)? Would that have hurt her? What if he'd shouted at her? That would have been unpleasant, but would it have hurt her? Probably not. Would it have had any long-term negative impact on her life? Absolutely not.

One of our principal goals in writing this book has been to help you grow more comfortable hearing no. Nobody likes rejection but research shows that women's self-esteem fluctuates more in response to feedback, whether positive or negative, than men's. A man who gets turned down when he asks for something may shake his head and think, *Better luck next time.* A woman may take the rejection as a judgment on the quality of her work—or, worse, as a reflection on her worth as a person. Studies also show that women feel less comfortable with social risk than men. Since there's always the chance that you'll get turned down no matter how well you prepare, negotiation by definition involves some degree of social risk.

Week 3 is designed to get you over this hump, so that you can take rejection in stride, as a calculated risk, and as part of discovering your full potential. Learning that you can ask for something (even something big), get turned down, and be okay with that—this is a great thing to learn. Finding that you can continue to interact comfortably with the person who turned you down can be a great relief. If you avoid negotiating for anything you may not get, you might not discover that rather than being offended, or thinking less of you, many people won't think anything at all. You asked, they said no, end of story.

With this in mind, thinking of it as a game with very low stakes, try negotiating the price of apples at the supermarket, the price of a suit in a department store, the price of a forty-two-inch plasma screen TV at an electronics store. Ask your personnel office if they can make a special exception and let you change your health insurance plan midyear. Ask if anyone in your office would mind if you brought in your dog during the day so he won't be lonely at home. Call up the assessor's office in your town and ask them to lower the tax assessment of your house. The answers to most of these requests will probably be no, but even if someone yells at you or treats you rudely, you'll have lost nothing and you'll suffer no lasting damage. (To prove this to yourself, you might consider asking for something that you *know* will get you yelled at. Then hang on tight and prepare to laugh about it afterward.)

Here are a few examples of things students in Linda's class tried to negotiate during this week.

- A student came to Linda's office and said she knew that she was only doing B work in the class but she really wanted to get an A because it would improve her GPA. As Linda had taught her, she made her pitch and waited for Linda's reaction. Linda hesitated because she couldn't figure out whether the student was serious or she was just, as Linda likes to say, "gyming" her. The student stayed calm during Linda's silence—she didn't laugh, take it back, or give away that she expected to be turned down. Linda said no. Afterward, the student said she really felt proud of herself for going through with it.

- Another student brought her car in for its state inspection, which in Pennsylvania costs about $40 if the car passes in every category. Assuming that the inspection price is set by the state, she nevertheless asked the mechanic if he'd perform the service for free since she and her husband both bring their cars into him for repairs. She thought he was going to get mad, laugh, or just say no. He actually said yes.

- A student asked the manager of a fast-food restaurant if she would give him forty vouchers for a free burrito or taco so that he could give one to each of his classmates in his negotiation class. She said no—but she did give him two vouchers for himself.

- A student asked one of the other tenants in his apartment building (whom he really didn't know) if she'd allow him to use her wireless Internet for free. He'd been "surfing" on it until she passcode protected it and locked him out. She refused.

- One student was planning a trip to Iceland with two friends. She called Icelandair to see if they would give her a "group" discount. They said three friends did not qualify as a group and turned her down.

None of these students felt as though they suffered any lasting psychological damage, or hurt any of their personal relationships, for courting rejection in this way. A few of them were surprised to find that their requests were more successful than they expected.

WEEK 4:
STEP IT UP

Now, up the stakes. Choose a week in which you have some "breath-ing room"—time to focus on the negotiations you decide to pursue, and time to reflect on your experiences.

- On the first day of the week, make a list of four or five things to negotiate this week. Your list should contain at least one thing that is relatively big, something you care about that won't be a no-brainer to get, and several things that aren't obvious slam-dunks. These negotiations should require a little preparation and some good strategic choices. Commit yourself to asking for everything on your list and begin.

- Ask for at least two things on the first day. At the end of the day, make notes about each experience. Describe what you did well and where you still need practice.

- Over the next four days, negotiate for the rest of the things on your list.

- Save the biggest thing on the list for the end of the week when you've gotten some practice under your belt. (If possible, try to make this a multi-issue negotiation, one in which you have the potential to logroll to get what you want.)

- At the end of the week, look back on which negotiations went well and which didn't. Ask yourself the following questions:
  - What forms of preparation were most effective? What was un-necessary? Would more (or different) preparation have helped?
  - Did you correctly assess and use your bargaining power?
  - How well did you anticipate the interests and behavior of the other side?
  - Which negotiation strategies (e.g., your initial offer, your tim-ing, etc.) worked well? Were there situations in which a differ-

ent strategy would have been more effective? Were there situations in which you chose the right strategy but presented it badly or didn't follow through?

- Compare your assessment of your last three negotiations to the notes you made about your first two this week. Has anything changed? Have you improved in certain areas? Can you identify more clearly where you still need more practice?

Here are examples of the more complex and consequential negotiations that Linda's students have attempted during week 4.

- One student had a fifteen-hour-a-week job during the semester working as an intern for a nonprofit organization. The heads of the organization wanted her to spend all of her time fund-raising and she wasn't enjoying it much. She proposed that she split her time between fund-raising and program development and persuaded them to say yes.

- A student wanted to fix up his basement but was short of funds. The walls had already been framed (the basement had been roughly finished years earlier, but the drywall had rotted from the damp, so he'd torn it out and installed a dehumidifier). He had two friends, a husband-and-wife team, with a small home-renovation business. The husband was certified as an electrician and the wife was a carpenter. The student knew that the husband had just bought a used Macintosh computer and was having trouble getting it to function. Since the student had owned Macs for years, he was well versed in their quirks and capabilities. He asked if he could pay the wife to put up and tape the drywall, and trade Mac expertise for the needed electrical work, which was not extensive. He'd paint the walls himself. His friends agreed.

- One student was working part-time as a secretary in one of the university's administrative offices to help pay her way through school. She wanted to keep working at the university once she finished her degree but she didn't want to continue as a secretary. She had a lot of ideas about how the department could serve students more effectively, but putting her ideas into practice would require the creation of a new position. During week 4, she presented her ideas to the dean in whose office she worked and asked if he would consider creating a new job for her. Although he couldn't give her an immediate answer, he promised to consider her request when he planned his budget for the next fiscal year.

- A student wrote freelance articles for a Pittsburgh newspaper on the side and hoped to be hired full-time after she finished her degree. During week 4, she asked her editor about a permanent position—and was turned down. Although she was disappointed, she stopped waiting around for the paper to offer her a job and launched a job search. By graduation, she had landed a full-time position at another newspaper.

WEEK 5:
GO LONG

This week, ask for three things that you're pretty sure you *can't* get, either because you know they would be hard for the other side to give you or because they're things that aren't typically negotiated. Unlike week 3, however, ask for things you care about, from people with whom you have an ongoing relationship, and include at least one long shot that you'd love to get. For example, consider asking someone close to you for something that involves changing the way things have always been done—such as asking your spouse or partner to take on cooking dinner half the time.

In each case, be sure not to signal that you think you're going to be turned down. The goal is not to get everything you ask for. The goal is to tolerate the discomfort of asking for a lot, and watching someone take his or her time deciding how to respond. Again, if you get turned down, *don't apologize*. Smile and say, "It was worth a try," and leave it at that.

Caitlyn—A TRIP TO DO HER JOB BETTER

Caitlyn worked in sales for a company that manufactured high-end replacement windows. Recently, the firm had started receiving a lot of custom orders for unusual or distinctive windows designed by architects specifically for individual houses. Manufacturing these custom-built windows was enormously labor intensive and expensive, and the company was forced to charge astronomical rates for each window. Caitlyn noticed that none of their clients contested the prices, though, and as these clients showed off the beautiful windows to their equally wealthy friends, more and more custom orders rolled in. Caitlyn realized that the company had inadvertently developed a niche market for its products, and a niche market with the potential to become extremely profitable. No one at the company really understood this market, though.

Caitlyn had heard about an organization in New York that specialized in selling to the luxury market—people with a lot of disposable income to spend on expensive goods and services. Sure that her boss would refuse (the firm was family owned and cautious in all its business practices), she asked if she could fly to New York and meet with the head of this organization. "If we're going to make the most of this opportunity," she argued, "we need to learn as much as we can about this market in the shortest possible time." Her boss consulted with his brother, who was co-owner of the company, and they paid for her to make the trip.

WEEK 6:
PILE IT ON

It's time to test those muscles you've been building. This week, choose something big that you think it's really *not okay* to want, something you think would make you seem greedy or selfish if you asked for it. And make sure it's something you really do want. Then ask for it. Whether you get it or not, fight your impulse to apologize or feel bad. Tell yourself it's okay to want what you want. Combat the impulse to scale back out of fear that you're overreaching.

Celia—DECORATE MY OFFICE

Celia was the director of marketing for a successful software start-up based in Silicon Valley. When her husband took a job in Minneapolis and they decided to move, she offered to resign but her boss insisted she stay on. "You don't need to be on-site every day to do your job," he said. "Fly in a couple of times a month and you can work from home the rest of the time." Celia agreed, and after she and her husband bought a rambling old Victorian house in a Minneapolis suburb, she set up her office in an attic room on the third floor. She had a small computer table that she'd used in her California house, a small printer, and copy and fax machines but not much else. She thought about buying new furniture for the space but she kept putting it off. Since her boss was the one who'd decided she should work from home, she wanted him to pay to fix up her office—wire it for high-speed Internet, put in a carpet, and buy her a better printer and some decent office furniture. She even wanted a sink and a small refrigerator so she wouldn't have to run up and down two flights of stairs whenever she wanted a cup of tea or a bottle of water. She felt as though this was unreasonable—the office was in her house, after all, and it wasn't as though she couldn't afford to decorate it if she made up her mind to do it. But she really wanted him to fund the renovation. "Working from home and schlepping back and forth to California twice a month is hard enough," she said. "It's not like I couldn't have gotten a good job in Minneapolis or St. Paul. But he wanted me to keep working for him and I just thought he should make my office as comfortable and efficient as the one I'd had before I moved." Feeling guilty and uncomfortable and as though it was really too much to ask, she asked anyway. Her boss didn't hesitate. "How much do you need?" he said.

COOL DOWN

If you've finished your six-week program, congratulations. How did you do? Did you successfully change more things than you expected? Did you succeed in making bigger changes in certain situations than you'd hoped? Were you able to improve—even a little—an intractable situation that you thought would be impossible to budge? Do you feel differently about negotiating in general because you've now done it so many times?

We've designed this negotiation workout to be challenging, yet fun. And just like the endorphin high or rush you feel when you finish a physical workout, we hope you feel a sense of elation and accomplishment now that you're done, knowing that you've worked hard, improved your skills, and flexed your negotiation muscles. You should feel great not only about the things you asked for and got but— perhaps even more—about asking for the things you didn't get.

PHASE FOUR

Put It All Together

13

DRESS REHEARSAL

IN HER CLASSES, Linda has her students work through practice negotiations every week. She hands out role assignments in advance that
contain detailed information about positions, interests, and targets. In
class, she pairs up students and sets them loose (dozens of negotiations
going on at the same time makes for a very lively class). This process
allows students to try out different strategies, grow more comfortable
with negotiating, and experience many of the strong emotions that
can arise in a negotiation.

For you, role-playing ahead of time will provide many of the same
benefits. You can experiment with strategies, practice talking about the
issues, and explore different ways of saying what you mean—choose
different words or phrases, rearrange the order in which you present
your ideas, tweak points of emphasis, and eliminate extraneous obser-
vations that seem germane but turn out to be side issues or diversions
when you actually try them out.

Role-playing is especially useful for controlling the emotional di-
mensions of a negotiation. Emotions create problems when they interfere with your ability to think on your feet, react quickly and creatively
to new information, and hang in there when your negotiation runs

into rough territory. A certain amount of anger can propel you to act. But it can also cloud your thinking and can make you lose sight of your overall goals. When you get angry, it's easy to be distracted by peripheral issues or to focus excessively on one point while ignoring others that are equally or more important. You may cling to your initial position and resist any type of compromise, and fail to objectively evaluate the legitimate arguments made by the other side. Digging your feet in, you'll overlook options that could solve some of the problems you're stuck on. If you do reach an agreement, the chances are good that one or both sides will be unhappy with many of its terms. Or you may not reach any agreement at all. Not to mention that giving way to anger will make the negotiation more unpleasant for everybody.

Sadness can also cause problems because it's been shown to make people set lower goals for themselves. If another negotiator says something that dampens your mood—about changes in your organization that will make it a less fun place to work or about a likable colleague who's going to be transferred—you may decide to lower your goals or concede too quickly.

Finally, negative emotions can be contagious. Your anger may spark anger on the other side of the table, prompting a "conflict spiral." If you let your mood slump or your energy sag, the other negotiator may also lose momentum, feel less optimistic about the possibilities of a good resolution, and agree to a solution that's disappointing all around.

As Roger Fisher and Daniel Shapiro write in *Beyond Reason: Using Emotions as You Negotiate,* "The worst time to craft a strategy to deal with strong negative emotions is while experiencing them. . . . You want to be able to make a conscious choice—a smart choice—about what to do with strong emotions and how to deal with the event that caused them." If you're surprised by strong feelings, you're more likely to shift your focus to figuring out what to do with them—whether to conceal them, express them, or leave them simmering below the surface. Diverting a lot of mental energy to keep your emotions in check makes it harder to concentrate on the issues being discussed, listen closely, analyze options objectively, and look for creative ways to solve shared problems. This loss of cognitive clarity, of the ability to think quickly, clearly, and energetically, can seriously undermine your ability to do the real work of the negotiation. To save face or avoid conflict or appease someone on the other side of the table, you may find yourself backing away from your plan and giving up abruptly.

Rehearsing ahead of time can prevent this from happening. Once you've anticipated and experienced an emotion while role-playing, that emotion won't feel as raw and powerful when it strikes in your real negotiation. Furthermore, it won't take you by surprise, which is critical because it's often the surprise rather than the emotion itself that throws us off our game. If the other negotiator confronts you with an offer you didn't anticipate, turns down your request without giving you a chance to explain, says something that puts you on the defensive, or refuses to budge despite your well-reasoned approach, you'll have planned and practiced a constructive response. You'll be prepared to acknowledge the feeling ("Okay, here's the part where I start to get angry") and keep going. You'll feel much more control over the process, even if it's not going as well as you hoped, and you'll be more likely to turn it in your favor.

ROLE-PLAYING BASICS

Get help. Recruit a friend or colleague whom you trust to play the part of the other negotiator. It can help if this friend knows the person with whom you'll be negotiating but it's not essential. Make sure you feel comfortable showing your emotions to this person. Arrange a time when you can both devote an hour or more to the exercise and find a setting that resembles the space in which your actual negotiation will take place. (If you'll be sitting across a desk from the other negotiator, find a room with a desk, for example.)

Write down your plan. Jot down your BATNA, reservation value, and target. Write out what you know about the other side's interests, goals, BATNA, and reservation value. (Appendix A and additional tools on our Web site, www.askforit.org, will help you organize your thoughts and identify strategic issues.) Decide what you're going to ask for first and how much you want to concede on the first round. What adjustments will you make if you encounter stiff resistance? If you're engaged in a multi-issue negotiation and expect to do some logrolling, choose what to offer in trade early in the process and what to hold in reserve. Estimate how many rounds the negotiation will last and plot out a concession plan—a likely series of offers and counteroffers that leaves you enough room to end up in your target area.

Identify flash points. You should also take a few minutes to identify those elements in your proposal that are likely to elicit a strong negative response from the other negotiator(s). Make detailed notes about how you imagine they may respond. Go further and imagine the most crushing remark someone could make, comments that might make you lose your composure, stop you in your tracks, hurt your feelings, or make you doubt whether you really deserve what you're asking for. Don't hold back—be honest with yourself about the harshest judgments the other negotiators might make about your work or your personal qualities.

Decide what to say. Now begin composing your responses. These responses should serve two overarching purposes: to move the negotiation in a positive direction and to help you maintain your composure. Your goal should be to find ways to reframe the negotiation as a collaboration rather than a conflict, and a collaboration with a shared goal of finding a solution that makes you both happy.

To prevent negative emotions from erupting and ease rising tension in the room, try:

- "I can see that what I've said has really annoyed you and that wasn't my intention. Can you help me to understand your reaction?"

- "I was totally unprepared for such a negative response. What have I been missing?"

- "I can see that you're completely opposed to the idea. Would you explain how you see the situation?"

- "You really hate my plan, don't you?" (smiling) "Let's think about what else might work." (If using humor is comfortable for you, it's a great way to de-escalate a tense situation.)

- "I really didn't mean it as a joke. Can you tell me why my request seems funny to you?"

- "It looks like I've taken you by surprise and I didn't mean to. Do you mind if I give you a bit more background information?"

- "You seem frustrated. Would you explain why?"

- "I'd rather not see this as a fight. Let's try to work things out."

- "I'm sure you have a lot of good reasons for saying no. Would you mind talking about them a little?"

- "It seems like what I want would cause problems for you. Can you tell me how?"

To avoid a potential impasse and move the conversation in a positive direction, try:

- "I know we haven't figured this out yet but let's keep talking; I'm sure we can think of something that will work for both of us."

- "We have a lot of shared goals here. How can we capitalize on them?"

- "If none of these scenarios works, why don't we try something different? With a little imagination I know we can figure this out."

- "It feels like we're headed in the wrong direction. What can we do to get back on track?"

- "I can certainly be a bit flexible about the ways to accomplish this. What are our options?"

- "Let's take a step back and think about this a different way."

To put the ball in the other court and get the other side to make a counteroffer, try:

- "I didn't expect you to be so surprised. What do you think would be fair?"

- "I can see that you're unhappy with what I've suggested. Tell me what kind of agreement you'd like to see."

- "If that seems like too much, then how close can you come to my figure?"

- "Wow. We're really far apart. Maybe we can meet somewhere in the middle."

- "How do you think we should try to resolve this situation?"

- "It sounds like you can't give me all that I've asked for. Instead, is it possible to give me X [where X is slightly more modest]?"

Once you've put together your plan and assembled a variety of responses to move the negotiation forward, you're ready to practice.

Brief your partner. Begin by thoroughly summarizing the overall context of the situation, including information about your department, the company, and industry (whatever's relevant). Provide your partner with notes highlighting crucial issues if the situation is complicated. Describe the personality of the other negotiator and how you expect that person to perceive the situation. Identify the parts of your request that you think will be hardest for the other negotiator to give you and those you think will be easiest (and why). Note the obstacles that the other side may put in your way. Be sure to include the things that worry you most.

Rehearse several times. Ask your partner to try to surprise you, to change direction abruptly, to refuse to compromise. Make it clear that it's okay to say harsh things to you, even harsh things *you* haven't thought of (because you want to be surprised). Ask your partner to vary her approach; experiment with different responses yourself. The idea is to experience the full range of what might happen. Get angry because your partner is being uncooperative and combative, frustrated because you're not getting what you want, and insulted because she says something cutting and hurtful about your abilities. Don't turn it into a game. You and your partner need to take this process seriously so that it triggers real emotions in you. While you practice, pay attention to your reactions.

Debrief. What worked well? What could have gone more smoothly? What unsettled you most? Ask your partner to give you feedback on how he or she thought you performed. Did you seem confident? Was your argument persuasive? Were some of the points you made stronger than others? Did you communicate clearly? Did you listen? Did you adopt a positive, collaborative attitude? Did you work to keep emotions (on both sides) from erupting? Ask your partner to be frank about the impact of your personal style and body language. Did you talk too fast, twist your hair around your finger, slouch in your chair, or hunch forward in a way that felt a little in-your-face? Did you remember to smile?

Repeat. Using this information, practice the negotiation again. (You may need to give this friend a really nice present.) Keep practicing until you feel comfortable and ready.

GET IN THE MOOD

Emotions that arise *during* a negotiation are not the only ones that can get you into trouble. Incidental emotions, bad feelings that carry over from one setting to another, can be just as influential. Imagine that your day begins with a fight with your seven-year-old daughter. She won't get out of bed, dawdles over breakfast, puts on and takes off four or five outfits before she's satisfied, and then can't find her homework. After an hour of wrangling, you leave the house irritated and angry. She's late for school, you're late for work, and you rush into a meeting in which you plan to negotiate with your boss for a raise. Or, road crews have begun construction on the stretch of highway you use every day to drive to work. You get stuck in an endless line of stalled traffic, arrive late, and feel flustered and self-conscious when you go in to ask for an assistant to lighten your load. Or, you own your own business and you're flying to another city to negotiate a contract for your services. Your flight is delayed, the airline loses your luggage, and because of a mix-up the hotel has released your room. Exasperated and angry, you go straight to your meeting. Situations like these can interfere with your ability to make a good impression and persuasively argue for what you want.

Research shows that carryover negative feelings—emotional hangovers—can influence how you behave during the rest of the day and make it harder to remain calm under pressure. Part of your negotiation planning should be to anticipate and avoid them if at all possible.

You may never reach a point where negotiating feels like fun to you, and it makes perfect sense if you don't. Why shouldn't you feel nervous about something that's really important to you? Most people do. You don't need to banish your emotions completely, just make sure they don't trip you up. Emotion per se is not the enemy of a successful negotiation, in any case. Positive moods and emotions—an upbeat, optimistic outlook—can help you reach better agreements.

IF YOU'RE HAPPY AND YOU KNOW IT

In one study, researchers showed participants one of two five-minute films. One film was funny and had been shown to produce happy feelings in viewers; the other was about math and had a neutral effect (it didn't change how viewers were feeling). After participants had viewed one of the two films, the researchers gave them a creativity problem called the Duncker task (named for its creator, Karl Duncker). Using a box of tacks, a match, and a candle, participants were asked to find a way to attach the candle to a wall-mounted corkboard so that it would burn without dripping wax onto the table or the floor. Each person had ten minutes to try to solve the problem. (The solution is to empty the tack box, affix it to the corkboard with the tacks, and use it as a platform for the candle.) Of the people who saw the funny film, 75 percent solved the problem. Of those who saw the neutral film, only 20 percent did. This suggests that happy feelings may stimulate creative problem solving and even productive teamwork.

Positive emotions are also contagious. If you walk into your negotiation feeling upbeat, relaxed, and confident, your mood may influence the feelings of the other negotiator, freeing both of you to look for imaginative, outside-the-box solutions. If you're part of a team working together toward a common goal, being in a good mood can increase your chances of getting to do the work that interests you most.

What Makes You Feel Most Confident and Relaxed?

With this in mind, start thinking about what makes you feel self-possessed, composed, and confident. There's no one magic bullet that works for everyone. Many people feel great after they exercise, some people find that meditation or yoga helps them feel confident, others are at their best after a long night's sleep. Hundreds of books, Web sites, and mind/body training programs recommend other techniques such as breathing exercises and self-hypnosis. Physical activities known to trigger hormones that help you feel calm include exercising, laughing, crying, and having sex. We can't tell you which one to choose, and for you, none of these may work. The key is to reflect on those times when you remember feeling most confident and sure of yourself. Then identify what was happening at the time. Here are some questions to ask yourself:

- Do you feel at your best in the morning or in the afternoon? Schedule your negotiation for the time of day when you feel most alert, calm, and focused.
- Does exercise help? (It does for most people.) Find a way to fit in an exercise session before your negotiation (take a swim before work, play tennis with a friend at lunchtime, take a midafternoon break for fifteen minutes of yoga and stretching).
- Do you feel most confident when you know you look great? Buy a new suit for the occasion, get a manicure, treat yourself to a great pair of earrings, or get your hair cut before your negotiation.

Once you've identified an activity that makes you feel composed and secure, try to use this activity to begin your negotiation feeling positive and upbeat.

Adele—PLEASURABLE DISTRACTION

Adele was a reporter for a local news station in a midsize media market. During her three years with the station she'd progressed from reporting on sewer committee meetings to covering the State House. Although she received steady praise from her boss, she hadn't received a promotion since she'd been hired and her annual raises had been pitifully small. She researched the pay rates for reporters at her level in similar markets and decided that she was due for a raise and a new title.

As she contemplated sitting down to negotiate with the station's managing editor, however, she found herself getting nervous. "I have no problem speaking to thousands of strangers on TV every night," she said. "But I felt queasy at the thought of sitting down with one man to ask for something I knew I deserved." What could she do to calm her nerves? Adele had played the piano very seriously as a child. Every night when she got home from work, usually after midnight, she put on earphones and listened to classical music for half an hour before turning in. She decided to see if this could help her. Shortly before she and her boss were scheduled to meet, she found a small conference room that wasn't being used. She turned off the lights, put up her feet, and boomed a particularly difficult piano concerto into her head for twenty minutes. "The fact that it was a difficult piece was important," she told us. "Because it required my total concentration to follow it. But it was also such a magnificent piece, and I was really moved by it. So when I went into my boss's office, I was smiling. I hadn't had time to get nervous. I was still in thrall to the music."

By finding something she could do before her negotiation that had a positive impact on her mood, Adele was able to enter her negotiation feeling optimistic and calm. She asked for more than she thought she could get, the managing editor pushed back, and after a few rounds of discussion, she got what she wanted.

Carrie—FRIENDLY ENDORPHINS

Carrie worked as an apprentice to a seasoned real estate agent. She liked her boss but after eighteen months she was itching to take on a few clients, and a few listings, of her own. Even though she'd earned her license, she dreaded bringing up the subject with her boss. He was unpredictable—extraordinarily charming when he needed to be but also prone to temperamental outbursts and dark moods. She knew he wouldn't want to lose her as an assistant, which would force him to hire and train someone new. But the office could clearly support another agent, there was plenty of business to go around, and Carrie thought she deserved the chance to move up.

At least four mornings a week, Carrie took a forty-minute run through a wildlife preserve near her house. The soothing effect of running through such beautiful surroundings combined with the mood benefits of exercise helped her start her day feeling calm and ready to go. Hoping that those feelings would help her, she made an appointment to talk to her boss first thing in the morning, right after her run.

As she feared, as soon as she broached the subject her boss started shouting at her. "I taught you everything you know!" he said. "And now you want to steal business from me? What kind of loyalty is that?"

Expecting her boss to react this way, Carrie had planned what to say and the calming effects of her run enabled her to respond without losing her composure. "I'm incredibly grateful for everything you've taught me," she said. "I hope you know that. You're the best mentor anyone in this business could have. And I love working for you. But I need to feel as though I'm moving forward professionally. Since you're that type of person too—you like to keep moving—I know you can understand. I was hoping you'd help me take this next step."

By appealing to her boss's generous side—and she knew he was fundamentally a generous man—and by presenting herself as someone like him, someone with whose ambitions he could identify, she'd won most of the battle. Presenting her case calmly and positively, even in the face of his angry outburst, won the rest. "His first instinct was to bully me," she said. "But when he saw that that wasn't going to work, he settled down and we mapped out a plan to get me started with my own clients. He even threw me several clients during the next six months when he was really busy. I helped train his new assistant, and everything worked out. Taking that run right before I talked to him was the smartest thing I did," she added. "Those endorphins pumping in my system—what an advantage!"

What Makes You Feel Powerful?

In a lab study, Linda and her colleagues asked men and women to rate on a scale of 1 to 7 how they felt about negotiating. Women reported perceiving negotiation as more scary, difficult, and even agonizing than men, who reported finding negotiation easier, less threatening, and more fun. The researchers then reran the experiment but made a subtle change. They first asked a new group of participants to recall an experience in which they'd exercised power over another person and controlled the outcome of the situation in which both were involved. Only then did the researchers ask how these participants felt about negotiation. For the men, recollecting events in which they felt powerful had no impact on their feelings about negotiation, perhaps because the experience of feeling powerful in this way is fairly ordinary for most men. But the women's negative feelings about negotiation dropped dramatically, to the same levels as those of the men. This study suggests that making yourself feel more powerful, effective, and in control beforehand, by whatever means, will send you into your negotiation feeling more confident and optimistic.

Don't feel as though you need to work yourself into an imperturbable Zen state, however. Instead, try to draw on experiences that make you feel strong and sure of yourself. Can you harness some of that positive energy to get in the mood for your negotiation? If you can, when your anxiety begins to stir, you'll be able to say, "Of course I'm anxious, but I'm also ready and I feel good."

Leila—SOCIAL SUPPORT

Leila worked in the publicity department of a major league soccer team. She'd started as an administrative assistant doing clerical work but had gradually taken on more and more responsibility. After four years in the job, she was performing the role of a public relations associate but still earning the salary of an administrative assistant.

After doing some legwork and deciding what to ask for, Leila felt ready to talk to her boss. But the prospect made her jumpy. "I was afraid I'd blow it by acting all twitchy," she said. Leila had grown up in the city where she worked, and she was still close to several friends whom she'd known since grade school. They were all big sports fans, and along with Leila's younger brother and one of her cousins they got together at a sports bar every month to watch a big game, catch up, talk, eat, and laugh. Leila always felt great after seeing her friends. "They think my job is really cool," she said, "and I tell stories about the team and my coworkers and it's like I'm Jerry Seinfeld—I'm hilarious." After a night out with these friends, she said, she'd sail into the office the next morning feeling on top of the world.

With this in mind, she asked her friends if they could meet her for lunch on the day she'd arranged to talk to her boss. Everyone loyally showed up at a pub close to the team's offices. Although she refrained from having a drink herself, by the time she left the table she was relaxed and laughing. When she sat down with her boss an hour later she was still smiling and feeling great. She laid out the data she'd collected, said how eager she was to take on more responsibility, and told him what she wanted. He agreed to change her title and increase her salary—not as much as she wanted but pretty close. "I might have done as well anyway," she told us. "I'll never know. But my friends made me feel great, and the whole thing went so smoothly. Next time I don't think it will be so hard."

GO FOR THE GOLD

One final idea for sustaining a good mood during a challenging negotiation: Promise yourself a big reward when it's over. Give yourself another reason to carry on if things get sticky. Is there something you've been wanting to do for yourself? Buy a new pair of shoes or a cocktail dress by a designer you like? Take rock-climbing lessons, get your favorite chair reupholstered, go to the Super Bowl? Splurge on a great vacation or hire someone else to do the spring cleanup in your yard? Buy yourself a new car (or a motorcycle!)? The possibilities are endless. Just be sure to choose something or a series of things that have no relation to the issues you'll be discussing in the negotiation.

Although this may sound silly, economists have repeatedly demonstrated the power of incentives to motivate behavior. Psychologists studying dieters and drug addicts have also shown that setting concrete but ambitious goals can help people stay motivated. You already have one concrete but ambitious goal—your target, what you want to get out of the negotiation. Adding a second goal—a special treat for yourself—not only gives you further reason to hang in there, it can actually provide a genuine physiological assist during the negotiation. If remembering the reward in store makes you smile, simply using the facial muscles involved in smiling has been shown to make people feel more upbeat. And that good mood may be catching.

Used all together, the tools we've recommended here have been shown to produce great results. In one revealing study, researchers taught a group of negotiators (both men and women) to set higher targets for their negotiations. They trained another group to use the following self-management techniques:

- Setting performance goals
- Anticipating obstacles and planning strategies to overcome them
- Role-playing with a partner
- Rewarding themselves for reaching their goals

The training to set higher goals improved the performance of both men and women, they found, but the gap between their performance didn't change—men still negotiated better agreements. The self-management training, however, improved the women's performance more than it improved the men's, and closed the gap between them. This study suggests that developing a comprehensive plan for your negotiation, role-playing in advance, and creating incentives for yourself can significantly increase your feelings of control during a negotiation, and increase your success too.

14

THE LIKABILITY FACTOR

ALEXANDRA WAS A design consultant for a retail chain that served consumers who were remodeling their kitchens and baths. Although she was one of the most popular designers at the store, with a constant stream of referrals, after seven years she wanted a change. Her store attracted clients with traditional tastes and she wanted a job that would allow her to be a little more creative. She applied for a job at another firm that catered to a more bohemian, artsy clientele, and after several rounds of interviews, she was offered the job. When she first applied, the position description had said the salary range was between $42,000 and $60,000. The company offered her $50,000, which was only $2,000 more than she was currently making. She thought that her credentials and experience merited a salary closer to the top of the range—$57,000 to $59,000. She also had great interpersonal skills, which made her especially adept at working with clients. Those skills had helped her to get the job offer because the people who interviewed her had liked her so much.

When Alexandra met with her future boss to discuss her salary, she decided to present her request for more money in a direct and forceful way. "I understand that the salary for the position could be as high as

$60,000," she said. "My popularity with my clients, my clearly demonstrated skills, and my years of experience qualify me to earn that top figure, $60,000. I'm sure that I'm worth it." Alexandra explained to us later that she wanted to communicate how confident she was about the value she was bringing to the firm. To her surprise, her future boss reacted badly to this change in Alexandra's manner. "He actually pushed his chair back from his desk as though he was pulling away from me," she said. "I swear I saw it flash through his eyes that maybe he'd made a mistake about me. In a very cold voice, he said, 'When we offered you this job, we thought you would fit in well with our team-oriented style. We work in a very collaborative way here.'" He refused to budge on his original offer of $50,000.

Alexandra was confused by his response. She didn't see how asking for more money meant she was not going to work collaboratively. "There's no link," she later told us. "Other designers who work there make more and they're still 'team-oriented.'"

Research about women and likability suggests that the link in her boss's mind was probably not between her ability to work collaboratively and *how much* she was paid, but between her ability to work collaboratively and *the way in which she asked* to be paid more. In presenting her request forcefully, Alexandra had stepped outside the bounds of expected behavior for women. Her boss couldn't reconcile this behavior with the impression he'd formed of her during the interview process—as a pleasant, sociable woman who could work well with anyone. Suddenly, she seemed like a different sort of person altogether.

There are a couple of important things to note about this story. First, had Alexandra's name been Alexander (if she'd been a man, that is), the story probably would have ended differently. A man would have been able to express his wish to earn more money in forceful terms without violating his new boss's expectations for male behavior. Second, it probably wouldn't have mattered if Alexandra's prospective boss had been a woman instead of a man. Both sexes penalize women when they stray beyond prescribed norms.

Like Alexandra, many people believe that to succeed in a negotiation they need to state their position clearly and confidently, affirm the quality of their work, and declare unequivocally that they deserve what they want. Unfortunately, behavior that seems too aggressive typically doesn't work for women and often backfires. This places an extra burden on women—on you—to control and monitor the impression you're making when you ask for what you want. We're not just guessing here. Multiple studies have shown that using a "softer" style can improve a woman's chances for success when she negotiates. As long as you behave in ways that don't seem too aggressive while making your request, you can still ask for what you want and hold firm against pressure to concede too much or too soon. Using a "softer" style when you negotiate, in other words, will allow you to remain tough on the issues.

RELENTLESSLY PLEASANT

What does this mean at a practical level? What exactly is a "softer" style? Should you wear an angora sweater, flutter your eyelashes, and act demure and admiring? Should you make sure every hair is in place, cross your ankles, speak in a quiet, ladylike voice, and offer to get coffee? No, no, and absolutely no. Instead, you need to behave in a way that Mary Sue Coleman, president of the University of Michigan, calls "relentlessly pleasant." This involves choosing your words carefully, using a nonthreatening tone of voice, and making sure your nonverbal behavior communicates what a nice, friendly person you are. Pleasant.

Really? We've got to be kidding, right? We didn't want to believe it either, so Linda and her colleagues decided to construct a study to see if this were really true. Using four actors, two men and two women, Linda and her colleagues created a series of videotapes. The videotapes show an employee who's just finished a management intern program being interviewed by the head of human resources for a permanent placement in one of the company's divisions. The division heads were then going to watch the videos and decide whom to hire for their sections. In some versions both parts were played by men, in others both parts were played by women, and in others they mixed it up: The division head was male and the intern was female and vice versa. In half the tapes, the freshly minted employees simply answered questions from the interviewers about their experience in the management intern program. In the other half, the actors used the same script and answered the same questions, but the intern also brought up the compensation package in a fairly aggressive way. Saying that he or she deserved to be paid at the top of the range for the position, the intern asked for a performance bonus at the end of the year that would add between 25 and 50 percent to the job's base salary. "I would certainly be more motivated if I could look forward to a performance bonus at the end of the year," the intern said.

Men who viewed the tapes, when asked how likely they were to hire the intern, said they'd be willing to hire the male candidate whether or not they saw the version in which he tried to boost his salary. Even using pretty aggressive language didn't hurt him with other men. But men reacted very differently to the female candidates: They were 50 percent more likely to hire a woman if she did *not* ask for the salary increase. In other words, the men's feelings about the woman changed as soon as she declared that she deserved to be paid more—and changed for the worse.

Like the men, women who viewed the tapes were also much more likely to hire a woman if she did not press for more money. But women's responses differed from those of men in one striking and revealing way. Women were also significantly less likely to hire the *male* candidate if he demanded a high salary. These results suggest two important differences between men and women who negotiate for themselves:

- Women risk being penalized when they negotiate aggressively, whether they're negotiating with another woman or with a man.

- Men can get away with negotiating aggressively as long as they're negotiating with another man.

This tells us that men enjoy a huge advantage in the workplace, since in this country the vast majority of supervisors, managers, and senior executives—most people's bosses—are men. Because men do not react badly to other men asking for what they want, even in pretty aggressive ways, men are freer to push hard to promote their own interests and much less likely than women to be penalized for doing so. Women, in contrast, always run the risk of being penalized when they negotiate in an aggressive way. This type of backlash can take many forms. Not only won't she get what she wants, a woman who negotiates using aggressive-seeming language may also develop a reputation for being difficult and not a team player, which could prevent her from advancing. She may find herself excluded from social and professional networks, left out of the loop when important decisions are being made, not given referrals by her colleagues, or held back in other ways.

While you may think that this response to a woman being forthright and direct sounds outdated, research has shown that it is surprisingly current—even among men and women in their late teens and early twenties. The average age of people who participated in this study was twenty-nine, which means that it's not just baby boomers who react negatively to women negotiating in an aggressive manner. Only 20 percent of the subjects were over forty.

YOU NEED TO BE LIKED

These results may make you mad (they make us mad) but that doesn't mean they're not useful. How? Linda and her colleagues asked participants in the study why they didn't want to hire the woman who negotiated. Their answer: *They didn't like her.* But it was the same woman, you may be thinking, the same woman using the same script, and what does being likable have to do with it anyway? Actually, quite a lot. Despite all the gains we've made, one double standard (at least) persists: In our society we expect women to be nice. And it's not just that we like nice women. We think women *should* be nice—warm, pleasant, friendly. When women behave in ways that we don't perceive as warm, pleasant, and friendly—when they engage in activities such as the aggressive negotiating that the actors demonstrated in the videos—we react negatively. Research shows that men can be influential and effective even if people don't like them. They can be persuasive and get what they want as long as they're perceived as competent. If they behave in aggressive ways or use aggressive language we call them no-nonsense, focused, a go-getter, ambitious (good things in a man). We use very different words to describe women who behave in similar ways, words that aren't so nice: bossy, pushy, overbearing, haughty, difficult, dragon lady, barracuda, bitch, or ice queen.

What's the solution? Make an extra effort to appear likable during your negotiation. This doesn't mean that you should change the substance of what you're asking for or soft-pedal your ambitions and goals. You can still be relentless in going after what you want. What we're talking about here is personal style. By setting the right tone for your negotiation, you can protect yourself from being turned down, even when what you're asking for is reasonable, because the other negotiator thinks you're coming on too strong. The language you use to frame your request and the tone you set for the interaction can strongly influence the ability of other negotiators to *hear* what you're actually saying.

- Start the meeting (or discussion) with phrases such as "Thanks so much for meeting with me" and "I'm glad we have a chance to talk about this." Show that you appreciate the opportunity to discuss the issues, that the issues are important to you, and that you value your relationship with the other side.

- Communicate polite concern for the other negotiator and members of the other team (but don't get coffee). Is this a good time to talk? Are they comfortable? Does everyone have what he or she needs? Does anyone need to take a break?

- Just because you're in a negotiation doesn't mean you should act formal and reserved. (Don't wear your most intimidating power suit.)

- Choose a location or setting (if you have a choice) that promotes collegiality and working together: sitting side by side, or at a round table, or in a more social setting. (Remember to take the setting into account when you're role-playing.)

- If you have a common interest outside the sphere of the negotiation, consider mentioning it. This can range from complimenting another woman on a piece of jewelry she's wearing, her bag, or the color of her living room (you have the same taste), sharing a sports enthusiasm ("How 'bout them Red Sox!"), or mentioning a family member ("I saw your son the other day and he's getting so big!"). Casual conversation like this can build a sense of alliance, but use it judiciously. Make sure it's not perceived as inappropriate.

- Avoid focusing solely on your own goals. As often as you can, reiterate what the other side will get out of the deal and how you're committed to addressing their interests.

- Actively solicit feedback as you go along. Make sure you're conducting a dialogue rather than presenting a request or demand and waiting for a decision. Use phrases such as: "I'm eager to hear your thoughts about this," and "What do you think we should do?"

- Take a problem-solving approach rather than a this-is-war approach; use persuasion rather than threats or coercion. This promotes cooperative bargaining and can prevent the other side from feeling forced into a decision. Use phrases such as "Let's work together...."; "How can we fix this?" and "Can you help me to...?"

- Frame your comments in positive rather than negative terms: "I'm ready for additional opportunities" rather than "I'm sick of doing the same old thing." Or "I've got an idea about how to improve the situation" rather than "This situation isn't working." Or "I'd feel more like equal partners if we split things more evenly" rather than "I'm doing more than my share and it's time for you to pick up some slack."

- Avoid giving ultimatums, such as "That's my best offer, take it or leave it," or "If you don't give me what I want, I'll . . ." or "If you want to get lucky tonight you'd better say yes."

- Start sentences with "I understand that you . . ."; "This can work for you because . . ."; and "My solution helps you to . . ."

- Ask questions about their concerns and interests; this communicates your willingness to look for solutions that work for both sides.

Describe what you want without acting overly aggressive, overbearing, or threatening; make it clear that you're prepared to discuss a variety of options for getting what you want. But don't go too far in the opposite direction. Being open and flexible doesn't mean conceding too readily or turning into a pushover. Avoid the vocal patterns and phraseology that make many women sound tentative and apologetic. (Ending all your sentences with an upward lilt that makes them sound more like questions than statements, for example.)

Avoid starting out with phrases like these:

- "You probably won't agree to this . . ."
- "I know this might be difficult for you to do . . ."
- "I'm not sure this is a good idea . . ."
- "This is just off the top of my head . . ."
- "I'm no expert, but . . ."

- "This may be a dumb question . . ."
- "I may be way out of line . . ."
- "Stop me if I'm wasting your time . . ."

All of these openings set up the other side to react negatively to your request. Don't dismiss your own ideas before anyone else can, and resist the impulse to tone down your approach by being self-deprecating. Don't apologize for asking for what you want.

FRAMING

Presenting your request in a positive way can make a huge difference to how the other side responds. Let's say you've received a job offer from another company for a lot more money than you're currently making. You don't want to leave your job but you can't pass up the higher salary. If your boss can't, or won't, match the other company's offer, you'll have no choice but to leave. In this situation, to give yourself the best chance of getting what you want, you should approach your boss carefully. She may already feel defensive when she discovers that you've been looking for another job. You don't want to sound as though you're presenting an ultimatum or making a threat.

Instead of saying
"If you don't match this offer I'm going to leave."

Say
"This is a great company. I think you're a great boss and I love my job. But I've received this other offer and I need to take it seriously because it's for more money."
or
"I've received another job offer—a good offer. But I love working here and I don't want to go. Before accepting, I

wanted to talk to you to see if there's some way to make it possible for me to stay."

or

"I've worked here for ten years and this place feels like home. I have a lot more I'd like to contribute. Is there any chance you could match the other offer so I can continue working here?"

or

"I can't imagine having a better boss or a better environment in which to work. I'm hoping that we might be able to find a solution that works for me and for the company so that I can stay."

This approach allows you to highlight the positive aspects of the situation (you want to stay; she's a good boss) and displays a let's-work-together attitude while still asking for what you want.

Here's another example: You're working on a team project and one of your colleagues isn't doing his share of the work.

Instead of saying

"If we're going to get this project done on schedule, I can't continue doing most of the work. You need to start pulling your own weight."

Say

"I'm worried that we're not going to meet our deadlines. Let's look at where we are and make a plan."

or

"We've accomplished a lot on this project. Let's assess what's left to do and decide who's going to do what."

or

"We're falling behind. Why don't we see if we can shift things around so that we're both working to our strengths."

Rather than criticizing his past behavior, this focuses on a productive direction for the future.

One more example: You want to ask for a promotion. You know you deserve it, but stating this outright may come off as too aggressive.

Instead of saying

> "I'm the best person for the job and I've earned it."
>
> *or*
>
> "I paid my dues and now I want to be promoted."

Say

> "I've learned so much in this job and I'd love a chance to do more. I'm ready to move to the next level."
>
> *or*
>
> "I'm sure I could contribute more if I had more responsibility. Can we talk about what's next for me? I'd like to be promoted."
>
> *or*
>
> "I'd like to show how much more I can do. I know there's a job open and I'd appreciate a chance to persuade you that I'm the right person for the job."

This approach draws attention to your joint goals (helping the company) and illustrates that you're a team player. But the underlying message is still the same: You want the promotion.

In each of these situations, you don't need to soften what you want. You just modulate the way in which you ask for it. You don't back down from your goals; you just present them in a positive, nonthreatening way.

THE SMILE GAME

Nonverbal behavior also plays a big part in how you're perceived. Consider the impact of your tone of voice, posture, facial expressions, and other body language. Make sure that they reinforce what you say rather than undercut it. The image you want to present is professional and capable but not competitive and aloof; upbeat and poised but not hyper or "wired"; warm, friendly, and cooperative but not flirtatious or a pushover. Focused but not obsessed. Calm. Here are some tips:

- Smile, make warm eye contact, use inclusive body language and hand gestures. These can include leaning toward the other person rather than away and nodding while they're speaking to show you're attentive and listening to them. Don't cross your arms (this is a defensive position). Rest your arms at your sides; if you gesture, turn your palms up.

- Avoid frowning, shaking your head, raising your eyebrows skeptically, and pointing.

- Don't lean back or sit partly turned away from the other negotiator(s).

- Adopt a pose that expresses interest and engagement but don't lean so far forward that you seem as though you're trying to impose your point of view. Don't invade the other negotiator's personal space.

- Gently mimic the other negotiator's gestures. If he nods his head, you nod too. If she brushes back her hair, brush back yours. Research shows that being mimicked increases (subconsciously) your liking of the person who's mimicking you. This is kind of weird but true. But tread carefully. If you try this, do so in a low-key, unostentatious way. You don't want the other negotiator to think you're making fun of him or her or being manipulative.

- Try not to fidget, play with your hair, fiddle with a ring or watch, bounce your leg nervously, chew your lip, or use other mannerisms that make you appear nervous.

STYLE MAKEOVER

If you think your usual office demeanor is a little cool, con-sider tweaking your personal style to convey more warmth. Ask your friends and family what your face looks like when you're deep in thought, tense, angry, frustrated, confused, or simply serious. Practice controlling your expressions to avoid giving the wrong impression (if you look severe when you're trying to make a decision, for example). Find ways to prevent negative feelings from showing on your face. If you tend to look out a window or up at the ceiling or off into space when you're processing information, try to break this habit. It can make you look as though you're not listening or don't respect the other speaker's views. Include this kind of practice in your role-playing when you prepare for your negotiation.

Alexandra—FIXING THE PROBLEM

Remember Alexandra, the kitchen and bath designer, who asked for more money in a forceful way and saw her friendly new boss turn cold and judgmental? Research shows that many women hang back from negotiating because they're worried about finding themselves in this situation. They fear that asking for anything at all will backfire. Fortunately, there's another way around this seeming dilemma.

When her first attempt to negotiate her salary met with such strong resistance, Alexandra didn't give up. She thought about the sit-uation overnight and tried again. The second time around, she pre-sented her salary proposal the way she did most other things, in her naturally friendly, easygoing way. She said to her future boss, "I'm looking forward to working with all of you—I love the company and everyone here does such great work. And I don't want to put you on the spot. But earning the higher salary would mean a lot to me so I'd appreciate your reconsidering my request. You said you can't pay me $60,000 [her initial request]. Is there anything I can do—anything the company needs—that would make it possible for you to come a little closer to $60,000? Could we meet halfway?"

The head of the design firm acted a little flustered, hemmed and hawed, and said he could probably give her $52,000.

"Wow, thanks so much," she replied. "I really appreciate your being open to this discussion. If there were any way you could pay me $56,000, I'd be thrilled. It would be such a great vote of confidence!"

The head of the firm said he wasn't sure he had that much in his budget for her position.

"Would you mind thinking about it overnight?" Alexandra said. "I don't need an answer this minute. I could start sooner if that would help."

He agreed to think about it and the next day called and said they could raise their offer to $54,000 but that was the highest they could go.

Alexandra thanked him, and decided to accept the job. Although she'd fallen short of her target, she'd persuaded him to raise his offer by $4,000. She did really like the firm, and his flexibility around the salary issue reassured her that she could work with him. She suspected (and we do too) that she might have done better if she hadn't started out by violating her future boss's expectations for how she, and every woman, should behave. He might have been more receptive to her proposal the first time around, and he might have given her more. Still, she salvaged the situation by rethinking her approach.

STYLE AND SUBSTANCE

If, like many women, you're more at ease acting friendly, engaged, and interested in the well-being of the people around you, draw on your natural warmth and personal engagement when you negotiate. Look on your personal style as an advantage rather than a weakness, and one that allows you to focus on the content of your negotiation without being perceived as a threat. If, on the other hand, you grew up wrestling with your brothers, playing competitive sports, or following the advice of a parent or mentor who told you that you need to fight for whatever you want (and this has worked pretty well so far), only you can be the judge of what works and what doesn't in your particular situation. You may be thinking, this is really going too far. Why should I have to tread so carefully around other people's sensitivities, change my personal style, and expend so much energy controlling the impression I create, especially when I'm asking for something I've worked hard for and earned? And you're right. It isn't fair that women should have to worry so much about how they ask. It's bad for women, bad for the businesses that employ them, and bad for little girls who grow up watching the women around them struggle against these outdated social constraints. Our society still needs to break down these barriers for women and we should all be striving to make that happen. But until that happens, you may find that taking a softer approach is the pragmatic choice.

CHANGE YOURSELF, CHANGE THE WORLD

Whether we realize it or not, we're all complicit in our society's requirement that women behave in likable, nonthreatening ways. To combat this problem, monitor how you yourself react to other women who behave in a direct, forthright manner and express their ambitions frankly. Have you ever criticized another woman for acting pushy or coming on too strong? Think about what she did that made you react this way. Start paying attention to how you react to men's and women's styles and notice your own negative reactions to women who act aggressively. Make an effort to be more accepting of assertive female styles and encourage others to do so as

well. Rather than roll your eyes at a woman for behaving in a
forceful way, say out loud, "That's great that she's going after
what she wants." Little by little, we *can* change the outdated
norms for how society wants women to behave.

In the meantime, using a sociable, friendly style may help you get
more of what you want and deserve. It may help you rise into senior
positions where you'll have more influence over the culture of your organization, your profession, and perhaps even the larger business
world. And then you can use your influence to make it more acceptable for women to ask for what they want in whatever way suits them.

15

THE CLOSER

On a television show called *The Closer,* the actress Kyra Sedgwick plays Deputy Chief Brenda Leigh Johnson, head of a squad of police detectives who investigate high-profile crimes in L.A. She's called the Closer because she's so talented at closing investigations—solving crimes and locking up the perpetrators. Although she's good at interpreting evidence and "reading" the details of a crime scene, her real gift is for interrogations—interviewing witnesses and persuading them to tell her what she wants to know. She asks a lot of questions, listens closely to what people say (and don't say), controls the pace of an interview by asking suspects to slow down or repeat themselves, and frequently stops an interrogation partway through and leaves the room for a while. She often expresses sympathy for a witness's point of view and motives. Throughout, she remains focused on her goal: getting the truth.

While we don't recommend some of Brenda Leigh Johnson's more extreme tactics, such as bringing in a burly associate to intimidate the other side, Brenda's strategies and her record of success can provide a useful model when you're negotiating.

FOCUS ON YOUR TARGET

The most important lesson to be learned from Deputy Chief Inspector Brenda Leigh Johnson: Always keep your eye on your target. Remember what you really want, what you've identified as your goal, and keep that idea squarely in front of you as you proceed. If you focus on the minimum you'll accept—your reservation value—rather than on your target, as soon as you're offered that minimum (or a little more), you might say yes. Research shows that this is a sure way to leave money, or more of whatever you're negotiating for, on the table. People who were instructed to focus on their targets in practice negotiations consistently negotiated better agreements than people who focused on their reservation values instead. The people who focused on their targets did two things differently. They asked for more at the outset, and they hung in there a little longer. They resisted agreeing until they received an offer that was close to their goal. In one study, participants who focused on their targets reached agreements that were 13 percent higher than those achieved by people negotiating about the same issues who focused instead on the minimum they would accept.

Here's an idea of the difference this can make in just one salary negotiation.

FOCUS ON YOUR TARGET

- Barbara and Catherine are both offered the same job for $28,000. Their research tells them that the job should pay between $28,000 and $40,000.

- Both decide that their reservation value for the job is $30,000—they won't accept it for less. Both want $35,000.

- They each ask for $38,000 and the employer counteroffers with $31,000.

- Barbara, pleased to get $1,000 more than her reservation value and $3,000 more than the bottom of the range, accepts the $31,000.

- Catherine, focused on her target of $35,000, asks for $36,000. The employer counteroffers again: "Will you take $33,000?" Catherine tries one more time: "Is there any way you can give me $36,000?" The employer goes up to $34,500. Catherine accepts.

- Focusing on her reservation value led Barbara to accept a salary that was $4,000 less than her target while Catherine persisted and negotiated a salary that was only $500 less than her target. Because she focused on her target, Catherine also started out earning $3,500 (about 11 percent) more than Barbara for doing the same job.

The bottom line is that using your research to establish a high, yet doable, target and striving for that higher amount will help you reach better agreements. If you're in a profession in which the sky's the limit—one in which, if you're good and keep progressing, there's no cap on how much you can earn—the long-term benefits can be astronomical. But even if, like most of us, you work in a field in which raises are calculated as a percentage increase over your previous salary, and there's a limit on how much you'll ever be able to earn doing what you do, you'll fare better throughout your career if you set your sights high and keep your eyes on your goal every time.

TAKE YOUR TIME

Don't let yourself be rushed. Professional negotiators know that managing the pace of a negotiation prevents confusion. It ensures that both sides get to describe all their issues and interests and have time to process the information and respond. You don't want to forget or jettison important points you want to discuss, and you want to be sure you understand the other side's point of view. A negotiation that's too rushed may prompt one or both sides to make ill-conceived concessions and can lead to an unproductive agreement.

Start by presenting your proposal or request clearly and calmly (practice this when you role-play), listen closely to the other negotiator's response, take a breath, and think carefully before you speak. Give yourself time to say exactly what you want to say. If you sense the other negotiator speeding up the pace, pressing you to make a quick decision, or rushing you simply because he or she has something else to do, slow things down. If for any reason you feel as though you're losing control of the process (or your feelings), again, slow things down. Say,

- "I could really use a bottle of water—can I get you one?"
- "I'm feeling a little rushed. I want to make a good decision here. Can we take a minute to review where we are?"
- "Let's back up. Would you clarify what you mean?"
- "I don't want to misunderstand. Would you explain that last point?"
- "We should stop and make sure we're on the same page. Would you mind recapping what we've agreed to so far?"

Or ask the other negotiator an open-ended question:

- "What are your thoughts about what I've just said?"
- "How do you see the situation?"

Remember not to ask a simple yes or no question. Ask a question that will require some thought for the other negotiator to answer. This will elicit more information and buy you some time.

TAKE A BREAK

Many women tell us that it never occurred to them that they could just say "stop" in the middle of a negotiation, that they can ask to take a break if they feel the process veering off course. But this is a perfectly appropriate thing to do, and far better than letting a negotiation become sidetracked. Use a break to collect yourself, gather more information, consult with others, and plan your response. For some of your negotiations, you'll anticipate every turn, every roadblock, and even every opening toward a new opportunity. But inevitably there will be times when you're presented with an alternative, an offer, or a refusal that you didn't expect. Saying, "Can we continue this conversation in half an hour (or tomorrow, or next week)?" is not only perfectly reasonable, it can yield enormous benefits. If the other negotiator says he's in a hurry to get this settled or she has a meeting in five minutes and will be tied up for the rest of the day, don't be deterred. Say that you want to be as flexible as possible, and offer to resume whenever he or she wants, even if it's at a time that's not especially convenient for you. Enduring a little inconvenience is not nearly as bad as feeling railroaded into making a decision you'll regret.

Here are some phrases you can use:

- "Can we talk again tomorrow when I've had some time to consider what you've said?"
- "This is obviously a bad time. Why don't we resume this discussion when things calm down?"
- "You probably need some time to think this over."
- "I'm not sure about the right course of action here. Can you give me a day or two to collect my thoughts?"
- "I see I've surprised you. Why don't we get back to this a little later?"

Asking for time to think before you make a decision is a particularly useful strategy when you're faced with "job creep"—your boss keeps dumping extra work on you. If you want to do the extra work or it's clear you have no choice, ask if you can take a day to think about what changes you'd need to make in your current responsibilities for this to be manageable.

Trina—WHEN THE NEGOTIATION TAKES AN UNEXPECTED TURN

Trina worked as a programmer for a company that designed video and computer games. After her team completed the testing phase for a new game and handed it over to manufacturing, Trina was assigned to another team that was developing a game very much like the one she'd just completed. The prospect depressed her. She'd been hoping to work on a company partnership with the local children's museum designing software to teach kids the rudiments of computer game design.

When Trina asked her boss if she could change her assignment, her boss's response surprised her. He said her skills were too valuable to waste on such a small job. If she wanted to work on the museum project she'd have to work overtime. He offered to pay her for ten extra hours a week until the museum project was completed as long as she devoted at least eight hours a day to the video game team. Trina hadn't anticipated this proposal, and she became flustered and a little angry. Why should she have to work overtime on a project the company was getting paid to do and that was bringing in good publicity to boot? She didn't need the money. Did she really want to work more than she was already working? She had to say something—either agree with her boss's proposal or offer a new one—but she was caught off guard. Just as she was about to open her mouth, her boss said, "Hey, why don't you think about it? We can talk more about it tomorrow." Trina nodded and agreed.

As Trina considered the proposal, she realized that she rarely worked an eight-hour day anyway. Like most game designers, she ate pizza at her desk several nights a week and worked most weekends.

"We have no lives," she laughed. Rather than imposing a greater time commitment on her, her boss's offer actually meant she'd be earning more money for working the same number of hours. "Taking that break was really helpful," she said. "It gave me a chance to recognize the positive aspects of his proposal."

Trina was lucky to have such a smart boss. It hadn't occurred to her that she didn't need to answer him right away. But she was a valuable employee, with a lot of experience and talent, and her boss wanted to keep her happy. He knew it wasn't in his interest for her to make a rash decision.

Angelica—WHEN YOU'VE SURPRISED THE OTHER SIDE AND DON'T WANT A REFLEXIVE NO

Angelica worked in the marketing department of a company that manufactured fine stationery products. For decades, the firm's papers had been the first choice for important society announcements: births and weddings, debutante balls, and elegant parties. But the firm's sales had declined abruptly as parties became more informal, people began printing out their own invitations on color printers, and using e-vites became popular. The company put together a task force to figure out why this was happening. Angelica was included to add a fresh perspective—she was the only person in marketing under forty.

At the first meeting, everyone agreed that they needed to shake off the company's fusty image and develop a trendier line meant for more casual communications. Angelica listened and waited, looking for the right moment. Finally, during a brief lull in the discussion, she raised her hand, and said, "We need a blog." Sensing that not everyone at the table understood, she described the nature of a blog. "It'll help us reach millions of younger customers who go to the Web to learn what's cool and what's new," she told them. She proposed writing the blog herself to give it a youthful, contemporary-sounding voice. When she stopped, "Everyone at the table had a totally blank look," she said.

"They had absolutely no idea what I was talking about and I could tell they were going to say no. It was too far out for them." Fortunately, Angelica had come prepared: She distributed printouts of half a dozen blogs started by other companies, data sheets showing the number of hits those blogs received every day, and copies of several articles from business magazines describing the success of corporate blogging. "Why don't you all think it over?" she said.

Three days later her boss told her that the task force had decided to let her write the blog on a trial basis for three months, but she had to show him everything she intended to post before she put it up on the Web. As soon as the new stationery line reached stores, Angelica began posting. "I wrote it as myself," she said. "You know—hip young marketing executive trying to shake things up at a stuck-in-the-past company. Luckily, the company hired an amazing designer and the new line was totally cool or it wouldn't have worked." The new line rapidly became a big seller, Angelica's boss gave her the go-ahead to keep writing the blog, and a year later one of the leading business magazines wrote up the company in its "innovative marketing" column.

In both of these situations, women benefited by interrupting a negotiation at a critical moment, before they said something they might have regretted or heard an answer they didn't want to hear. For some people, the thought of stretching out the negotiation process rather than getting it over as quickly as possible sounds dreadful. But in certain situations it can greatly improve your chances for success. You should never make a commitment without giving it careful thought, and your manager—or your partner, parent, coworker, neighbor, or anyone else on the other side of the table—shouldn't want you feeling bulldozed into doing something you don't want to do.

CURB YOUR ENTHUSIASM

Taking a break can be important even when you're not upset or angry. Sometimes feeling really happy can get you into trouble too. Many of us, when we receive a job offer, especially if it's a job we've been dying to get, bubble over with excitement and immediately accept. Unfortunately, once you say yes you've sacrificed most (if not all) of your power to negotiate the terms of your employment. You've signaled how badly you want the job, giving your employer little incentive to sweeten the offer. Rather than accept immediately, try to conceal your delight for a little while. Absolutely say you're excited but request an offer letter explaining all the details of the compensation package and make an appointment to discuss the offer in a day or two. If this is not realistic, ask your future employer to describe the offer in detail over the phone. Take notes, and say you'll call back in a few hours or the following day. Or, if you think it would work, ask to come in and talk about the offer face-to-face. This will give you time to plan your strategy (and calm down).

Step Away from the Fray

Sometimes what you need is not a physical break from the negotiation but a mental one. In one of the classic negotiating texts, *Getting Past No,* the author, William Ury, recommends a technique called "going to the balcony":

> Imagine you are negotiating on a stage and then imagine yourself climbing onto a balcony overlooking the stage. The "balcony" is a metaphor for a mental attitude of detachment. From the balcony

you can calmly evaluate the conflict almost as if you were a third party. You can think constructively for both sides and look for a mutually satisfactory way to resolve the problem.

Detaching yourself in this way allows you to move away from emotions that may be justified but still harmful to your interests if expressed, such as anger. It can help defuse potentially destructive emotions and give you a chance to remember some of the responses you practiced while role-playing. You can make your next move based on the realities of the situation rather than on the rush of your feelings.

"Going to the balcony" can also be effective when you're confronted by negative feelings on the other side of the table. If the other negotiator has a bad temper or rudely rejects your request, you might reflexively respond with anger, or fear. Although it sometimes feels great to yell back at someone who's abusing you, the satisfaction is short-lived and the damage can last a lot longer. If your response is to shut down completely, that's not constructive either. Better to take the high road, step back mentally, and evaluate the situation coolly before you speak. For example, say you're long overdue for a raise and you finally approach your boss about an increase. He responds with a lecture about something that is not at all pertinent. You could let yourself get defensive—and sidetracked by this unrelated issue—and you'd probably walk out of his office with no raise or a smaller one than you wanted. If instead you take a moment to step away from your anger, you might feel able to say that this other issue is extremely important and you absolutely want to discuss it as soon as possible, but at this meeting you were hoping to focus on your salary increase. If he agrees, you can make your case. If he's still too worked up about the other issue, your emotional distance will help you judge whether it would be better to reschedule the meeting after your boss calms down.

Sandy—FROM RIVAL TO MENTOR

Sandy, a hairstylist, was moving with her husband to another state and leaving the salon where she'd worked for five years. She'd been happy at her job and extremely popular among the salon's clientele—even more popular than the salon's owner, Aya, who wasn't in such high demand. To apply for jobs after she moved, Sandy needed a letter of reference from her previous employer. Since she'd brought in so much business, it never occurred to Sandy that Aya wouldn't give her a glowing recommendation. She was shocked and hurt as a result when Aya told her that she would write a letter saying that Sandy was "capable and experienced" but that this was the most she felt she could honestly say.

Aya proceeded to describe several areas in which she thought Sandy's skills were deficient. Listening, Sandy felt a surge of anger. She wanted to say that she thought Aya was jealous and petty. But instead of losing her cool, Sandy tried to look at the situation as if she were outside it. "I actually thought," she told us, "what can Sandy do to get that letter out of Aya?" If Aya was jealous, Sandy realized, then she needed to find a way to make Aya feel less threatened. With this goal in mind, she said, "I had no idea you felt that way. I'd really like your help improving my skills. Are you free later?"

Aya agreed to meet Sandy for coffee later in the afternoon, and by the time they sat down together Aya's attitude had changed. Playing the role of teacher and mentor made her feel invested in Sandy's future success. Two weeks later, Sandy left with an enthusiastic letter of reference in her hand.

WAIT, LISTEN, GO SLOW

When there is silence in the discussion, don't feel as though you need to jump in to fill it. Many people feel uncomfortable with silence and talk to break the tension, and end up saying too much or backtracking from what they want. Instead of rushing in, take advantage of moments like this to plan your next move. Don't rashly answer for the other negotiator if he's taking his time responding; give him time to reflect and wait to hear what he has to say.

It's also okay to go slowly even when it's your turn to speak. In addition to gaining time to collect your thoughts, this shows respect for the other side and signals that you're listening to them (an essential piece of cooperative bargaining).

SEAL THE DEAL

What do you do if you can't seem to get closure on your negotiation? You've discussed the issues but you haven't been able to reach an agreement or get a firm commitment? In this situation, try to figure out the underlying reasons for your impasse.

They're not getting enough of what they want. Make sure that you understand all of the other side's underlying interests, including intangibles like feeling respected and enjoying creative autonomy. Now think about what interests might not be met by your proposed solution. How could you alter your offer to meet those interests or deal with them in another way? If you think they may have interests that they haven't revealed or that you don't understand, ask them about their remaining concerns. You may learn about some hidden factor that's holding things up.

They're not sure they can justify the agreement. In what way will the agreement reflect on the other negotiator's abilities, potential, or status? Who's watching closely and likely to have an opinion, positive or negative, about the result? What will those people's reactions be? Don't forget about linkage: If you get the agreement you want, what are the implications for other people whose interests may be linked to yours? Could this cause problems? The agreement may be easier for the other negotiator to justify if you add one issue to your proposal or change a detail. Perhaps it would help to show that the agreement is consistent with company policy or doesn't impinge on the interests of third parties. Pointing to precedents or external standards might help justify or validate your proposed solution.

They're afraid of repercussions or unexpected results. Think about their worst fears associated with saying yes. How can you work to alleviate them?

They're still taking an adversarial approach. If they seem determined to "win," and won't agree to anything that doesn't involve significant concessions from you, try again to move them to a joint problem-solving mode using the cooperative bargaining techniques in Chapter 10. If this fails, think hard about (1) whether or not your BATNA is better than the deal or offer; and (2) if you're sure you want to be in a relationship, professional or personal, with someone who has such a winner-takes-all approach.

They have a strong BATNA. They know they're in a strong bargaining position because they have great alternatives to making this agreement with you. Even if it's a good agreement for them, they may want more. They want you to really make it worth their while. Ask them what else they need to accept your offer. If it seems appropriate, ask them about the other offers they're considering so you can evaluate where you stand in comparison. Then give them what you need if you can, provided that it's better than *your* BATNA.

They're stalling. Why? They need approval from "higher-ups" and are still waiting to hear? They're waiting for more information (last quarter's sales figures, news of a planned merger, a consultant's recommendations for strategy changes, a reshuffling of the executive management team, cost projections for the upcoming year, the provisions of a new shipping contract)? They like your ideas but have other options for solving the problem and can't decide? They're busy and just haven't had a chance to focus on the issue? The solutions being discussed just don't work for the other side and rather than saying no they're avoiding the issue? Regardless of the cause for delay, you need to take steps to keep the process moving forward.

If you suspect that the other side just hasn't made a decision about what you want, give them a reasonable amount of time to think about it, but don't allow them to delay indefinitely. Once a sufficient time has passed, revisit the issue. If they need approval from someone else, ask when they expect this to arrive. If you suspect they're waiting for more information, find out if this is the case and ask when they expect that information to become available. If they have other options or just haven't focused on the issue, prod them gently. Send an e-mail, mention it after a group meeting, bring it up after dinner—whatever context is appropriate for your situation.

Even if you fear that the answer will be no or there's no room for an agreement, you don't want to be left hanging indefinitely. Remind the other negotiator that you'd like some closure:

- "What are your thoughts about our conversation last week? I'd like to move the process forward."
- "I enjoyed our discussion the other day. When can we talk more about it?"
- "I'm eager to get your feedback—what's your timetable for making a decision?"

Once again, be sure to ask an open-ended question. "Have you had some time to think about what we talked about?" may elicit a simple no.

They don't fully appreciate the benefits of your proposal.
If you're convinced that the proposal on the table meets the other side's
interests but they don't seem to see it, try restating the details. Say
something like, "These are the ways in which I think the proposal
meets your interests. The benefits to you are X, Y, and Z. In my view,
the agreement would be superior to these other alternatives [name
them] in the following ways [describe them]."

There's no room for a deal. There will be cases, however, when
after a lot of reflection and analysis you can only reach one conclusion:
You're not going to agree. When this happens, rather than compromis-
ing too much and accepting an agreement that doesn't serve your interests, you may be better off going with your BATNA, and this is a
perfectly legitimate choice. Don't feel as though you've failed as a negotiator if you faithfully work through the process and find that you
can't agree. Keep your eye on your goal, but don't forget your BATNA.
Sometimes walking away truly is the best choice.

DON'T LEAVE AFTER THE FIRST ACT

Some women, as soon as they hear no, back down fast. They think,
Now I've gone too far. Or, *I don't want this to turn into a conflict.* Women
often have the same response to low counteroffers. They've asked for a
lot, the other negotiator offers much less, and they think, *Okay, that'll
be fine. I don't want to fight about it.* (Remember, not backing down is
not the same as starting a fight.) Other women decide not to negotiate
because they've received a surprisingly good offer or their confidence
wavers when they get in the room. In the middle of a negotiation, what
they planned to ask for suddenly seems ridiculous, excessive, too
much. If this happens to you, hold on tight to the information you've
collected, and don't suddenly revise your goals downward. Focus on

your target and fight the impulse to concede too quickly. After all your hard work, don't make the mistake of walking away too soon.

Kellie—MADE HERSELF A PROMISE

After a search, Kellie was offered a job she really wanted. Reading *Women Don't Ask* and attending one of Linda's workshops had convinced her to ask for more money regardless of the salary she was offered. Although the salary offer was much higher than she expected, Kellie kept her resolve and reminded herself that they wouldn't offer the most they could pay. She asked for 10 percent more. The human resources associate who made the offer told Kellie that with a 10 percent increase she'd be earning the same salary as a much more senior member of the staff. Kellie knew, however, that this staff member had reduced his project load recently and was working fewer hours, and that his salary had been reduced accordingly. She decided not to back down. She simply said, "I understand that this is a sensitive issue, and I would very much appreciate your taking some time to consider my request." Five minutes later, the HR associate called Kellie to say, "Done." Kellie wrote to tell us not only that she'd increased her base salary but that she was enjoying "the simple satisfaction of having asserted myself when otherwise I wouldn't have."

Latanya—SMILED AND KEPT GOING

Latanya earned her associate degree in criminal psychology right after high school and then worked for ten years as a police officer in San Diego. She left the police department to complete her bachelor's degree (in business) and six months later she was hired by a small private security company in Los Angeles. The company grew quickly and within five years Latanya had moved up from being a case manager to taking charge of the company's San Francisco office. The firm was still expanding, and a year later the partners asked Latanya to relocate to the East Coast and open an office in New York.

The New York office was a success from the start and at the end of her first year the partners made Latanya a managing director of the firm and gave her a 30 percent raise. As her second year in New York neared its end, she began to prepare for her annual review. She knew that her counterpart in the firm's Washington, D.C., office was being paid $60,000 more than she was earning. The New York office was more profitable than the D.C. office, and she knew that she'd been instrumental in that success. She decided that she wanted a 40 percent increase, which would bring her salary in line with that of the managing director in D.C. She planned to ask for a 45 percent increase so that she'd have room to back down to her real target during the negotiation.

As soon as her review began, Latanya's boss, who'd flown in from Los Angeles, told Latanya what good work she'd been doing and said he was going to give her a 20 percent raise. He explained why he thought 20 percent was appropriate, and Latanya almost forgot about all the research she'd done. She started thinking, *Wow, twenty percent is a lot. I got a huge raise last year. I should just be pleased that my work is appreciated and take it.* As her turn to speak approached, self-doubt intervened and threatened to override all her careful preparation. Happily, Latanya didn't heed the voice in her head. Instead she smiled and decided to ignore it. She trusted the objective evidence she'd compiled, asked for 45 percent more, explained why she thought she deserved that much, and got the 40 percent she wanted.

CONCLUSION:

IF YOU NEVER HEAR NO, YOU'RE NOT ASKING ENOUGH

HANNAH, A VIOLINIST, was offered a teaching job at a conservatory for $40,000 a year. Hannah asked for $42,000 and got it, making her wonder if she could have gotten more if she'd asked. The answer is, probably. Because she didn't aim high, and didn't risk having her first request turned down, she'll never know what her boss was really willing to pay her and how much she left on the table.

We've heard dozens of stories like this from women we've met:

"I finally asked for a raise and my boss said okay right away. Now I feel stupid for not asking for more."

"I thought I was aiming really high and I never thought he'd give me what I asked for. When he said yes immediately, I realized I'd aimed too low *again*."

"I'd never gotten a bonus before but I'd put in a killer year—my sales figures were monstrous—so I marched in and asked for one. I thought I was being pretty nervy. But my boss didn't even look up from his desk. 'Okay,' he said. I should have asked for twice as much."

Researchers call this phenomenon the winner's curse. We call it the downside of yes. If the other side can easily give you what you want, in most cases they could have given you more. Always getting what you ask for in a negotiation—always hearing yes and never risking no—means that you *never ask for enough*. Excessive caution, rather than protecting you from rejection or losing face, can actually prevent you from getting all that you're worth, all you deserve, and all that's available.

Pushing the boundaries pays off in other ways, as well. When you aim high in a negotiation, you adjust other people's perceptions of you. (Remember, most people assume that more expensive things are superior to less expensive things.) You communicate that you expect to be treated fairly and that you're willing to stand up for yourself (in a friendly and likable way, of course).

Now and then one of your requests may elicit a no that stings. But you may discover that this too is not necessarily so bad. Sometimes a no means a relationship won't survive, not because the other party is offended but because you discover that you no longer want to continue under the status quo. Achieving this kind of clarity can be painful but worth it. Elizabeth spent ten years in a relationship with a man whom she eventually hoped to marry. She'd already been divorced once, she was in her forties, and she wanted to have a child, but when she pressed him he said he didn't want to marry her. Elizabeth could have stayed with him and given up her chance to be a mother but his refusal to marry her made her decision easy. She left him and immediately began the application process for an overseas adoption. A week before she left for Russia to pick up her daughter, she met the man who would later become her husband and the father of her adopted child. Her previous boyfriend's rejection, ironically, saved her years of heartache.

Boys learn in Little League (and now more and more girls are learning this too) that if they never get tagged out stealing a base, they're not trying to steal enough bases. In other words, they'll gain more ground, score more runs, and win more games if they take chances, if they try to steal bases even when they're not sure they can make it. They also refine their ability to gauge when to take those risks—they get better at stealing bases. They improve their skills and get used to failing sometimes, and they learn to celebrate those failures as risks well taken.

The same lesson can be applied to negotiating. By asking a lot and setting high targets, you'll gain more than if you hold back out of fear that you might be turned down. Yes, you'll get thrown out at second base sometimes. But you'll still do better than if you never ask or you always ask for less. You'll also learn what can and can't be negotiated. Taking greater risks helps you map out what is possible, negotiable, and flexible, and what is not. Like the Little Leaguer, you'll learn what works and what doesn't, when to run and when to hold. You'll gain valuable experience and get better at negotiating.

You'll also form new habits and new ways of thinking, and soon negotiating will become a reflex rather than an effort. The day-to-day negotiations—for a table by the window instead of one by the kitchen door, for a better cut of meat than the first one the butcher grabs, for half an hour to run an errand in the middle of the workday, for your partner to take the kids to an amusement park on a summer weekend when you need a break—will become second nature. You'll know you can ask for both the big and the little changes, and you'll feel calm, confident, and comfortable in your skin while doing so. Life will open its doors a little more easily to you, and it's worth hearing no now and then for that, isn't it?

APPENDIX A

Negotiation Prep Worksheet

(Downloadable and PDF versions of this worksheet can be found at www.askforit.org.)

DECIDE WHAT YOU WANT

What is your ideal job?
When were you happiest in your work or at home? Why? How are things different now?
Is there something that you love but have stopped doing?
Whom do you admire or envy? Why?
Are you good at something that you never get to do?
What drives you crazy or could be better?

What will you regret if you never do?

What do you need to feel happy? Are any of these missing from your life?

Stimulating, challenging work

Likable colleagues

Feeling that you're part of a team—not isolated

Power and responsibility

Autonomy

Flexibility

Clear evidence that your work is respected

Freedom to be creative

Feeling that you're making a contribution/doing something worthwhile

Potential for widespread recognition—in your field or among the public at large

Opportunities to learn new things

Rewarding friendships

A stable, happy private life

Who are your role models?

What would you want if you were certain you could get it?

SHORT TERM GOALS

Personal

Financial

Athletic

Hobbies and free time
Self-improvement
Material
Philanthropic
Political
Just fun
LONG TERM GOALS
Personal
Financial
Athletic
Hobbies and free time
Self-improvement
Material
Philanthropic

Political
Just fun

FACTOR IN FAIRNESS

Are you being paid what you're worth?	Are you being given assignments that use all your talents?
Have you been promoted to the level you deserve?	Are you doing work commensurate with your abilities?
Does your title describe your level of responsibility and authority?	Do you feel recognized for the full scope of your contribution?
Are you progressing in your career at a brisk pace?	Are you doing more than your share of the household chores?

DO YOUR HOMEWORK

SIZE UP THE SITUATION
Number of issues
Number of parties
Nature of your relationship
Will the contract be binding?
Costs and benefits of delay

Is there linkage (will outcome affect negotiations with others)? If so, who will be affected and how?
Will the process and/or outcome be public or private?
Behavioral norms for negotiation in this situation
Are there precedents for what you're asking?

IDENTIFY SOURCES OF THE INFORMATION YOU NEED

Web sites
Trade publications
Business press (local and national)
Professional associations
Mentors
Supervisor or manager
Networks
Colleagues
Friends

FIND OUT WHAT YOU CAN ABOUT THE OTHER SIDE
How well is the organization doing?
What are the organization's short- and long-term plans?

What are the other side's:
 	
    Interests
 	
    Concerns
 	
    Priorities over the issues
 	
    Likely target(s)
 	
    Likely BATNA

How do decisions get made?
 	
    Who has influence over the decision-making process?
 	
    Relevant policies, procedures, precedents
 	
    Internal political issues that may influence outcome

What common goals do you share with the other side?
Where do your interests conflict with those of the other side?
What problems might prevent them from giving you what you want?

ASSESS YOUR BARGAINING POWER
Education
Training
Special skills, unique strengths
Work history
Depth of knowledge or expertise
Years of experience
Demonstrated performance excellence
Reputation in your field
Awards won
Important outside contacts
Support of a powerful mentor
Social or interpersonal skills
Leadership or team-building abilities
Internal alliances (if you're employed)
Knowledge of the organization's culture, processes, history
Flexibility (re: timing, scheduling, etc.)
Alternatives (another offer?)
Strong BATNA
Weak BATNA on other side of table
Preparation
What sets you apart from your peers?
Why does the other side need you?

BOOST YOUR BARGAINING POWER
Improve your credentials
Improve your BATNA (get another offer?)
Make yourself indispensable
Think creatively about ways to help your organization
Can you give something up?   *Can you do something extra?*

ESTABLISH YOUR NEGOTIATION PARAMETERS
Rank your goals in order of their priority—most important to least important
List your underlying interests
What else would you like (not vital but desirable)?
BATNA—your best alternative or fall-back position if you fail to reach an agreement
Reservation value (RV), your bottom line, the minimum you'll accept or the most you'll concede (or pay)
Target or aspiration value (TV or AV). What would you love to get? Remember to aim high.

MAKE STRATEGIC DECISIONS

APPROACH
Competitive (single-issue negotiation, relationship will not continue)
Cooperative (multi-issue negotiation or one that involves a long-term relationship)
What information will you reveal (and in what order) and what will you conceal?

MODE OF COMMUNICATION (PROS AND CONS)
Face-to-face
Telephone
E-mail
Letter

TIMING
How much time do you need to prepare?
When will your bargaining power be highest?
When is the best time for the other side?

LOCATION
Find a location that will be free of distractions.
Choose a room setup that promotes cooperative discussion.

Decide whether aids such as a whiteboard, flip-chart, blackboard, or projector would be useful.

OPENING

Should you make the first offer?

How much information do you have about the other side's reservation value?

Can you anchor the negotiation and influence the other side's estimates of your reservation value if you go first?

How can you "punt" if the other side wants you to go first and you don't want to?

How will you put the negotiation on hold if you realize you've asked at the wrong time?

Estimate the number of rounds the negotiation is likely to go.

CHOOSE YOUR TACTICS

OFFERS AND CONCESSIONS

Decide on a first offer that anchors the negotiation above your target.

Choose counteroffers that will position your target halfway between each of their offers and yours.

Plan to concede less in each round, and to use the amount you concede on each round to influence their perception of your reservation value.

—

—

—

—

Develop phrases to put the ball back in the other court.

Identify a proposal from the other side that's close enough to your target for you to offer to split the difference.

WIN/WIN

Ways to initiate the negotiation that convey a cooperative approach

Descriptions of your interests (not positions)

Questions that will allow you to identify their basic interests

Information to share that will illustrate your interests and perspective

Identify pairs of issues that you think you can logroll—lower priority items you'd be willing to trade in return for things you want more.

Techniques and phrases that you can use to deescalate conflict

Methods for generating creative solutions that address both sides' interests

Ways to move the other side away from defending his or her position and over to problem-solving
Comments, actions, or gestures that will build trust and promote the alliance
STYLE
Mannerisms that will help you present yourself as "relentlessly pleasant"
Nonverbal behavior that will reinforce your cooperative approach
Phrases that suggest a "let's work together" attitude
Positive ways to frame your argument

GET READY

Role-play *Choose a partner* *Schedule a time* *Find a room* *Rehearse and repeat*
Figure out what will put you in an upbeat, positive mood beforehand.
Choose incentives to reward yourself with after it's over.

STAY CALM AND CLOSE THE DEAL

Compose constructive responses to roadblocks.
Plan strategies to delay or take a break if necessary.
Consider ways to get the negotiation back on track if it loses focus or veers toward impasse.
Imagine ways to prevent yourself from compromising in the heat of the moment.
Design open-ended questions to slow things down and get the other side to clarify its point of view.
Develop questions to ask if you don't understand why they're resisting giving you what you want: *Are they worried about how they will justify the agreement to others?*_____ *Is there not enough in it for them?*_____ *Are they afraid to set a new precedent that will influence future negotiations with others?*_____ *Is your negotiation a low priority for them?*_____ *Are they waiting for more information or to see how other issues resolve themselves?*_____
Keep your BATNA in mind. Know when to walk away.

APPENDIX B

PROGRESS: Teaching Girls to Negotiate

In 2006, Linda Babcock founded a research center at Carnegie Mellon called PROGRESS (Program for Research and Outreach on Gender Equity and Society; www.heinz.cmu.edu/progress), whose mission it is to teach women and girls to negotiate. PROGRESS's first project, with the Girl Scouts Trillium Council (serving 22,000 Girl Scouts in western Pennsylvania and parts of Ohio, West Virginia, and Maryland), created a badge for negotiation. To earn the badge, called "Win/Win: How to Get What You Want," junior Scouts (ages 8–12) must read a story designed as a primer on negotiations and then complete ten activities, including practice negotiations with other troop members and negotiations at home. In response to enthusiastic feedback from girls, troop leaders, and parents, Girl Scout troops from all over the country have begun to incorporate the Win/Win badge into their programs.

Partnering with the Entertainment Technology Center at Carnegie Mellon, Linda and her PROGRESS colleagues have also developed "The Reign of Aquaria," a computer game that teaches girls to negotiate (www.heinz.cmu.edu/progress/reignofaquaria). In the game, the player wakes up in a foreign land and must learn to negotiate in order to find her way home. The game teaches girls how to recognize opportunities to negotiate, how to use cooperative bargaining strategies, how to make good decisions about what to offer, and how to communicate effectively what they want. As a girl becomes more skillful at negotiating, she advances to the next stage of the game. When she reaches the highest level of play she must negotiate with Queen Aquaria for her freedom.

PROGRESS is currently developing a portfolio of materials to be used by after-school programs and other educational and social organizations that serve girls. These include role-playing scripts, a film, and interactive games that make learning to negotiate fun. PROGRESS staff members also train teachers and other leaders of girls' programs how to teach negotiation skills to young girls.

For more information, please go to www.heinz.cmu.edu/progress.

NOTES

Chapter 1

Page 4: *Linda and several colleagues launched a research program to explore these questions:* The research team consisted of Michele Gelfand, Deborah Small, Hillary Gettman, and Heidi Stayn. For publications see: Babcock, L., M. Gelfand, D. Small, and H. Stayn. 2006. "Propensity to initiate negotiations: A new look at gender variation in negotiation behavior." In D. De Cremer, M. Zeelenberg, and J.K. Murnighan (Eds.). *Social Psychology and Economics* (pp. 239–262). Mahwah, New Jersey: Lawrence Erlbaum Associates; Small, D., M. Gelfand, L. Babcock, and H. Gettman. 2007. "Who goes to the bargaining table? The influence of gender and framing on the initiation of negotiation." *Journal of Personality and Social Psychology* 93(4), 600–613.

Page 8: *the gap in the frequency with which younger men and women negotiate is about the same as the gap between older men and women:* Babcock's calculation based on data reported in Babcock, L., M. Gelfand, D. Small, and H. Stayn. 2006. "Propensity to initiate negotiations: A new look at gender variation in negotiation behavior." In D. De Cremer, M. Zeelenberg, and J.K. Murnighan (Eds.). *Social Psychology and Economics* (pp. 239–262). Mahway, New Jersey: Lawrence Erlbaum Associates.

Page 8: *Married women who work full-time still perform two-thirds of the housework and childcare:* Lennon, M.C., and S. Rosenfield. 1994. "Relative fairness and the division of household work: The importance of options." *American Journal of Sociology* 100:506–531; Blair, S.L., and D.T. Lichter. 1991. "Measuring the division of household labor: Gender segregation of housework among American couples." *Journal of Family Issues* 12:91–113.

Page 8: *experience a dramatic upward spike in their stress levels at the end of the workday:*
Frankenhaeuser, M., U. Lundberg, M. Frederickson, B. Melin, M. Tuomisto, A.L.
Myrsten, M. Hedman, B. Bergman-Losman, and L. Wallin. 1989. "Stress on and off
the job as related to sex and occupational status in white-collar workers." *Journal of
Organizational Behavior* 10(4):321–346.

Page 14: *In 2002, only 12.5 of the women had negotiated their offers while four times as
many men, 51.5 percent, negotiated theirs:* Data collected from Heinz School career services by Linda Babcock. Statistical analyses available upon request from Linda.

Chapter 2

Page 32: *This is true when it comes to physical risks:* Rowland, G.L., R.E. Franken, and
K. Harrison. 1986. "Sensation-seeking and participating in sporting activities." *Journal
of Sport Psychology* 8:212–220; Svebak, S., and J.H. Kerr. 1989. "The role of impulsiv-
ity in preference for sports." *Personality and Individual Differences* 10(1):51–58;
Jelalian, E., A. Spirito, D. Raile, L. Vinnick, C. Rohrbeck, and M. Aarrigan. 1997.
"Risk-taking, reported injury, and perception of future injury among adolescents."
Journal of Pediatric Psychology 22:512–531.

Page 32: *and just as true when it comes to economic risks:* Croson, R., and U. Gneezy.
2004. "Gender differences in preferences," unpublished manuscript; Eckel, C.
"Experiments on gender differences." Forthcoming in *The New Palgrave Dictionary of
Economics,* 2nd edition (S.N. Durlauf and L.E. Blume, Eds.). New York: Palgrave
Macmillan; Jianakoplos, N.A., and A. Bernasek. 1998. "Are women more risk averse?"
Economic Inquiry 36:620–630; Sunden, A.E., and B.J. Surette. 1998. "Gender differ-
ences in the allocation of assets in retirement savings plans." *American Economic
Review, Paper and Proceedings* 88:207–211.

Page 32: *Men also tend to view most situations as inherently less risky than women do:*
Lerner, J., R. Gonzalez, D. Small, and B. Fischhoff. 2003. "Effects of fear and anger on
perceived risks of terrorism: A national field experiment." *Psychological Science*
14:144–150; Slovic, P. 2000. *The perception of risk.* London: Earthscan Publications.

Page 32: *because men take too many risks and trade too much:* Barber, B., and T. Odean.
2000. "Boys will be boys: Gender, overconfidence, and common stock investment."
Quarterly Journal of Economics 116(1):261–292.

Page 32: *Women also tend to refrain from actions that put their relationships at risk:*
Arch, E. 1993. "Risk-taking: A motivational basis for sex differences," *Psychological
Reports* 73(3):6–11.

Page 34: *two to three times more likely to describe something they didn't do instead of something they did:* Gilovich, T., and V.H. Medvec. 1994. "The temporal pattern to the experience of regret." *Journal of Personality and Social Psychology* 67(3):357–365;
Gilovich, T., and V.H. Medvec. 1995. "The experience of regret: What, when, and
why." *Psychological Review* 102(2):379–395.

Chapter 3

Page 40: *Men . . . believe that the locus of control in their lives is internal. . . . Women are far more likely to believe that "life happens to them":* Kunhikrishna, K., and K. Manikandan. 1995. "Sex difference in locus of control: An analysis based on Calicut L.O.C. Scale." *Psychological Studies* 37:121–125; Parkes, K.R. 1985. "Dimensionality of Rotter's Locus of Control Scale: An application of the 'Very Simple Structure' techniques." *Personality and Individual Differences* 6:115–119; Strickland, B.R., and W.E. Haley. 1980. "Sex differences on the Rotter I-E Scale." *Journal of Personality and Social Psychology* 39(5):930–939; Wade, T.J. 1996. "An examination of locus of control/fatalism for blacks, whites, boys, and girls over a two-year period of adolescence." *Social Behavior and Personality* 24:239–248.

Page 40: *and not just in the United States . . . :* Smith, P.B., S. Dugan, and F. Trompennaars. 1997. "Locus of control and affectivity by gender and occupational status: A 14-nation study." *Sex Roles* 36:51–57.

Page 41 box: *Women were 45 percent more likely than men to score low on this scale:* Babcock, L., M. Gelfand, D. Small, and H. Stayn. 2006. "Propensity to initiate negotiations: A new look at gender variation in negotiation behavior." In D. De Cremer, M. Zeelenberg, and J.K. Murnighan (Eds.). *Social Psychology and Economics* (pp. 239–262). Mahwah, New Jersey: Lawrence Erlbaum Associates.

Page 41: *Organizational psychologist Lisa Barron . . . :* Barron, L.A. 2003. "Ask and you shall receive: Gender differences in negotiators' beliefs about requests for a higher salary." *Human Relations* 56(6):635–662.

Page 46: *He asked a class of adults working toward their MBAs at night to "go negotiate something in the real world":* Malhotra, D. 2002. "Let's take this outside: Some striking results of students negotiating in the real world." Paper presentation at the International Association for Conflict Management annual meeting, June.

Chapter 4

Page 57: *a phenomenon that the social psychologist Faye Crosby calls "the denial of personal disadvantage":* Crosby, F. 1984. "The denial of personal discrimination." *American Behavioral Scientist* 27:371–386.

Pages 58–59: *cause well-intentioned people to devalue the work of women simply because they're women:* For a good review of this literature, see: Heilman, M. 1995. "Sex stereotypes and their effects in the workplace: What we know and what we don't know." *Journal of Social Behavior and Personality* 10(6):3–26.

Page 59: *A group of prominent psychologists, Mahzarin Banaji, Anthony Greenwald, and Brian Nosek . . . :* For a list of their publications, see www.projectimplicit.net/articles.php.

Page 59: *When we last looked, over 83,000 people had taken this particular test with similar results:* We took the gender/work-family test in October 2006.

Page 60: *psychologists believe that these subconscious biases influence our behavior in ways we don't realize . . . :* For a review see: Poehlman, T.A., E.L. Uhlmann, A.G. Greenwald, and M.R. Banaji. "Understanding and using the implicit association test: III. Meta-analysis of predictive validity," available at www.projectimplicit.net/articles.php.

Page 60 box: *Two economists found that the use of a screen to hide the identity . . . :* Goldin, C., and C. Rouse. 2000. "Orchestrating impartiality: The impact of 'blind' auditions on female musicians." *American Economic Review* 90(4):715–742.

Page 61: *Schein assembled ninety-two words and phrases commonly used to describe people's characteristics:* Schein, V.E. 1973. "The relationship between sex role stereotypes and requisite management characteristics." *Journal of Applied Psychology* 57:95–100; Schein, V.E. 1975. "Relationships between sex role stereotypes and requisite management characteristics among female managers." *Journal of Applied Psychology* 60:340–344. For more recent research on the Schein Descriptive Index, see: Deal, J.J., and M.A. Stevenson. 1998. "Perceptions of female and male managers in the 1990s: *Plus ça change . . .*" *Sex Roles* 38:287–300; Schein, V.E., and R. Mueller. 1992. "Sex-role stereotyping and requisite management characteristics: A cross-cultural look." *Journal of Organizational Behavior* 13:439–447; Schein, V.E., R. Mueller, T. Lituchy, and J. Liu. 1996. "Think manager—think male: A global phenomenon?" *Journal of Organizational Behavior* 17:33–41.

Page 61 box: *To study whether people respond differently to men and women who exhibit "leadership behavior":* Butler, D., and F.L. Geis. 1990. "Nonverbal affect responses to male and female leadership: Implications for leadership evaluation." *Journal of Personality and Social Psychology* 58:48–59.

Page 62: *the women typically receive the least credit for the team's success:* Heilman, M.E., and M.C Haynes. 2005. "No credit where credit is due: Attributional rationalization of women's successes in male-female teams." *Journal of Applied Psychology* 90(5): 905–916.

Page 62: *Evaluations of a woman's work may also be skewed if she's working in an area in which there are very few other women:* Heilman, M.E. 1980. "The impact of situational factors on personnel decisions concerning women: Varying the sex composition of the applicant pool." *Organizational Behavior and Human Performance* 26:286–295.

Page 67: *They're typically excluded from men's social and professional networks:* Mehra, A., M. Kilduff, and D.J. Bass. 1998. "At the margins: A distinctiveness approach to the social identity and social networks of underrepresented groups." *Academy of Management Journal* 41(4):441–452.

Page 71: *This is increasingly true with the rise of "I-deals":* Rousseau, D. 2005. *I-Deals: Idiosyncratic Deals Workers Bargain for Themselves.* Armonk, NY: M.E. Sharpe.

Page 71: *contract provision required by Jennifer Lopez..."* Rousseau, D. 2005. *I-Deals: Idiosyncratic Deals Workers Bargain for Themselves.* Armonk, NY: M.E. Sharpe.

Chapter 5

Page 77: *experts call this assessing the negotiation environment:* We are indebted to Howard Raiffa's wonderful book, *The Art and Science of Negotiation* (Belknap Press, reprint edition, 2005), for outlining some of the features of the negotiation environment that we describe here.

Page 83: *BATNA:* This term was originally coined by Roger Fisher and William Ury in their book *Getting to Yes: Negotiating Agreement Without Giving In.* New York: Houghton Mifflin, 1981.

Chapter 6

Page 90: *With two colleagues, Linda analyzed the starting salaries...:* Bowles, H.R., L. Babcock, and K.L. McGinn. 2005. "Constraints and triggers: Situational mechanics of gender in negotiation." *Journal of Personality and Social Psychology* 89(6):951–965.

Pages 90–91 box: *Researchers asked people to review college application folders and predict the success of incoming college freshmen:* Major, B., D.B. McFarlin, and D. Gagnon. 1984. "Overworked and underpaid: On the nature of gender differences in personal entitlement." *Journal of Personality and Social Psychology* 47(6):1399–1412.

Chapter 7

Page 103: *a short video made by the Visual Cognition Lab at the University of Illinois:* For information about the lab, visit http://viscog.beckman.uiuc.edu/djs_lab/index.html.

Chapter 8

Page 127: *Ninety-five percent of my assets drive out the front gate every evening:* Quotation from interview on *60 Minutes,* available at: www.cbsnews.com/stories/2003/04/18/60minutes/main550102.shtml.

Page 127 box: *The U.S. Bureau of Labor Statistics reports that 23.1 percent of the 134 million nonfarm workers in the United States... voluntarily quit each year:* Data available at http://www.bls.gov/opub/ted/2006/mar/wk2/art03.htm.

Page 127 box: *The Hay Group estimates that a quit costs a company between 50 percent and 150 percent of a worker's annual salary:* "The retention dilemma: Why productive workers leave—seven suggestions for keeping them." HayGroup Working Paper, available at www.haygroup.com/downloads/ww/Retention_Dilemma.pdf.

Page 127 box: *The U.S. Bureau of Labor Statistics reports that in 2006, median annual earnings were approximately $35,000:* http://data.bls.gov/PDQ/servlet/SurveyOutput Servlet.

Page 127: *reduced annual turnover at SAS to just 3 percent, saving his company between $60 and $80 million a year:* www.cbsnews.com/stories/2003/04/18/60minutes/main 550102.shtml.

Page 128 box: *annual attrition costs for a midsize company:* Example from: "The retention dilemma: Why productive workers leave—seven suggestions for keeping them." HayGroup Working Paper, available at www.haygroup.com/downloads/ww/Retention _Dilemma.pdf.

Page 130: *Business leaders have begun to realize that they need to make special efforts to retain female employees, many of whom leave organizations before reaching the upper ranks:* Hewlett, S.A., and Buck Luce, C. in: "Off-roads and on-ramps: Keeping talented women on the road to success." In *Harvard Business Review Ideas with Impact Series: On Women in Business.* Cambridge, MA: Harvard Business School Press, 2005, pp. 1–27.

Page 130: *In the article "Winning the Talent War for Women":* McCracken, D.M. 2005. "Winning the talent war for women: Sometimes it takes a revolution." In *Harvard Business Review Ideas with Impact Series: On Women in Business.* Cambridge, MA: Harvard Business School Press, pp. 51–67.

Page 130: *Women currently represent 57 percent of entering college freshman (and men only 43 percent):* Report from the American Council on Education (July 11, 2006), available at: http://www.acenet.edu/AM/Template.cfm?Section=HENA&TEMPLATE=/CM/ ContentDisplay.cfm&CONTENTID=17251.

Page 130: *In "Off-Ramps and On-Ramps: Keeping Talented Women on the Road to Success," Sylvia Ann Hewlett and Carolyn Buck Luce report that:* In *Harvard Business Review Ideas with Impact Series: On Women in Business.* Cambridge, MA: Harvard Business School Press, 2005, pp. 1–27.

Page 130: *Felice N. Schwartz, author of "Women as a Business Imperative," explains that:* In *Harvard Business Review Ideas with Impact Series: On Women in Business.* Cambridge, MA: Harvard Business School Press, 2005, pp. 159–184.

Pages 130–31: *J. Michael Cook, the CEO of Deloitte Consulting who created the firm's famous Women's Initiative, wrote:* McCracken, D.M. 2005. "Winning the talent war for women: Sometimes it takes a revolution." In *Harvard Business Review Ideas with Impact Series: On Women in Business,* Cambridge, MA: Harvard Business School Press, pp. 51–67.

Page 131: *Studies have shown that women's leadership style, often called "transformational leadership":* Eagly, A.H., M.C. Johannesen-Schmidt, and M. van Engen. 2003.

"Transformational, transactional, and laissez-faire leadership styles: A meta-analysis comparing men and women." *Psychological Bulletin* 129:569–591.

Page 131: *Other research suggests that achieving greater gender diversity in the upper echelons of an organization may increase productivity and profitability:* "The Bottom Line: Connecting Corporate Performance and Gender Diversity," Catalyst research report, 2004.

Page 131: *As Schwartz writes in "Women as a Business Imperative":* In *Harvard Business Review Ideas with Impact Series: On Women in Business.* Cambridge, MA: Harvard Business School Press, 2005, pp. 159–184.

Page 131: *Schwartz concludes, "A company's reputation for good human values is as valuable an asset as capital equipment":* In *Harvard Business Review Ideas with Impact Series: On Women in Business.* Cambridge, MA: Harvard Business School Press, 2005, pp. 159–184.

Page 142: *Eugene Carr, the founder and president of Patron Technologies, an e-mail marketing service for arts organizations, says that:* personal interview with Sara Laschever.

Chapter 9

Page 146: *Research has consistently shown that there's a direct correlation between your target—what you aim for in a negotiation—and what you get:* White, S.B., and M.A. Neale. 1994. "The role of negotiator aspirations and settlement expectancies in bargaining outcomes." *Organizational Behavior and Human Decision Processes* 57:303–317; Blount, S., M.C. Thomas-Hunt, and M.A. Neale. 1996. "The price is right–or is it? A reference point model of two-party price negotiations." *Organizational Behavior and Human Decision Processes* 68:1–12; Stevens, C.K, A.G. Bavetta, and M.E. Gist. 1993. "Gender differences in the acquisition of salary negotiation skills: The role of goals, self-efficacy, and perceived control." *Journal of Applied Psychology* 78(5):723–735.

Page 149: *In study after study, researchers have found that women have a low sense of what psychologists call "personal entitlement":* Callahan-Levy, C.M., and L.A. Messe. 1979. "Sex differences in the allocation of pay." *Journal of Personality and Social Psychology* 37(3):433–446; Jost, J. 1997. "An experimental replication of the depressed-entitlement effect among women." *Psychology of Women Quarterly* 21:387–393; Major, B, D.B. McFarlin, and D. Gagnon. 1984. "Overworked and underpaid: On the nature of gender differences in personal entitlement." *Journal of Personality and Social Psychology* 47(6):1399–1412.

Page 149: *One study asked undergraduate business students applying for similar jobs to predict two things:* Major, B., and E. Konar. 1984. "An investigation of sex differences in pay expectations and their possible causes." *Academy of Management Journal* 27:777–792.

Page 149: *In another study, researchers compared women's and men's estimates of what would be fair pay for a variety of jobs:* Jackson, L.A., P.D. Gardner, and L.A. Sullivan.

1992. "Explaining gender differences in self-pay expectations: Social comparison standards and perceptions of fair pay." *Journal of Applied Psychology* 77(5):651–663.

Page 149: *A 2007 study published by CNN/*Money *asked thousands of MBA students about their expected future earnings:* CNN/*Money* study results available at: http://money.cnn.com/magazines/fortune/mba100/2007/pay/index.html

Page 150: *Similar studies have been conducted with schoolchildren:* Callahan-Levy, C.M., and L.A. Messe. 1979. "Sex differences in the allocation of pay." *Journal of Personality and Social Psychology* 37(3):433–446

Page 153 box: *Researchers asked participants to negotiate in pairs over the price of a single item:* Bowles, H.R., L. Babcock, and K.L. McGinn. 2005. "Constraints and triggers: Situational mechanics of gender in negotiation." *Journal of Personality and Social Psychology* 89(6):951–965.

Page 155 box: *In one research study, students were asked to write a series of opinions about campus-related issues:* Callahan-Levy, C.M., and L.A. Messe. 1979. "Sex differences in the allocation of pay." *Journal of Personality and Social Psychology* 37(3):433–446.

Page 156: *One of Linda's studies looked specifically at senior executives:* Bowles, H.R., L. Babcock, and K.L. McGinn. 2005. "Constraints and triggers: Situational mechanics of gender in negotiation." *Journal of Personality and Social Psychology* 89(6):951–965.

Chapter 10

Page 166: *This assumption is so common that experts have named it the fixed-pie bias:* For a good discussion of the fixed-pie bias, see Neale, M.A., and M.H. Bazerman. 1991. *Cognition and Rationality in Negotiation.* New York: The Free Press.

Page 174: *In a lab study, participants were paired up to attempt a multi-issue negotiation:* Thompson, L. 1991. "Information exchange in negotiation." *Journal of Experimental Social Psychology* 27(2):161–179.

Page 184: *Four years ago, Laura founded a small New York–based dance company:* The idea for this example comes from a teaching case called *Oceania!,* written by Leigh Thompson and Jennifer Bloniarz for the Dispute Resolution Research Center (DRRC) at Northwestern University.

Chapter 11

Page 201: *In new research on how people experience dread:* Berns, G.S., J. Chappelow, M. Cekic, C.F. Zink, G. Pagnoni, M.E. Martin-Skurski. 2006. "Neurobiologic substrates of dread." *Science* 312 (May 5).

Chapter 12

Page 223: *Nobody likes rejection but research shows that women's self-esteem fluctuates more in response to feedback, whether positive or negative, than men's:* Lenny, E. 1977. "Women's self-confidence in achievement settings." *Psychological Bulletin* 84:1–13.

Pages 223–224: *Studies also show that women feel less comfortable with social risk than men:* Arch, E. 1993. "Risk-taking: A motivational basis for sex differences." *Psychological Reports* 73(3):6–11.

Chapter 13

Page 236: *But it can also cloud your thinking:* Allred, K.G., J.S. Mallozzi, F. Matsui, and C.P. Raia. 1997. "The influence of anger and compassion on negotiation performance." *Organizational Behavior and Human Decision Processes* 70(3):175–187; Bodenhausen, G.V., L.A. Sheppard, and G.P. Kramer. 1994. "Negative affect and social judgment: The differential impact of anger and sadness." *European Journal of Social Psychology* 24:45–62; Tiedens, L. Z., and S. Linton. 2001. "Judgment under emotional certainty and uncertainty: The effects of specific emotions on information processing." *Journal of Personality and Social Psychology* 81(6):973–988.

Page 236: *Sadness can also cause problems because it's been shown to make people set lower goals for themselves:* Small, D., J.S. Lerner, and G. Loewenstein. 2004. "Heart strings and purse strings: Effects of specific emotions on economic transactions." *Psychological Science* 15(5):337–341.

Page 236: *Finally, negative emotions can be contagious:* Hatfield, E., J.T. Cacioppo, and Rapson, R.L. 1993. *Emotional Contagion.* Cambridge University Press.

Page 236: *As Roger Fisher and Daniel Shapiro write: Beyond Reason: Using Emotions as You Negotiate.* Penguin Books, 2006.

Page 242: *Research shows that carryover negative feelings—emotional hangovers—can influence...:* Bodenhausen, G.V., L.A. Sheppard, and G.P. Kramer. 1994. "Negative affect and social judgment: The differential impact of anger and sadness." *European Journal of Social Psychology* 24:45–62; Lerner, J.S., R.M. Gonzalez, D.A. Small, and B. Fischhoff. 2003. "Effects of fear and anger on perceived risks of terrorism: A national field experiment." *Psychological Science* 14(2):144–150; Lerner, J.S., and D. Keltner. 2001. "Fear, anger, and risk." *Journal of Personality and Social Psychology* 81(1):146–159; Lerner, J.S. 2005. "Negotiating under the influence." *Negotiation* 8(6):1–3.

Page 243 box: *In one study, researchers showed participants one of two five-minute films:* Carnevale, P. J. D., and A.M. Isen. 1986. "The influence of positive affect and visual access on the discovery of integrative solutions in bilateral negotiation." *Organizational Behavior and Human Decision Processes* 37:1–13.

Page 243: *Positive emotions are also contagious:* Barsade, S.G. 2002. "The ripple effect: Emotional contagion and its influence on group behavior." *Administrative Science Quarterly* 47:644–675.

Page 247: *In a lab study, Linda and her colleagues asked men and women to rate on a scale of 1 to 7 how they felt about negotiating:* Small, D., M. Gelfand, L. Babcock, and H. Gettman. 2007. "Who goes to the bargaining table? The influence of gender and framing on the initiation of negotiation." *Journal of Personality and Social Psychology,* 93(4), 600–613.

Page 249: *Psychologists studying dieters:* Locke, E.A, and G. Latham. 1990. *A theory of goal setting and task performance.* Englewood Cliffs, N.J.: Prentice-Hall.

Page 249: *In one revealing study, researchers taught a group of negotiators (both men and women) to set higher targets for their negotiations:* Stevens, C.K, A.G Bavetta, and M.E. Gist. 1993. "Gender differences in the acquisition of salary negotiation skills: The role of goals, self-efficacy, and perceived control." *Journal of Applied Psychology* 78(5):723–735.

Chapter 14

Page 253: *Multiple studies have shown that using a "softer" style can improve a woman's chances for success when she negotiates:* Carli, L.L., S.J. LaFleur, and C.C. Loeber. 1995. "Nonverbal behavior, gender, and influence." *Journal of Personality and Social Psychology* 68:1030–1041; Ridgeway, C. 1982. "Status in groups: The importance of motivation." *American Sociological Review* 47:76–88; Rudman, L. 1998. "Self-promotion as a risk factor for women: The costs and benefits of counterstereotypical impression management." *Journal of Personality and Social Psychology* 74(3):629–646; Rudman, L., and P. Glick. 1999. "Feminized management and backlash toward agentic women: The hidden costs to women of a kinder, gentler image of middle managers." *Journal of Personality and Social Psychology* 77(5):1004–1010.

Page 253: *Using four actors, two men and two women, Linda and her colleagues created a series of videotapes.* Bowles, H.R., L. Babcock, and L. Lei. 2007. "Social incentives for gender differences in the propensity to initiate negotiations: Sometimes it does hurt to ask." *Organizational Behavior and Human Decision Processes* 103(1):84–103.

Page 256: *Research shows that men can be influential and effective even if people don't like them:* Carli., L. 1990. "Gender, language, and influence." *Journal of Personality and Social Psychology* 59:941–951; Wade, M.E. 2001. "Women and salary negotiation: The costs of self-advocacy." *Psychology of Women Quarterly* 25:65–76.

Page 262: *Research shows that being mimicked increases (subconsciously) your liking of the person who's mimicking you:* Chartrand, T.L., and J.A. Bargh. 1999. "The chameleon effect: The perception-behavior link and social interaction." *Journal of Personality and Social Psychology* 76:893–910.

Chapter 15

Page 268: *People who were instructed to focus on their targets in practice negotiations consistently negotiated better agreements than people who focused on their reservation values instead:* Galinsky, A.D., T. Mussweiler, and V.H. Medvec. 2002. "Disconnecting outcomes and evaluations: The role of negotiator focus." *Journal of Personality and Social Psychology* 83(5):1131–1140.

Page 275: *In one of the classic negotiating texts:* Ury, W. 1991. *Getting Past No: Negotiating Your Way from Confrontation to Cooperation.* New York: Bantam Books.

ACKNOWLEDGMENTS

Linda would like to thank her research collaborators: Julia Bear, Hannah Riley Bowles, Michele Gelfand, Hillary Gettman, Lei Lai, Kathleen McGinn, Deborah Small, and Heidi Stayn. Their work studying women and negotiation as well as their support, inspiration, and enthusiasm for this book have added immeasurably to its scope and rigor. She's especially grateful to her students at the Heinz School—guinea pigs, crash-test dummies, and willing collaborators—for their energy, constant questioning, and imaginative commitment to the ideas and principles embodied in the *Ask For It* program. Emily Lyman Sturman read an early draft and made numerous useful suggestions.

She would like to extend special thanks to the National Science Foundation, the Heinz Family Foundation, and the Heinz School at Carnegie Mellon for their generous financial support of her research.

We're both blessed with wonderful and patient families, friends who humor and encourage us, and kids who make us laugh and keep us sane. Linda asks special forgiveness from her daughter, Alexandra, for writing another book when she promised she wouldn't. Sara promises her two boys, Moses and Adam, that someday she'll write a book that's not about girls.

We owe special thanks to Jill Kneerim, our agent, who gave us superb advice and guided us to our wonderful editor, Toni Burbank. Toni's savvy and nuanced understanding of the predicaments that befall many working women helped us frame our discussion and structure this program to make it useful for the broadest possible audience. Her zeal and high standards made it a far better book.

Finally, thanks to all of you who wrote to us, shared your stories, and asked for our advice. We hope that, in return, *Ask for It* helps you get much more of what you really want out of your lives, beginning now.

INDEX

ABOUT THE AUTHORS

LINDA BABCOCK is the James M. Walton Professor of Economics and the former acting dean of the H. John Heinz III School of Public Policy and Management at Carnegie Mellon University. She has twice received the Heinz School's award for teaching excellence, in 1991 and again in 2001.

A member of the Russell Sage Foundation's Behavioral Economics Roundtable, Dr. Babcock has also served on the economics review panel for the National Science Foundation. Her research has been published in the most prestigious economics, industrial relations, psychology, and law journals, including the *American Economic Review,* the *Quarterly Journal of Economics,* the *Journal of Economic Perspectives,* the *Journal of Personality and Social Psychology, Organizational Behavior and Human Decision Processes, Industrial and Labor Relations Review, Industrial Relations,* and the *Journal of Legal Studies.* She has received numerous research grants from the National Science Foundation and been a visiting professor at the University of Chicago's Graduate School of Business, the Harvard Business School, and the California Institute of Technology.

In 2006, Dr. Babcock founded the Program for Research and Outreach on Gender Equity in Society (PROGRESS), www.heinz.cmu.edu/progress. The mission of PROGRESS is to foster positive social change for women and girls through education, partnership, and research. One of PROGRESS's first initiatives was to develop a a Girl Scout badge for negotiation called "Win–Win: How to Get What You Want." PROGRESS has also developed a video game, the Reign of Aquaria, to teach girls how to negotiate (www .heinz.cmu.edu/progress/reignofaquaria).

Dr. Babcock's research on women and negotiation has been discussed in hundreds of newspapers and magazines in the United States and abroad. She is a frequent guest on television and radio news and talk show programs.

Linda Babcock lives in Pittsburgh with her husband and daughter.

SARA LASCHEVER is a writer with a long-standing interest in women's life and career obstacles. Her work has been published by the *New York Times,* the *New York Review of Books,* the *Harvard Business Review, Vogue, Glamour, Mademoiselle, WomensBiz,* the *Boston Globe,* the *Boston Phoenix,* the *Village Voice,* and many other publications. She has taught writing at Boston University, and privately edited books published by the Harvard Business School Press, Perseus Books, Hyperion, St. Martin's Press, and Alfred A. Knopf.

Ms. Laschever also served as principal interviewer for Project Access, a landmark Harvard University study funded by the National Science Foundation. Project Access explored impediments to women's careers in science—the hindrances, both internal and external, that prevent women from rising to the tops of their fields. Ms. Laschever's work contributed to the publication of two seminal studies in this field, *Gender Differences in Science Careers: The Project Access Study* and *Who Succeeds in Science? The Gender Dimension,* both by G. Sonnert, assisted by G. Holton.

Ms. Laschever has lectured about women and negotiation for the Microsoft Corporation, Bristol-Myers Squibb, Procter & Gamble, the Aon Corporation, Deloitte Consulting, DuPont, the Forbes Executive Women's Forum, the Employment Management Association, the Program on Negotiation at Harvard University, the Woodrow Wilson School of Public and International Affairs at Princeton University, the British-American Trade Association, the Committee for the Advancement of Women Chemists, and many other nonprofit professional associations and women's leadership groups.

Sara Laschever lives in Concord, Massachusetts, with her husband and two sons.

OUR WEBSITE, www.askforit.org, contains both printable and PDF versions of the personal inventory, fairness assessment, negotiation prep worksheet, and information search tools in this book, as well as links to numerous other useful sites.